THE HEIRS OF MOLIÈRE

FOUR FRENCH COMEDIES

OF THE 17TH AND 18TH CENTURIES

Le Glorieux (*The Conceited Count*)

THE HEIRS OF MOLIÈRE

FOUR FRENCH COMEDIES OF THE
17th AND 18th CENTURIES

BY

JEAN-FRANÇOIS REGNARD
PHILIPPE NÉRICAULT DESTOUCHES
PIERRE NIVELLE DE LA CHAUSSÉE
JEAN-LOUIS LAYA

TRANSLATED AND EDITED BY
MARVIN CARLSON

LIBRARY OF CONGRESS CATALOGING-IN PUBLICATION DATA
Regnard, Destouches, La Chausée, Laya
[Plays. English. Selections]
The Heirs of Molière/ by Regnard, Destouches, La Chaussée, Laya ;
translated and edited by Marvin Carlson
p. cm.
Includes bibliographical references.
Contents: The Absent-Minded Lover by Regnard -- The Conceited Count by Destouches -- The Fashionable Prejudice by La Chaussée -- The Friend of the Laws by Laya.
ISBN 0-9666152-5-5 (pbk.)
1. Jean-François Regnard, 1655-1709; Philippe Néricault Destouches, 1680-1754; Pierre Nivelle de La Chaussée, 1691-1754; Jean-Louis Laya, 1761-1833 I. Title: The Heirs of Molière. II. Carlson, Marvin A., 1935-
2003
2002020900

Copy-editing and typography by Kurt Taroff
Design and graphics by Kimon Keramidas

TABLE OF CONTENTS

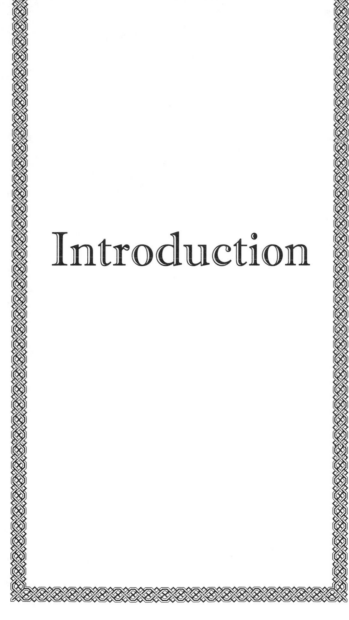

Introduction

The Heirs of Molière

The figure of Molière has dominated the French comic stage since the seventeenth century, but never was his influence stronger than in the somewhat more than a century between his death and the French Revolution, which brought to an end the society which his comedies reflected and the theatrical system within which they were created.

In the aftermath of the Revolution, the French theatre developed new forms and adjusted to new structures of organization and to new audiences, reflecting a new social order. During the previous century, however, despite some occasional and modest experimentation, tradition ruled the French stage. The genres of tragedy and comedy remained distinct and highly predictable in terms of subject matter, style, and construction, and the models for each were the masters of the "great century" — Racine and Corneille in tragedy, Molière in comedy. The heirs of Molière, those comic dramatists who worked in the tradition and the shadow of the master during the century after his death, have on the whole not been treated very kindly by theatre history. Today only two French comic authors of this period are widely known, even in France, and each is a rather special case. These are Marivaux and Beaumarchais.

Marivaux's delicate style and subtle emotionality links him closely to the rococo. His dramatic world seems peopled with figures from paintings by his contemporaries Watteau or Boucher, but in the dramatic world of his own time he was a distinct anomaly. He worked primarily not for the Comédie Française, already popularly known as the "house of Molière" and dedicated to the work of the French classic dramatists and their faithful followers, but for the more marginal Comédie Italienne, created for the performance of commedia dell'arte and thus much less dominated by the Molière tradition. Today Marivaux is one of the pillars of the Comédie Française, but it was not until the early nineteenth century that his work was considered proper for that theatre, and he still remained much less highly regarded than other eighteenth-century comic authors such as Regnard and Dancourt. In more recent times his reputation has steadily grown and theirs decreased, especially after Patrice Chereau and other modern directors found in him a dark psychological dimension that suited well the taste of the late twentieth century.

Beaumarchais is quite a different case. Far more widely known and admired in his own time than Marivaux, his work achieved its early high visibility not for its comic craft, among the best Europe has ever seen, but for the close association of his character Figaro, and especially the play *The Marriage of Figaro* to the political dynamics of the early years of the Revolution. For later generations, the familiarity of Beaumarchais's two "Figaro" plays, *The Barber of Seville* and *The Marriage of Figaro*, has primarily been due to the fact that they inspired popular operas by Rossini and Mozart, two of the greatest operatic composers of all time. The number of revivals of the plays that inspired these operas is today totally overshadowed by the operas themselves. The fact that Beaumarchais created other dramatic works, indeed even a third Figaro play, *The Guilty Mother*, is now almost totally forgotten.

In different ways, then, the dynamics of dramatic and theatre history have been relatively kind to Marivaux and Beaumarchais, but far less so to the many other French comic dramatists of their century, not a few of them more popular nationally and internationally in their own time than either of these now much more familiar authors. There are a variety of reasons for this neglect. Perhaps the most important is the overwhelming dominance of Molière in the French comic tradition, indeed in the French theatre in general. Almost any theatergoer, anywhere in the world, asked to name a single French dramatist, is most likely to name Molière, just as they would be likely to name Shakespeare for England. This dominance has naturally created serious problems for subsequent dramatists, who frequently are regarded, and frequently regarded themselves, primarily as inferior followers of the great master. This attitude has been institutionalized in critical and historical writings on the theatre, and, equally important, in subsequent production history, so that today one is far more likely to see a production of one of the least interesting works of Shakespeare or Molière than of considerably more interesting and accomplished works by their overshadowed contemporaries or followers, such as Beaumont and Fletcher or Regnard.

Nor is the dominance of the canonical figures the only reason for the relative neglect of most eighteenth-century dramatists in later periods. Time is not generally kind to comic works. Often directed toward the concerns and follies of their own society, comedies often seem quaint and faded to audiences who look back upon them when social conditions have changed, and new customs and new follies have replaced the old. Moreover, comedies of the eighteenth century tend to suffer not only from the disappearance of the entire society which they reflected but also from a change in what sort of emotional tonality audiences expect from comedy. The emotional appeals and strong sentimentality that characterize much eighteenth-century comedy throughout Europe usually seem to modern audiences mawkish and overdrawn, the appeals to emotion too obvious to be convincing. The general tradition of comedy in France, as in England, has been to emphasize laughter and wit over sentiment, and such popular eighteenth-century genres as the English "sentimental comedy" or the French "weeping comedy" seem to modern audiences, who expect a much sharper emotional edge, almost contradictions in terms.

Yet what such works may have lost in immediate social relevance they have gained by offering to later viewers or readers lively pictures of another time, engaging glimpses into another social world. The specific social rules and emotional valences may have changed, but the struggles between classes, between generations, between value systems are so much a part of human society in general that one can still appreciate the dynamics, and a good deal of the humor of these plays in recognizing familiar human relationships working themselves out in another key.

In general, French classic comedies, most of them written in rhymed verse, have been translated into English in prose, which in fact adds another barrier to their appreciation. As Richard Wilbur's delightful verse translations of Molière have demonstrated, an important part of the appeal of these plays is in the way that the rhythm and turns of the verse support the wit and the flow of the scenes. Both long individual speeches and rapid exchanges that seem rather flat in prose can often take on a surprising life when sympathetically rendered in verse. Each of the translations in this volume therefore seeks to achieve for its original something of the liveliness and flavor Wilbur has brought to their great inspirer, Molière.

The death of Molière in 1673 left his theatre for a time without a major living comic dramatist, but in the middle of the next decade two playwrights appeared who were widely regarded, in France and abroad, as legitimate heirs of the master and whose works dominated the French comic theatre into the first decades of the next century.   These were Dancourt and Regnard.   Since Dancourt used prose for his major comedies, he has been omitted from this collection of verse comedies, but he rivaled Regnard (and far surpassed Marivaux, Beaumarchais, and even Corneille) in productions at the Comédie Française up until modern times. Regnard, on the other hand, worked primarily in verse, as in the amusing *The Absent-Minded Lover* (*Le Distrait*) from the closing years of the century, which shows clearly how the tradition of Molière comedy is being continued a generation after his death. Indifferently received when first presented in 1697, it was withdrawn by its author and only revived in 1731, more than twenty years after his death. It then enjoyed a great success and was often revived in France and abroad for the rest of the century. Haydn composed a delightful set of incidental music for its German version.

The title of Regnard's play refers, in the manner of Molière, to a defect in the central character which drives much of the comic action. In Molière this defect is most commonly found in the older character who serves as a barrier to the union of the sympathetic young lovers (as in *The Miser* or *The Imaginary Invalid*). Regnard, by making it a defect in his romantic lead, looks more to the eighteenth-century interest in internal conflicts (the works of Marivaux provide clear examples of this), although a Molière model could be cited, if a much darker one, in *The Misanthrope*.

After the major works of Dancourt and Regnard at the turn of the century, another generation passed before a flurry of important new comic works appeared during the 1730s. If Regnard and Dancourt look clearly back to the previous century, these new works, while certainly within the same tradition, are very clearly eighteenth-century in tone. In this generation Marivaux has already been mentioned, but his popularity and influence in his own century was very slight.   Two of his contemporaries, however, enjoyed enormous success and strongly influenced the course of comedy for the rest of the century. These were Nericault Destouches and Pierre

Nivelle de La Chaussée.

Destouches, like his younger contemporary Voltaire, spent time as a young man in England and was strongly influenced by the English theatrical scene, then dominated by the Augustan authors Addison, Steele, and Cibber. In the works of Destouches, then, are found the first clear indications of the sentimentality and moralizing tone that characterized much French and English drama of the mid-eighteenth century. Oliver Goldsmith's famous essay "On Sentimental and Laughing Comedy" depicts English comic drama of the mid-eighteenth century as a kind of sentimentalized wasteland between the witty comedy of the Restoration and the revival of "laughing" comedy by such authors as himself and Sheridan. Although Goldsmith's case is overstated on at least two counts — laughing comedy never really disappeared, nor was sentimental comedy so devoid of laughter as he implies — it is certainly true that a distinctly more sentimental and moral tone dominated both English and French (and thereby European) comedy during the mid-eighteenth century. Modern readers and spectators, more in sympathy with the approach of Goldsmith than that of Steele, or of Beaumarchais than that of Destouches, must be willing in some measure to enter the emotional world of that period in order to appreciate its comic production.

In his own time Destouches was generally seen as a faithful follower of Molière (unlike Marivaux, who was generally thought to be taking comedy in a different and less attractive dimension). This was in part due to his practice of building a play around a central "ruling passion," as in his most famous and successful work, *Le Glorieux* (*The Conceited Count*). Destouches in fact saw himself as more innovative, and it is true that he did bring a variety of new elements into the Molière comedy of character, elements probably inspired by his admiration of the English theatre. In addition to a new emphasis upon morality and sentiment, Destouches is thought to have borrowed from the English the sort of romantic elements represented in this play by the hidden relationship of Lycandre and his children (although perhaps only the sentimental treatment of this relationship is really new, since Molière also used the common Plautine device of lost and reunited parents, children, and spouses, as in the conclusion of *The Miser*). Another mark of the new century, though by no means original with Destouches, is the tension between the newly rich but unsophisticated representatives of the bourgeoisie and the proud but nearly destitute members of the aristocracy, with marriage as the shifting and unstable point of negotiation between the two. The rising influence of the middle class brought this tension to the forefront of French comedy during this century, and the ongoing tensions between old families and new money continued to fuel French comic plots until well into the twentieth century.

French historians of the drama have long debated whether Destouches or his younger contemporary La Chaussée should be credited with inventing the *comédie larmoyante*, or "comedy of tears," which became a major element in the mid-eighteenth-century dramatic repertoire. Perhaps it is best to say that Destouches adds to the Molière tradition a distinctly eighteenth-century moral tone and emotionality, much more in harmony with the contemporary British stage, while La Chaussée moves much further in the direction of serious or at least sentimental comedy, truly establishing this as a new comic form. La Chaussée's first great success, *The False Antipathy*, appeared the year following *The Conceited Count*, and clearly left the traditional Molière comedy of character for the comedy of sentimentalized relationships. *Le Préjugé à la Mode* (*The Fashionable Prejudice*), attacking by emotion the prejudice that it was unbecoming and middle-class for a husband openly to express love for his wife, in both message and tone so precisely suited the taste of the times that it became a great success and one of the most influential plays not only in establishing the new "comedy of tears," but in establishing middle-class concerns and values as suitable subjects for serious drama as well.

In France, as in England, there was a reaction against the now well-established tradition of sentimental comedy in the 1770s, led in England by Goldsmith and Sheridan, and in France by Beaumarchais, with *The Barber of Seville* and *The Marriage of Figaro*. During the Revolutionary years Beaumarchais returned to the sentimental tradition with his third Figaro play, *The Guilty Mother*, but the most famous of the many Revolutionary comedies was Jean-Louis Laya's *L'Ami des lois* (*The Friend of the Laws*), which ends this volume and comes from the final days of the political and social system in which the Molière comic tradition was created and developed. Laya began writing plays in the 1780s and in 1793 presented this, his most famous work, at the Comédie during the trial of Louis XIV. The play is fascinating simply as an historical document, but particularly interesting in the context of this collection is how Laya has adapted the techniques of the comic tradition to make his political statement. Like most eighteenth-century French comedy, *The Friend of the Laws* is distinctly moral in tone, the moral norm here set by the protagonist Forlis, a former nobleman who supports the Revolution but condemns its excesses. This was a position which clearly recalled the moderate raisonneurs of the Molière comedies but simultaneously aligned the play with the moderate Revolutionaries, the Girondists, now locked in what literally became a death struggle with the more extreme Revolutionary elements. Representatives of the extremist party appear in Laya's play as clear descendants of characters like Tartuffe, ruthless hypocrites interested only in advancing their own ends under the guise of a higher good. The traditional Molière comedic structure also remains in place, with a foolish member of the older generation, here the mother, infatuated with the grotesque villain and determined to marry him to a daughter who clearly is destined for the sympathetic hero. Laya's play increases its topical relevance by making his Tartuffe, the evil Nomophage, clearly suggest Robespierre, while Duricrane, the ruthless journalist who supports Nomophage, is equally clearly modeled on the Jacobin spokesman Jean-Paul Marat. Enthusiastically cheered by the moderates and violently opposed by the extremists, the play was a center of public confrontation during its brief run, shut down by the Revolutionary Commune, reopened by the Convention, and again closed after a single additional performance as a source of public disorder. It directly resulted in the re-establishment of dramatic censorship, which had been outlawed in the early days of the Revolution, and it was unquestionably one of the major reasons for the continuing hostility of Robespierre's party toward the Comédie Française, which was closed soon after they came to power and all of its actors arrested. *The Friend of the Laws* was revived soon after the fall of Robespierre, clearly more for political than artistic reasons, and enjoyed only a modest success. It remains still a fascinating example of the Molière dramatic structure being adjusted by the writer who was arguably Molière's last direct heir, to address the rapidly changing social circumstances as Molière's social and political world was coming to an end.   As for Laya himself, he survived by going into hiding during the Terror and re-emerged during the Restoration as an important figure in the French literary and academic world. He was elected to the French Academy in 1817 and served as the royal censor for the theatres from that year until his death in 1833.

REGNARD.

The Absent-Minded Lover

by

Jean-François Regnard

Regnard and La Bruyère

Regnard did not write a preface to *Le Distrait*, but in the collected edition of his works, his editor provided by way of preface, the major source for the play, the character of Ménalque, or *Le Distrait* from La Bruyère's popular book of *Characters*. How Regnard converted that source material into the conventionalized structure and pattern of character relationships of French neoclassic comedy provides an excellent illustration of the operations of that tradition, so we here follow the example of Regnard's editor by providing, as preface, the relevant section of La Bruyère.

Ménalque, or The distracted person by La Bruyère

Ménalque descends the stairs, opens his door to go out, and shuts it again. He notices that he is still wearing his nightcap, and examining himself more closely, finds that he is only half-shaved. He sees that he is wearing his sword on the wrong side, that his stockings are hanging down over his heels and that his shirt is hanging down over his breeches. If he goes out walking, he suddenly feels a rude blow to his face or his stomach. He can't imagine what this might be until he opens his eyes and finds himself in front of the rails of a cart or behind a long piece of woodwork that a workman is carrying on his shoulder. He has been seen running directly into a blind man, getting entangled in his legs, and falling down with him, each one tumbling over the other. Often he has come face to face with a prince of the realm who wishes to get by him, and scarcely recognizes him in time to squeeze up against the wall to give him space. He runs about all worked up, shouting, becoming heated, calling his servants one after the other. He loses everything. Everything is mislaid. He asks for the gloves he is holding in his hands, like the woman who asks for the mask she is wearing on her face. He enters the royal apartments and as he passes beneath a chandelier, his wig is caught on it and remains hanging there, with all the courtiers observing and laughing. Ménalque also notices, and laughs more heartily than the others while looking about the whole assembly to see who has lost his wig and has his ears showing. If he goes into town, he barely enters a street before he becomes lost. Becoming uneasy, he asks passersby where he is and they give him the name of his own street. He then enters his own house, from which he immediately rushes forth, crying out that he has made a mistake. He comes out of the law courts and finding a coach waiting at the foot of the grand staircase, assumes it is his own and climbs in. The coachman flicks his whip, thinking he is taking his master home. Ménalque then hops out of the coach, crosses the courtyard, climbs the stairs, passes through the ante-chamber, the bedroom, the study. Everything seems familiar to him, nothing odd. He sits down and relaxes as if at home. The master arrives and he rises to receive him. He treats him most civilly, begs him to be seated, and believes he is doing the honors of his own rooms. He chats, he muses, he speaks again. The master of the house is both bored and astonished. Ménalque is also. He does not say what he is thinking, that this is a boring fellow with nothing to do who eventually will depart. At least he hopes so, and waits patiently. It is not until night that he is convinced of his error, and then only with difficulty.

Another time he calls on a lady and soon becomes convinced that she has called on him. He settles into his armchair with no thought of giving it up. He then decides that this woman makes rather long visits, and expects at every moment that she will go away and leave him at liberty. But as she remains, he grows hungry, and the day being far gone, he invites her to supper, and then she bursts out laughing, which brings him to his senses. He gets married in the morning and has forgotten it by evening, and spends his wedding night away from home. Some years afterward he loses his wife, who dies in his arms. He attends her funeral and the next day when his servants come to tell him dinner is ready, he asks if his wife has been advised and if she is prepared to dine.

He is the one who, entering a church, mistakes a blind man standing by the door for a pillar and the plate he is holding for the basin with holy water. He dips in his hand and makes the sign of the cross on his forehead, upon which he hears the pillar speaking and asking for alms. He advances into the nave, and, thinking he sees a praying-chair, throws himself heavily upon it. The chair folds up, collapses, and tries to cry out. Ménalque is surprised to find himself kneeling on the legs of a very small man, leaning on his back with both arms on his shoulders, his folded hands stretched out, taking him by the nose and stopping his mouth. He retires in confusion and goes to kneel elsewhere. He thinks to take out his prayer-book but instead of that pulls out his slipper, which he put in his pocket as he left. He has scarcely left the church when a man in livery runs after him, asking, with laughter, if he has a slipper belonging to the bishop. Ménalque shows him his own, saying "This is the only slipper I have on me." However he rummages about and finds that of the bishop, whom he just visited, finding him indisposed at his hearth, and whose slipper he had picked up before taking his leave, thinking it one of his gloves which had fallen to the floor. So Ménalque returned home lacking one slipper.

One day having lost all the money in his purse while gambling yet wishing to continue playing, he entered his study, unlocked a cupboard, took out his cash box and drew out what he wished and thought he had restored it to its proper place. But then he heard a barking inside the closet he had just closed. Astonished at the prodigy, he opened it again, and burst out laughing to discover that he had put away his dog instead of his cash box. While playing backgammon he asked for something to drink, which was brought to him. It was his turn to play. He took the glass in one hand and the dice box in the other, and, being very thirsty, swallowed the dice and nearly the box as well, while throwing the water on the board and soaking his opponent.

In the home of a family he knew well, he spit on the bed and threw his hat on the floor, thinking he was doing just the opposite. On a river trip he asked what time it was. He was handed a watch, but scarcely had he received it when, thinking neither of the time nor of the watch, he tossed it into the river like something he found embarrassing. He wrote a long letter, poured some sand on several passages, then poured the sand into the inkstand. Nor was that all. Writing a second letter, he sealed them both and then confused their addresses. A duke and peer of the realm received one of them, and opened it to read the words: "Master Olivier, do not fail to send me, upon receipt of this letter, my provision of hay." His farmer received the other, and had someone read it to him. In it he found: "My Lord, I have received with total submission the orders which it has pleased your highness," and so on. He wrote another letter at night and, after having sealed it, extinguished the candle. Then he is astonished to find that he cannot see anything and cannot conceive how this has happened.

Coming down the Louvre staircase, Ménalque meets someone coming up to whom he says "I've been looking for you." He takes him by the hand, makes him go downstairs with him, crosses several courtyards and various rooms, and wanders hither and yon, even retracing his steps. Finally he looks closely at the man he has been dragging about with him for a quarter of an hour and is astonished to see him. He has nothing to say to him. He lets go of his hand and goes another way.

Often he will ask you a question and is already far away before you have time to respond, or he will ask you as he is running about how your father is faring, and if you tell him he is seriously ill, he cries out that he is delighted to hear it. Another time he meets you on the street and is enchanted to see you. He has just come from your house to talk to you about a certain matter. Then, looking at your hand, he comments: "That's a nice ruby you have there. Is it a balass?" and then leaves you to go on his way. So much for the important matter he wanted to talk about.

If he is in the country, he says to someone that he must be happy to have been able to get away from the court during the fall and to have passed the time at his estate while the King was at Fontainebleau. Then, after speaking to others about something else, he returns to the first, saying "You had fine weather at Fontainebleau; doubtless you spent a lot of time hunting." He then starts out on some story that he forgets to finish. He laughs to himself, and then aloud, at something that is passing through his mind. He replies to his own thoughts. He sings under his breath, he whistles, he throws himself down into a chair, he utters a painful sigh, he yawns, all the while thinking himself alone. If he finds himself at dinner, he unconsciously gathers all the bread onto his own plate, leaving his neighbors with none, and he does the same with the knives and the forks, which they have little chance to use. He takes one of those large spoons that have been invented to serve more efficiently, plunges it into the dish, fills it, carries it to his mouth, and then is astonished to see the soup he was trying to swallow spreading all over his linen and clothing. He forgets entirely to drink at dinner, or, if he remembers, thinks that he has been given too much wine, and flings more than half of it into the face of the person seated to his right, then quietly drinks the rest, not understanding why everyone has burst out laughing when he has merely poured his excess wine on the floor. One time he was confined to his bed by some indisposition. A group of ladies and gentlemen came to visit him and were seated around the bed chatting with him. In their presence he lifted up the blankets and spat in the sheets.

He was taken to the Convent of the Carthusians and shown a cloister filled with works, all executed by the hand of an excellent painter. The monk showing him around spoke at length of Saint Bruno and of his adventure with the canon, which was the subject of one of the paintings.

Ménalque, whose thoughts have wandered out of the cloister and far beyond it during this narration, finally comes back to it, and asks the father if it were Saint Bruno or the canon who was damned. By chance he found himself with a woman recently widowed. He spoke with her about her departed husband and asked how he died. The woman, whose sorrows were renewed by this conversation, with sobs and tears recounted in detail all the sufferings of her husband, from the evening when he was first taken with a fever until his final agony. "Madam," inquired Ménalque, who seemed to have been paying close attention, "was he the only one you had?"

One morning it occurred to him to hurry up everything in his kitchen. He got up before dessert and left his guests at the table. During that day he was to be seen everywhere in town except at the one spot where he had arranged a meeting to complete the business which prevented him from finishing his dinner and forced him to depart on foot for fear that fitting up his carriage would take too much time. Do you hear him shouting, growling, raging against one of his servants? He is astonished not to see him. "Where can he be?" he cries. "What is he doing? What has become of him? Let him never appear before me, I dismiss him this instant." The valet arrives, and is asked, in an imperious tone, where he has been. He replies that he has just returned from where he was sent, and gives a faithful account of his errand.

You would often take him for a fool, which he is not, since he does not listen, and speaks even less, or for a madman, since he talks to himself and is subject to certain grimaces and involuntary movements of the head, or for a proud and discourteous fellow, since when you greet him he will go right past without looking at you or regard you without returning your greeting, or for a man without any consideration, since he talks about bankruptcy while with a family that bears that stain, or about executions or the scaffold in front of a man whose father was condemned, or of plebians in front of plebians who have become rich and are trying to pass themselves off as aristocrats. He hatched a plan to bring up his own illegitimate son in his home while passing him off as a servant, and although he wanted to hide this fact from his wife and his legitimate children, he could not avoid hailing him as his son ten times a day. Moreover, he decided to marry his daughter to the son of a businessman, yet cannot avoid talking from time to time about his house and his ancestors, and remarking that the Ménalques have never married beneath themselves.

In short, he never seems to be present nor attentive to the conversation that is going on about him. He thinks and speaks at the same time, yet the thing he speaks about is rarely the same as what he is thinking about, so there is rarely any coherence or sequence to what he says. He often says "Yes" when he means to say "No," and "No" when what he wants you to understand is "Yes." He may answer you pertinently, with his eyes wide open, but that does not mean anything. He is not looking at you, or at anyone, or at anything in the world. All that you can get out of him, even when he is the most attentive and sociable, are such words as "Yes, indeed! Very true! Good! Really? Ah, yes, I think so. Certainly! Oh, Heavens!" and a variety of other monosyllables, often not even appropriate to the occasion. He is never with those he appears to be; he calls his footmen very seriously "Sir," cannot recall the names of friends, says "Your Reverence" to a prince of the royal blood and "Your Highness" to a Jesuit. When he is at Mass, if the priest sneezes, he cries out "God bless you!" In the company of a magistrate, grave in character and venerable in age and dignity, who asks him whether a certain event happened in a certain way, Ménalque responds "Yes, mademoiselle!"

One day as he was coming home from the country his footmen planned to rob him and succeeded. They jumped down from his carriage and holding a torch under his chin demanded his purse, which he surrendered. When he arrived home he told his friends what had happened, and when they asked for more details he said to them "Ask my men. They were present."

THE ABSENT-MINDED LOVER

by

Jean-François Regnard

Premiered at the Comédie-Française
December 2, 1697

CAST OF CHARACTERS

LEANDER, an absent-minded young man

CLARICE, beloved of Leander

MME GROGNAC, a well-to-do woman of Paris

ISABELLE, Mme Grognac's daughter

THE CHEVALIER, Clarice's brother, in love with Isabelle

VALERE, the uncle of Clarice and The Chevalier

LISETTE, Isabelle's maid

CARLIN, Leander's valet

A LACKEY

Scene: The Grognac apartments in Paris.

ACT I

(*Enter* VALERE *and* MME GROGNAC.)

VALERE: The family's wishes, then, are not your own?

MME GROGNAC: No.

VALERE: Must your daughter spend her life alone?

MME GROGNAC: Yes.

VALERE: Merely speaking of it angers you?

MME GROGNAC: Yes.

VALERE: Maybe, though, in time a gentler view . . .

MME GROGNAC: No.

VALERE: Good! Yes! No! A pleasant conversation,
Though too laconic for my inclination.
Perhaps if you could just elaborate
We'd profit rather more from this debate.
Why not begin by telling me the cause
You have for turning down all son-in-laws?
That well-known banker, for example, why . . .

MME GROGNAC: I must assume, Monsieur, you're joking. Fie!
He is too rich.

VALERE: Now there's a new complaint!

MME GROGNAC: Such wealth could not be gathered without taint.
Fortunes like his, we may find to our sorrow,
Seem great today, and can't be seen tomorrow.

VALERE: The marquis, then, has hardly a defect.
There's nothing in his background to suspect.
He sings and dances, mixes well at court,
Has wit and spirit of a pleasant sort . . .

MME GROGNAC: He is too poor.

VALERE   Of course. I should have known
You'd hit on some defect — to each his own.
You have two choices, both of them you shun
Because this one has money, that one none.
Is there some pattern here I can't detect?
What sort of son-in-law do you expect?

MME GROGNAC: The sort of one you don't find nowadays . . .
Accomplished in all, discreet and poised always,
With modest fortune and with honest birth,
But lacking all those airs of little worth . . .
Vapors and folly and a manner rude,
As if the man's wits had become unglued . . .
To women he should give due deference;
His discourse should reveal a man of sense;
In short, he should be, in my estimation,
Like no one in the younger generation.

VALERE: I must admit you clearly have defined
The sort of son-in-law you have in mind.
If you succeed, and I don't think you will,
In finding him, then I'll salute your skill.
Despite your daughter's name and her estate,
She'd better not expect to find a mate.

MME GROGNAC: Nonsense! Leander is the perfect choice.

VALERE: Leander!

MME GROGNAC: There is something in your voice
That I don't care for, but he suits my vision
Of son-in-law, and that is my decision.

He isn't perfect, as I'm well aware;
I don't approve of his distracted air.
He can't contribute to a conversation;
Some part of him seems always on vacation.
But this is not a crime, one often finds
The wisest men have the most absent minds.

VALERE: But what about Clarice? Frankly, I thought
It was my niece's hand Leander sought.

MME GROGNAC: A natural error. Put it now aside.
My Isabelle will be Leander's bride.
His wealthy uncle has agreed with me
That he or I must give indemnity
If either house withdraw from this alliance.
And poor Leander can't afford defiance.
He's gone, half-heartedly, to state his case,
And when he's back, the wedding can take place.
He's half-committed now to my design
By taking the apartment next to mine.
Haven't you recently seen some decrease
In the attention he has paid your niece?

VALERE: Can you assure me he's not thinking of
Your contract with his uncle, not his love?
And that your Isabelle might not prefer
To wed a man who's not been picked for her?

MME GROGNAC: Leander loves my daughter, and she'll do
Whatever I decide to tell her to.
My wish is her command, as you'll discover,
And my wish now is that she take a lover.

VALERE: Why don't we ask her to express her feeling?
A heart-to-heart talk might be quite revealing.

MME GROGNAC: Of course! Lisette! Lisette! She's never by.
No one in Paris is worse served than I.
Lisette!

LISETTE (*entering*):   Lisette! Yes, Madame, that's my name.

MME GROGNAC: Where's Isabelle?

LISETTE: What! Do you mean I came
               Down here for that? I should be more discerning.
               The noise led me to think the house was burning.

MME GROGNAC: Answer my question, if you've finished balking.

LISETTE: You're always scolding.

MME GROGNAC: And you're always talking
               Beside the point. You haven't answered yet.
               Where is my daughter?

LISETTE: She's at her toilette.

MME GROGNAC: At her toilette! She's there for days on end.
               I'd swear her mirror is her only friend!

LISETTE: Complaining's easy, but a coiffure may
               Require adjustment several times a day.
               You've no idea how much time can be spent
               In railing at a hook that's gotten bent!

MME GROGNAC:Time well spent, truly! Get upstairs, you dunce,
               And tell her I demand she come at once.

LISETTE: I'll fetch her. (*She goes.*)

VALERE: Hold your anger until later
               I pray you, Madam. Don't intimidate her.

MME GROGNAC: By heaven, I think I know as well as you
               Just what one should and what one shouldn't do.
               You'll find out how she feels. She's coming now.

(*Enter* LISETTE *and* ISABELLE.)

MME GROGNAC: Come, Mademoiselle, and don't forget to bow.
　　　　　　　(ISABELLE *makes a curtsey.*)
　　　　　　　Lower, still lower! God, what ignorance!
　　　　　　　To think she's had a teacher in the dance
　　　　　　　For some three years, and still moves like a stick.

LISETTE:　　She practices, but Mademoiselle's not quick.
　　　　　　　What can one learn in three years?

MME GROGNAC:　　　　　　　　　　　　　　To be still.

LISETTE (*aside*): Oh, she can be sarcastic when she will.
　　　　　　　(*aloud*) The new Italian master comes today.
　　　　　　　He'll show her how . . .

MME GROGNAC:　　　　　　　　Not if I have my way.
　　　　　　　I know these Southerners and their instruction;
　　　　　　　The only art they're skilled in is seduction!
　　　　　　　(*To* ISABELLE)
　　　　　　　Keep up your head still more. Come here. Don't droop.
　　　　　　　Can't you attempt to walk without a stoop?
　　　　　　　Keep your chest out, and hold your chin in tight.

LISETTE (*aside*): It's like parade drill here from morn to night.

MME GROGNAC (*to* ISABELLE):
　　　　　　　Two paces forward! Speak! No hesitation!
　　　　　　　This wedding, does it suit your inclination?
　　　　　　　(ISABELLE *laughs.*)

VALERE:　　She laughs. That is at least a hopeful start.

LISETTE:　　It is a laugh, one might say, from the heart.

MME GROGNAC: Hussy! You dare to laugh? A well-intentioned
　　　　　　　Young girl should blush when marriages are mentioned.

ISABELLE:　　Excuse me, but I didn't know the word
　　　　　　　Of marriage was so shameful to be heard.

Tell me what's wanted. If you should desire
My blushes, then my cheeks will be afire.

LISETTE (*aside*): How unaffected!

MME GROGNAC: Husbands are a pain . . .
Capricious, arbitrary, brutal, vain . . .
We're often all too anxious to get married.

LISETTE: I don't remember hearing that you tarried
When you were young. Or were men better then?

MME GROGNAC: Your father was just like all other men.
Despite his title and a noble name,
De Coupille was a scoundrel all the same.
He bore me off by night and by surprise;
I would have had no master otherwise.

ISABELLE: I see. You'd rather that I was abducted.

LISETTE (*aside*): You can't say that she's not been well instructed.

MME GROGNAC: Could I have spawned this imbecilic creature,
This dolt, without a sole redeeming feature,
This reptile, totally deprived of sense?

LISETTE: The family likeness is indeed immense.

MME GROGNAC: What's that?

LISETTE: I'm being silent, as requested.

MME GROGNAC: That's wise. My patience has been sorely tested.

VALERE (*to* MME GROGNAC):
Let me approach her gently on this question.
(*To* ISABELLE) Would you accept a husband?

ISABELLE: The suggestion

Is new — but surely if I had a bid
From someone pleasant, I'd accept, as mother did.

MME GROGNAC: What's that?

VALERE: Remember, gently, for the present.
            (*To* ISABELLE)
            And tell me, have you met that someone pleasant?

ISABELLE: Ah!

LISETTE: Courage!

VALERE: Have you something to reveal?

ISABELLE: There's a young man. When I see him I feel . . .

VALERE: What?

ISABELLE: . . . certain feelings. Just what they may be
            I don't know, but I know it pleases me.

LISETTE: I know the feeling. It is love that stirs.

MME GROGNAC: See to your own affairs; I'll see to hers.
            (*To* ISABELLE)
            Could you please give the rest of us some notion
            Of what sweet youth has stirred all this emotion?

ISABELLE: Oh, if you knew him, you'd feel as I do.
            He tells me daily that he loves me too.
            He often weeps. Lisette, why don't you tell
            Them what he's like, you also know him well.

LISETTE: He's of good family, he's a veteran,
            A short but yet a quite well-built young man;
            He leaps and dances, though he rarely walks;
            Talks as he whistles, whistles as he talks;
            Sings, gestures, is in constant agitation

To prove to all his high self-estimation;
He blossoms in a lady's company . . .

VALERE: Why, it's the Chevalier!

LISETTE: Yes, it is he.

MME GROGNAC: That fool?

VALERE: Please, Madam, he is my relation.
I'm sorry you're not pleased. His situation
Is very good. He's welcome at the court.

MME GROGNAC: Let him stay there.

VALERE: I grant you that he's short.
But he has wit, he's young, and he'll inherit
A tidy fortune . . .

ISABELLE: No one has such merit,
At least in my opinion . . .

MME GROGNAC: What is this?
What right have you to an opinion, Miss?
Without consulting me, how could you dare. . .

VALERE: It is, I'm sure, an innocent affair.

MME GROGNAC: Perhaps, but that's no reason to rejoice.
The fact is, I have made a different choice,
And further, pledged a forfeit which insures
My daughter shall wed my choice and not yours.
I've never met your nephew, but I trust
His reputation as a fool is just.
(*To* ISABELLE)
You're not to see him, do you understand?

ISABELLE: As always, I will do as you command.
I won't see him, you have my guarantee,

But how can I prevent him seeing me?

MME GROGNAC: In any other person, I'd suspect
A naivete so open and direct.
I warn you, daughter, I'll be watching you.

ISABELLE: You disagree with everything I do.
I get confused and stupid when you're fussy
And I start losing weight.

MME GROGNAC: Be still, you hussy!
Go to your room, and stay there `til I'm through!

VALERE: If I might interject a word or two . . .

MME GROGNAC: I am the mistress here, sir. That is all.

VALERE: Yes, but . . .

MME GROGNAC: Good-bye. So nice of you to call.

VALERE: But, Madam, just between us, are you sure . . .

MME GROGNAC: Sir, just between us, if you could procure
A daughter or a son still at your age,
You wouldn't see me running to engage
In their upbringing. Your advice is fine
For your own children. I'll take care of mine.
(*To* ISABELLE)
Get upstairs! When I speak, you will obey!
(*Exit* ISABELLE *and* MME GROGNAC.)

LISETTE: Madam is stubborn. She will have her way.
You won't gain her consent, I can assure it;
We'll have to wed Leander and endure it.

VALERE: Four youngsters ready to proclaim their banns,
And one damned forfeit cancels all their plans!
Leander loves my Clarice, I can tell,

And if he feigns some warmth for Isabelle,
It's just because he has no other choice
Than to obey his rich old uncle's voice.

LISETTE: Without his uncle we would still be lost.
Madam's the very devil when she's crossed.

VALERE: Perhaps in time we'll change her mind somehow.
My nephew might . . . but look, he's coming now.

THE CHEVALIER (*enters, laughing*):
Good evening, uncle . . ha! ha! . . and Lisette.
I've just seen something I won't soon forget.

VALERE: Pray, share it with us, even though we two
May not laugh quite so readily as you.

THE CHEVALIER: I've reason for my laughter as a rule.
Leander, that poor absent-minded fool,
That fuddled dreamer, just arrived by post
Covered with mud, but what amused me most
Was that he'd lost one of his boots somewhere
And came ahead without it unaware.

LISETTE: I fear he's often prey to such distractions.

THE CHEVALIER: I've nearly died of laughter at his actions.
But what I saw was nothing. His valet
Affirms (and I believe it) that the day
His dying uncle, out in Normandy
Called for him, he set out for Picardy
And stayed there several days, consumed with shame,
Unable to remember why he came.

LISETTE: The way he took was rather indirect.

THE CHEVALIER: Why aren't you laughing, uncle, I suspect
If we descended straight from Heraclitus,
Father to son, such antics would delight us!

Enjoy them, uncle, laughter's no depravity!

VALERE: And neither, nephew, is a bit of gravity.
            Your foolish airs can be amusing too.
            You laugh at him, but others laugh at you.

THE CHEVALIER: And I at others, so on down the line,
            I don't like your faults, and you don't like mine.
            And most amusing in this gentle fight
            Is that we all are sure that we are right.
            I have to laugh, whatever you may say,
            At what I see around me every day.
            The clothier who boosts his prices higher
            To rob gallants, is robbed by his supplier.
            Cidalise, who has such a loving soul
            That with her lovers she has no control.
            Lucinda, who of parting has such fear,
            She'll follow you as far as the frontier.
            Now, don't you laugh at follies such as these?
            You're joking!

VALERE: No more satires, if you please,
            Or turn your wit upon your own defects.
            You've smirched the honor of the gentler sex
            By boasting of the favors you could get
            From women whom you've never even met.
            Can you deny this harmful failing in you?
            (THE CHEVALIER gives two or three ballet steps.)

THE CHEVALIER: A moving sermon, uncle. Please continue.
            I'm deeply touched. Is this dance to your liking,
            Lisette?

LISETTE: I find its timing rather striking.

VALERE: You're a great libertine, or so you think.
            You boast of your capacity for drink
            And when you've drained a bottle to the dregs,
            With reeking breath and half-collapsing legs

You go to the theatre, where you find
A company of others of your kind.
You sit on stage, salute each other, kiss,
And to insure the audience won't miss
Your antics, you debate, you fight, you bawl
Above the actors, back and forth you call
`Til everyone laughs at your follies more
Than at the play they paid their money for.

THE CHEVALIER: I hope your next complaining will be stronger,
        Or briefer . . . I can't stay awake much longer.
        Lisette's asleep already.

VALERE: Your excess
        Has caused me countless hours of distress.
        You'll force me into what I wouldn't do . . .
        Give to your sister money meant for you.
        Your dying parents gave into my care
        A nice inheritance. Your rightful share
        Should guarantee your future happiness
        If it's not forfeited by your excess.

THE CHEVALIER: Come, don't be angry, uncle. Let me know
        What I have done to irritate you so.
        I drink, I flirt, I gamble, I'll admit,
        But never thought I'd be condemned for it.
        I get up very late, but I give ear
        To all my creditors . . .

VALERE: Yes, but I fear
        That's all you give them.

THE CHEVALIER: Then I slip away
        In the last hours of the dying day
        With a few bottles and a few close friends,
        Gathered together as the evening ends
        In homes of quiet respectability
        With ladies known for their gentility.
        In warmest fellowship we pass the night . . .

Leave, so that tongues won't wag, in broad daylight
And in good order, quietly, each guest
Wends his way homeward to his well-earned rest.
A life more innocent you seldom see.
One meal a day is quite enough for me;
An invalid has no more strict existence.

LISETTE: You're like a monk.

THE CHEVALIER: Come, uncle, at a distance
You cannot judge. This evening five of us
Will take champagne together. Make no fuss
About it, simply join us if you will.
We'll even give you leave to pay the bill . . .
For, speaking frankly, I don't think all five
Have got enough to keep a cat alive.

LISETTE: Happy the tavern whose attraction lures
Five fine young men with assets such as yours.

VALERE: You are a fool.

THE CHEVALIER: I grant you that. As proof
I soon will take a wife beneath my roof.
Tell me, Lisette, how is the little miss?

LISETTE: Monsieur . . .

THE CHEVALIER: Dreaming, no doubt, of married bliss?
She is a little jewel, a sprite, an elf,
And I can't wait to get her to myself.
(*To* VALERE)
 She's young, she's rich . . I'll introduce you to her.
You'd be as charmed as I am if you knew her.

VALERE: I know her. Do you know her mother, too?
She claims that the affair will not go through.

THE CHEVALIER: She claims! I think it's time that we define

Just whose claims are the stronger . . hers or mine.
She claims! Then let her say so to my face.
It seems I need to show Madam her place.

LISETTE: You'll waste your time, Monsieur, I guarantee.
                You might as well try to control the sea.

THE CHEVALIER: Is that so? Follow me.

VALERE: Nephew! One minute!
                For once try something with some prudence in it.
                Boldness with Isabelle may be no fault
                But you won't take her mother by assault.

THE CHEVALIER: She claims! I trust you've told the ancient crone
                My manners are as polished as her own.
                I'm quite aware of how one plays these games.
                Insufferable arrogance. She claims!

VALERE: Believe me, I've done everything I could
                To make her recognize your claim as good.
                It's your task, nephew, now to carry through
                The image that I've given her of you.

THE CHEVALIER: I'll think about it, uncle. So, farewell.
                (VALERE *goes.*)
                Now, little mouse, convey to Isabelle
                My love and my regrets. I have to go,
                Since friends and wine won't wait for me, I know.
                And so she'll realize I'm thinking of her,
                Give her this kiss from her departed lover.
                (*He tries to embrace* LISETTE.)

LISETTE: Excuse me, sir, it wasn't my ambition
                To undertake so weighty a commission.
                Find someone else, or bear your own salute.

THE CHEVALIER: I know my Isabelle. A substitute
                Won't bother her.

LISETTE: But it would bother me.
I'm glad your mistress trusts your constancy.
Adieu, Monsieur. (THE CHEVALIER *leaves*.)
                         What sort of love is this?
A charming tête-à-tête he's forced to miss . . .
Since wine, not women, seems to stir his passion.
Is that the sort of feeling now in fashion?
Ah, men! Why do we women still continue
To go along with every whim that's in you?
How can such rascals keep us so enraptured?
Cursed be the first who let herself be captured!
But tit for tat, and lovers, make no fuss
If we treat you as you have treated us!

ACT II

(*Enter* LISETTE *and* CARLIN.)

LISETTE: It's pleasant, Carlin, seeing you again.

CARLIN: I hurried here as soon as we got in;
As you can see, my hair is still in papers.

LISETTE: Tell me about your master's latest capers.
Is he still shy a boot?

CARLIN: How did you know?

LISETTE: I know a lot.

CARLIN: He keeps me on the go,
I swear. At lunch he seems to have mistaken
His finger for an extra bit of bacon
And bit it to the bone.

LISETTE: That should suffice
To make sure he won't be distracted twice.

CARLIN: I fear he's past reform. You know, he's prone
To take another's carriage for his own.
The other day that caused a near disaster.
Some foolish coachman took him for his master
And carted him straight home all unawares.
Nobody stopped him; he went up the stairs,
Didn't observe the lady of the house
In bed already, waiting for her spouse,
And started getting ready to retire.
He put his outer clothing by the fire,
Then, nightgown on and nightcap on his head,
He was already making for the bed . . .
When in the husband came. He raged, he swore

He'd throw my master out . . not through the door
But from a window. He escaped the place
Without a broken neck, by God's good grace,
But running home, dressed only in a gown,
He scandalized the better half of town.

LISETTE: A charming tale, but now be serious, pray.
What business kept you two so long away?

CARLIN: We found a fortune to pursue, my sweet.

LISETTE: A fortune?

CARLIN: Yes, for laying at your feet.
But we were so frustrated, I'm suspicious
We must have gone against the devil's wishes.

LISETTE: What happened?

CARLIN: All our prospects were cut short;
Our hopes were shipwrecked practically in port.
We thought ourselves the heirs of an infernal
Old uncle, who turns out to be eternal.
Each new disease, each downward step restored
Our hope that he'd soon pass to his reward.
We thought the golden day had come at last
When we saw charitable heaven cast
Two or three pleurisies upon his head
Followed by apoplexy. We were led
To rush away in firmest expectation
Of witnessing the happy expiration . . .
Vain foolish mortals! What a worm is man!
How heaven laughs at our attempts to plan!
That old man's treachery was past belief!

LISETTE: You were too slow to come to his relief?
Someone else . . .

CARLIN: No.

LISETTE: Ah! When the will was read,
                  You found another heir preferred instead?

CARLIN: Not that.

LISETTE: Did he admit, before expiring,
                  Some secret marriage? Children he'd been siring?

CARLIN: No, he was too tight-fisted to create
                  New heirs.

LISETTE: What then?

CARLIN: The foul old reprobate
                  Maliciously made up his mind to live!

LISETTE: That's treachery indeed! Who could forgive
                  Such baseness!

CARLIN: With my own hands I fixed up
                  Emetics for him. Into every cup
                  I put a double dose in the belief
                  That this would bring the sufferer relief.
                  But every time inexorable fate
                  Thwarted my efforts to improve his state,
                  And now the gentleman, at eighty-nine,
                  Beset with every symptom of decline.
                  With intermittent fever, with thrombosis,
                  Pleurisies, gout, arteriosclerosis,
                  Fluxions, catarrah, his coffin at the door,
                  Seems far more healthy than he was before.

LISETTE: Your trip then wasn't much of a success.

CARLIN: Indeed, it cost us money, I confess.
                  We had a trusted friend to carry on
                  Our business here for us while we were gone
                  And happily he's kept us up to date
                  Or we'd be in a far more sorry state.

LISETTE: But if this business trip was a disaster
             Perhaps romance will compensate your master.
             How is that matter going?

CARLIN: Not too well.
             There's no doubt that he's in Clarice's spell,
             But since he gets distracted, she is not
             Always the foremost object of his thought.
             He loves to dream of her, but then he's swayed
             Considering the forfeit to be paid.
             Your mistress isn't lacking in allure,
             And she is well-to-do, Clarice is poor . . .
             My master's faithful, though, you'll never see
             A nobler specimen of gallantry.
             He's not like other lovers in his dealing;
             He has no art, but he's chock-full of feeling.

LISETTE: Too full, if anything. What can we do
             To further an affair thus split in two?
             Will he wed both?

CARLIN: Why not? There's nothing to it,
             And he's quite scatterbrained enough to do it.
             I've never known such an eccentric soul . . .
             He dreams of nothing, wanders without goal;
             He's always on some unexpected tack;
             Talk white to him and he will answer black;
             Says no to that when he means yes to this;
             Addresses ladies "sir," yet calls me "miss" . . .
             You never can be sure of his reaction;
             It's rather close to madness, this distraction.
             Yet he's an honest man, sincere and warm
             A generous soul, who'd do nobody harm.
             He loves the very person he affronts . . .
             In short, he is a sage and fool at once.

LISETTE: If tender feelings occupy Leander
             About Clarice, I must admit with candor
             My mistress feels drawn toward the Chevalier.

CARLIN: So much the better. Then our course is clear.
             That cursed forfeit we must do our best
             To get around, and love will do the rest.

LISETTE: Let's set to work then to arrange this mating.

CARLIN: Agreed. But I must go. My master's waiting.
             I only wanted from your lips to hear
             How you'd been faring when I wasn't near.

LISETTE: Thank you. I've no complaints. And you?

CARLIN: So-so.
             My health is good. I've an abrasion, though,
             Which I'm afraid may be a bit infected.

LISETTE: You came by coach? Then, that's to be expected.
             Goodby, poor sufferer, `til we meet again.
             (*She goes.*)

CARLIN (*alone*): Your eyes cause me more suffering than my skin.
             A harsh word from you fills me with regret,
             But wait, you rogue, I'll settle with you yet.
             Who's this? My master! And in conversation
             As usual, with his own imagination!

LEANDER (*Wandering about the stage dreamily. One of his
             stockings has come down*):
             Young love by absences should not be tested;
             I hope I'll find Clarice still interested.
             Few lovers really have the sort of heart
             That keeps its fire up when the lovers part . . .
             Most fires go out as fast as they arose.

CARLIN: Perhaps he'll see me if we're nose to nose.

LEANDER (*Bumping into CARLIN without noticing him*):
             But I love her; how pitiful I'd be
             If she preferred somebody else to me.

My love, but also my distress is growing;
I can remain no longer without knowing,
From her own lips, just who it is she loves.
Carlin! Fetch me my saber and my gloves!

CARLIN: I'll go, sir, and return in half a minute! (*He goes.*)

LEANDER: Our present state has little promise in it.
I thought on my return, my uncle dead,
I'd be quite free to chose whom I should wed.
But all my plans have fallen to the ground.

CARLIN (*returning*):
Your sword and gloves are nowhere to be found.

LEANDER: Not to be found? That shows what care you took!
You didn't find them since you didn't look!
I just now left them lying on a chair.

CARLIN: The devil take me! I looked everywhere.
Some rascal doubtless carried them away.
(*He notices* LEANDER *is wearing his gloves and
sword*)
What's this? Some trick? I could have looked all day
For them! Are you awake or sleeping?

LEANDER: What do you mean?

CARLIN: I mean there's no use keeping
Up the pretense. Are you prepared to laugh?
(*Aside*) He is a constant wonder. I'm not half
Prepared for each new turn.

LEANDER: Rascal, one word. . .

CARLIN: Monsieur, what charming gloves! Is this your sword?

LEANDER: Ah, ah.

CARLIN: Ah, ah.

LEANDER: A brief lapse of attention . . .

CARLIN: The eighth or ninth today that I could mention.

LEANDER: My heartache has disturbed my usual peace
             Of mind, Carlin. You know I love Clarice.
             But even so, my uncle may compel
             Me now to turn my suit toward Isabelle.
             Yet, Carlin, I burn with too pure a flame;
             Goods, fortune, interest, glory, power, fame . . .
             Nothing can banish Clarice from my heart.
             I must see her. We've been too long apart.
             What time is it?

CARLIN: About six forty-five.

LEANDER: Good. Who told you?

CARLIN: Who told me? Man alive,
             It was the clock!
             (*Aside*) He must have lost his mind!

LEANDER: I think I've left one of my boots behind.
             I know I had it getting on my horse.

CARLIN: Don't worry, just let matters take their course.
             Forget your boot. A kindly fate is leading
             Clarice to you in answer to your pleading.
             Just concentrate. Don't let some new delusion
             Develop now to add to the confusion.

(*Enter* CLARICE.)

LEANDER (*to her*): I hoped, alas, to bring some compensation
             To make up for our lengthy separation,
             You're even more attractive than before.
             Each day, each passing hour adds to your store

Of charms. Each hour adds also to my zest
For these delights . . .
(*To* CARLIN) An armchair for my guest!

(CARLIN *brings a chair.* LEANDER *sits in it.*)

CLARICE: All parting lovers speak so, but, returning,
They often find they can control their yearning.
Our sex used to be fickle, `twas the fashion
When we first learned how to control our passion;
But lately men have learned to do the same,
And threaten now to beat us at our game.

CARLIN (*carrying a stool to* CLARICE):
Don't be offended, madam, at this stool.
I'd offer you the armchair as a rule,
But as you see, my master's taken it.

CLARICE: I thank you, but I've no desire to sit.
(*To* LEANDER)
I would be happier if I loved you less,
But I am apprehensive, I confess.
My love is mixed with fear that my attractions
Can't always triumph over your distractions.
I worry that some rival may dispel . . .

LEANDER: I'm yours alone, my darling Isabelle.

CARLIN (*low, to* LEANDER): Clarice, not Isabelle.

LEANDER: My wants are few.
It is enough to live and die near you,
My Isabelle.

CARLIN (*low, to* LEANDER): Clarice.

LEANDER: I praise your charms.
In your eyes love finds his most powerful arms;
In Isabelle . . .

CARLIN (*low, to* LEANDER):   Clarice . . .

LEANDER: Heaven has made
   A model where all beauties are displayed.

CLARICE: (*to* CARLIN):
   His slips of tongue reveal what I suspected.
   It's Isabelle your master has selected.
   I'm in despair. I feel within my heart
   Fury appear, and outraged love depart.

LEANDER (*coming out of his reverie*):
   You're angry, madam. What's the reason, pray?
   This rogue, has he displeased you in some way?

CLARICE: If anyone displeased me, it was you.

LEANDER: I?

CLARICE: You.

LEANDER: You're mad at me? It can't be true.

CLARICE: You ingrate, cad, unfaithful wretch, farewell.
   Love, honor, and obey your Isabelle.

LEANDER (*to* CARLIN): Rascal, what have you said?

CARLIN: What? I, indeed!
   Is it my fault?

LEANDER: Clarice, it's you I need.
   My heaven's vengeance fall upon my head
   Before your eyes, may lightning strike me dead
   If I've a heart that someone else is sharing.

CARLIN: You are distracted, sir. Watch what you're swearing.

CLARICE: It's Isabelle you love. That hateful name

Was on your lips the moment that I came.

LEANDER: I spoke of Isabelle? Could you be testing
             My love for you, Clarice? Or are you jesting?
             I, mention someone else before your face,
             When in my heart you only have a place?

CARLIN: It's come at last. He's finally lost his mind.

LEANDER: Your doubts are unjust as they are unkind.
             Look at me, can you really think it true
             That I prefer somebody else to you?
             Oh, by the way, I'm in a legal tiff . . .
             You know one of the witnesses, and if
             You'd give me a good word, you'd save the day.

CLARICE: Gladly.

CARLIN: At least he phrased it "by the way."

CLARICE: My love for you still gives me apprehensions
             However you may plead your good intentions.
             Yet somehow it alleviates my fears
             To know with you I can't quite trust my ears.
             I'll trust your innocence. Your heart I've found
             Is good, although your wits may be unsound.

LEANDER: The criticism, I'll admit, is fair.

CARLIN: He really loves you, madam. That I'll swear,
             If there were just no forfeit to be paid . . .

CLARICE: I'm sure we can enlist my uncle's aid.
             He's tried to help my brother and has spent
             Much time in seeking him a regiment,
             Although he lacks much influence at court.

LEANDER: If he'll help us, I'll give him my support.

CARLIN: What could be better! Here's the Chevalier!

THE CHEVALIER (*entering and embracing* LEANDER):
                My friend! How fortunate to meet you here!

LEANDER: My pleasure, sir. Your name has slipped my mind.

CARLIN: The Chevalier!

THE CHEVALIER: My sister! So I find
                You here as well. Now, could it be by chance,
                Or did you smell someone's inheritance?

CLARICE: Monsieur, you always have some wit to spare.

THE CHEVALIER: What is more charming than a new-made heir?
                Lovers in mourning stimulate affection;
                Black somehow sets off anyone's complexion.
                One can be uglier than Carlin is,
                Yet if that one's an heir, romance is his.

CARLIN: As Carlin is? Pray, sir, don't be offended.
                Your odious parallel must be amended.
                Some Carlins, though you see them as absurd,
                To certain chevaliers might be preferred.

THE CHEVALIER: You're angry, friend! Enough! Let us embrace!
                The uncle's gone, I take it, with good grace?
                I trust you found his coffers full of gold?
                The coins he hoarded, were they new or old?

CARLIN: We didn't really notice. We decided
                To joyfully accept what God provided.

THE CHEVALIER: He's really dead then? (*sings*) "I am in despair."

CLARICE: That's evident.

CARLIN: It's an appropriate air.

THE CHEVALIER: I'll teach it to you. It's a thing of mine
That's like an epic poem in every line.
Song
In the tavern I seek consolation
When cruel Iris delights in my pains,
There I give way to Bacchus' temptation;
He succeeds to my mistress's claims.
There I give way . . .

CARLIN: The tavern is the ideal place for that.

THE CHEVALIER (*singing*):   . . . to Bacchus' temptation;
He succeeds, succeeds . . .
It goes straight to the heart, that well-placed flat!
. . . succeeds . . .
What do you think?

CARLIN: Bacchus, it seems to me,
Is far more likely to succeed than we.

THE CHEVALIER (*singing*) He succeeds to my mistress's claims.
(*To* LEANDER)
How do the words and music strike your ear?

LEANDER (*coming out of the reverie which has possessed him
since the beginning of the scene, he takes* CLARICE
by the arm, assuming that she is THE CHEVALIER,
and leads her to one corner of the stage):
I've always been concerned with your career.
Your father was my friend. Feel free to call
On me to aid you any way at all.

CLARICE: I see you're much more honest than I thought.

LEANDER (*fearing he might be heard, leads her to the other side
of the stage*): Here, let us find a more secluded spot.

THE CHEVALIER: (*following them, with* CARLIN)
It seems to me the thing that we are after

                              Is some diversion . . .

CARLIN: We could use the laughter.

LEANDER: I know the king. I'm sure he will supply
              You with the regiment you want.

CLARICE: What! I!

THE CHEVALIER: Your master seems a trifle disconnected.

CARLIN: You're rather more like him than I suspected.

LEANDER (*to* CLARICE):
              Any young man who's served as well as you
              Can surely claim such honor as his due.

CLARICE: Look at me!

LEANDER: Madame! I apologize!
              Apparently the sun was in my eyes.
              I thought you were . . .

THE CHEVALIER: Clarice! A regiment!

CARLIN: But just consider, what a supplement
              To our armed forces! If we just could get
              Each home to arm a girl, we'd be all set.

THE CHEVALIER (*to* CLARICE):
              This young man's lost his wits for love of you.

CLARICE: He says the same thing. I suppose it's true.

THE CHEVALIER (*to* LEANDER):
              It's marriage that will cure your discontent.
              My sister's lovely and intelligent . . .

LEANDER: No, not at all!

THE CHEVALIER: No? Please don't speak in haste.
　　　　　　　　Consider . . .

LEANDER:　　　　　　　　　Please, monsieur, respect my taste.

THE CHEVALIER: But if you love . . .

LEANDER:　　　　　　　　　　Ah, music, I adore it!
　　　　　　　But I have rather strict requirements for it.
　　　　　　　I would prefer a tune more gay and light,
　　　　　　　Your words, between us, seem a little trite.

THE CHEVALIER: What music do you mean?
　　　　　　　　　　　　　What words? What tune?
　　　　　　　Your lover, sister, is a great buffoon.

LEANDER:　　Didn't you just now ask for a suggestion
　　　　　　　About your song?

THE CHEVALIER:　　　　　　　No.

LEANDER:　　　　　　　　　　Then what was your question?

THE CHEVALIER: I wanted to discuss your state of mind
　　　　　　　About Clarice. I simply want to find
　　　　　　　How much you love . . .

LEANDER:　　　　　　　　　Don't ask! But I implore you,
　　　　　　　Look in her eyes. There is your answer for you.

THE CHEVALIER: I share your taste. If I were not her brother,
　　　　　　　I wouldn't see her won by any other.
　　　　　　　But I'm engaged elsewhere . . . a gentle soul
　　　　　　　Has made me play an unaccustomed role.
　　　　　　　For her I have pursued my suit in silence . . .
　　　　　　　Forsworn all uproar, swaggering, and violence;
　　　　　　　I go now to the object of my heart. (*He leaves.*)

LEANDER (*to* CLARICE): Since you are so determined to depart

Let me accompany you back, I pray.
(*He puts on one glove, and presents to her the other hand.*)

CLARICE: I think you want your glove the other way.

LEANDER: True. (*He takes off the glove and offers his hand*)

CLARICE: Please, it's not worth taking trouble for.

LEANDER: No trouble! I will show you to your door.
(*He accompanies her to the middle of the stage, then leaves her to speak to* CARLIN. CLARICE *exits alone.*)

LEANDER: Carlin, I have a secret to convey.
              Listen . . . Let's see, what did I start to say?
              Go ask the watchmaker if he'll repair
              This snuffbox . . . No, it just came back from there.

CARLIN (*aside*): Some secret!

(THE CHEVALIER *returns.* LEANDER *goes back and gives him his hand, thinking he is* CLARICE.)

LEANDER: Madame, pardon the delay.
              Let me accompany you on your way.

CHEVALIER (*imitating a woman's voice*):
              There is no need. You're really too kind-hearted.

LEANDER (*recognizing* the CHEVALIER):
              What, you're still here? I thought you had departed!
              She's gone without my help. What a disgrace!

THE CHEVALIER: Permit me, just this once, to take her place.
              And be advised, if marriage is your goal,
              Keep your distracted mind under control.
              One girl's enough, I warn you for your sake,

Don't get involved with others "by mistake."
I fear my sister, if put to the test,
Will likely pay you back with interest.
Adieu, monsieur. I am your humble servant. (*Goes.*)

LEANDER: Where has she gone? Am I so unobservant?

CARLIN: It's hard to see her when she isn't there.

LEANDER: Pity me, Carlin, I am in despair.
Everything's going wrong for me today.
There are a hundred things I ought to say
To you, but when Clarice is out of sight,
Then I can't think as clearly as I might. (*He goes.*)

CARLIN: And when she's present, then it's even worse!
Could hellebore, I wonder, cure this curse?
He's more distracted now than yesterday.
It's getting worse. I can't go on this way!
I've always heard it said that one should flee,
Whenever possible, bad company.
Yet he's my friend, and a true heart respects
A friend's good points, whatever his defects.

ACT III

LISETTE (*entering, with* ISABELLE):
>You're finished now with your toilette, you say?
>Your mother should be satisfied today!
>Keep speeding up and it's within your power
>To be quite dressed before the dinner hour.

ISABELLE: And yet, I've little hope of passing muster;
>My eyes have lost their customary luster.
>It's all my mother's fault. Her conversation
>Turns all my beauty into desolation.

LISETTE: She can't abide attractiveness in others.
>There should be laws against romantic mothers,
>Whose beauty and whose lovers have departed,
>Whose lives some fifty years or more have charted,
>Requiring them, if it must be, to spurn
>Romance, and let their daughters have a turn.

ISABELLE: That would be just. We all should have a chance,
>It seems to me, to find ourselves romance.

LISETTE: At least the songs say so. But let's be clear;
>Is your heart given to the Chevalier?
>It is love or esteem?

ISABELLE: How can I know?

LISETTE: What's that?

ISABELLE: The feeling that disturbs me so
>Might well be love; I know I am amazed
>To find how pleased I am to hear him praised.
>Perhaps it's fate, but it's a mystery . . .
>Whatever interests him then interests me.

I blush and then grow pale when he appears;
When he departs I find myself in tears.
My heart pursues him when my eyes cannot,
His manners and his airs invade my thought,
And often when I sleep his image seems
To be a part of my most pleasant dreams . . .
Is this esteem or love?

LISETTE: It's what you will.
In any case, there's no cure for this ill
Except a dose of marriage, and I swear
To bring that happy end to this affair.
Frankly, I much prefer the Chevalier.
Leander's witty, but I really fear
He's too distracted. You need someone sprightly
Who sings and dances well, who takes life lightly,
Devotes himself to pleasure without shame,
And leaves his wife quite free to do the same.
Who never worries whether what she spends
Actually comes from him, or from his friends.
Many Parisian husbands have these traits;
That's why Parisian ladies love their mates.

ISABELLE: But what about my mother's opposition?
You'll never win her mind to that position.
She told me not to see him or I'd rue it!

LISETTE: Wed with your eyes closed, if you're driven to it!
But keep your hopes up. We are sure to find
Some strategem; love stimulates the mind.
There's no way for your mother to prevent us.
Look here, you see who kindly Fate has sent us.

THE CHEVALIER (*enters dancing and whistling, to* ISABELLE):
At last I've found you, princess. I must say,
Your beauty's like a goddess's today!
Cupid's own mother, rising from her shell,
Could not in Heaven's eyes have looked so well!
Give me this token that my love's returned.

(*He kisses her hand.*)

ISABELLE: Monsieur . . .

LISETTE: She means, be good, now that you've earned
             Our trust.

THE CHEVALIER (*to* LISETTE): People like me, who live at court,
             Have learned to cut love's preparations short.
             Would you prefer some amateur in wooing
             Who didn't really know what he was doing?
             Who'd heave great sighs and chew his fingernails?
             Let bourgeois lovers tend to these details!
             I go straight to the heart!
             (*To* ISABELLE)   Could you believe
             I've sought ten years for someone to relieve
             My suffering, and that at last you can?

LISETTE: I could believe it; you're a dangerous man.

THE CHEVALIER (*to* ISABELLE):
             I've drunk a lot this evening, without boasting,
             I've drained more than a hundred bumpers toasting
             Your love. Wine sometimes quenches my desire,
             But this tonight was fuel to my fire;
             Now I'm extremely warm.
             (*He takes off his wig and combs it.*)

LISETTE: A charming way
             To put your natural beauties on display.
             How pleasant once again to see your hair!

ISABELLE: (*to* THE CHEVALIER)
             You can't be comfortable. Take a chair.
             (*To* LISETTE) Bring in an armchair.

THE CHEVALIER: Not that, if you please.

ISABELLE: Surely, Monsieur . . .

THE CHEVALIER: I'm never at my ease
                In armchairs. They restrict my liberty.
                A sofa is the only seat for me.
                (*To* LISETTE)
                Just pull one up, and I'll stretch out a bit.

LISETTE: Stay on your feet unless you want to sit.
                Forgive me, but it puts me out of sorts
                When young men, like old buildings, need supports.
                Stretched out in armchairs, thrusting out their feet
                Like barriers on some deserted street.
                For shame! Our fathers on their wooden chairs
                Sat upright. Aren't your bones as strong as theirs?

ISABELLE: Be quiet, Lisette. I fear he'll take offense.

LISETTE: Young folks today could stand to hear some sense.

THE CHEVALIER: Let's change the subject;
                              servants' manners bore me.
                Why don't you tell me how much you adore me?
                Has the old lady's grouchiness diminished?
                She's a real porcupine.

ISABELLE: I just now finished
                Speaking with her. She said we mustn't meet.

THE CHEVALIER: Absurd! My own virtues I won't repeat,
                But can she set your happiness aside?
                My heart, you know, has claimed you as my bride.

ISABELLE: Your bride, Monsieur? Forgive my being wary.
                I've been informed Chevaliers never marry.

THE CHEVALIER: What slander! Every day we take our brides
                From every sort of woman France provides.

LISETTE (*looking off*): Madame Grognac!

ISABELLE: Ah, Monsieur, disappear!
              Leave . . No, come back . . .

LISETTE: Where can we hide him here?

THE CHEVALIER: Go. Leave me here alone to face the storm.

LISETTE: Don't risk it. I've an idea taking form;
               We may escape from this dilemma yet.
               She knows your name, but you have never met.
               A teacher in Italian is expected;
               Pretend to be him, you won't be detected.

ISABELLE: Oh, heavens, she's upon us!

CHEVALIER: I confess
               Your wit is admirable under stress.
               Fortunately I've been in Italy.

MME GROGNAC (*entering*):
               Daughter, you're in good company, I see.
               Who is this man?

LISETTE: Nobody unexpected.
               Just the Italian master we selected
               To help us with his tongue.

MME GROGNAC: A foolish thought.
               You talk too much with the one tongue you've got.
               Learn silence, if it's learning that you seek.

THE CHEVALIER: A wise man said, use Spanish when you speak
               To God. Italian wins a lady's heart;
               Its accent lifts your words to works of art.
               French is the tongue for men, for horses, Swiss . . .
               Das dich der donder schlalcq!

LISETTE: What tongue is this?

MME GROGNAC: What use is all this language going to be,
        When I've forbidden you all company?

THE CHEVALIER: I'd just begun explaining, I believe,
        Agreement of the noun and adjective.
        La Isabella bella — that is you.
        (*Low*) Amante fedele — a lover true,
        That's me, your life-long suitor and defender.
        (MME GROGNAC *moves closer to listen.*)
        (*Louder*)
        Now let us speak of number, case, and gender.

MME GROGNAC: Gender! This tongue's impertinent! I object!

THE CHEVALIER: Please, Madame. Grammar merits our respect.
        We'll move right on to active verbs. You'll find
        My teaching is the very swiftest kind.
        Amo, I love, is where I like to start.
        If you agree.

ISABELLE: I do, with all my heart.

LISETTE (*to* THE CHEVALIER):
        She's an obedient pupil, as you see.

THE CHEVALIER: Let's test your accent. Conjugate with me:
        Io amo, I love.

ISABELLE: Io amo, I love.

THE CHEVALIER: That's not the accent that I want to hear.
        (*To* MME GROGNAC)
        Please pardon me if I'm a bit severe.
        (*To* ISABELLE)
        These words require a soft pronunciation.
        Io amo, I love.

ISABELLE (*very gently*):   Io amo, I love.

THE CHEVALIER: That's it. A really charming intonation!
　　　　　　I've never seen a pupil learning faster;
　　　　　　She'll soon be even better than her master.
　　　　　　(*To* ISABELLE)
　　　　　　I'm charmed. Let us continue with our session,
　　　　　　And see if you give plurals the same expression.

MME GROGNAC: She's too expressive now, Monsieur, therefore
　　　　　　We won't need your instruction any more.

THE CHEVALIER: She's so well started — that would be a shame!

VALERE (*entering, to* THE CHEVALIER):
　　　　　　Ah, nephew! I'm delighted that you came!
　　　　　　(*To* MME GROGNAC)
　　　　　　Madame, I have the highest expectation
　　　　　　For this young man — that's no exaggeration.
　　　　　　Your pleasure is his only happiness.

LISETTE (*aside*):　　　The devil take him!

ISABELLE: (*aside*)　　　　　　　　　　What an awful mess!

MME GROGNAC:　　　Your nephew? He?

VALERE:　　　　　　　　　　　Come, Monsieur, why rely
　　　　　　On me to introduce you. Don't be shy.

MME GROGNAC:　　Sir, do you teach Italian, yes or no?

VALERE:　　　　　What? He's the Chevalier.

THE CHEVALIER:　　　　　　　　　　Yes, that is so.
　　　　　　Although in several houses I could name
　　　　　　I've taught the girls Italian all the same.

MME GROGNAC (*to* ISABELLE): You shameless creature!

THE CHEVALIER (*to* MME GROGNAC):

Come, use some control.

MME GROGNAC (*to* ISABELLE): After I told you . . .

THE CHEVALIER (*to* MME GROGNAC):   Madam, on my soul,
Don't scold my pupil right before my face!

MME GROGNAC: I'd thank you, sir, if you'd recall your place!
(*To* ISABELLE) When I forbid you . . .

THE CHEVALIER: Let's avoid a fight.
Come, kiss me, mother.

MME GROGNAC: Get out of my sight!
You seem to think I'm joking, sir. I'm not!

(THE CHEVALIER *takes her by the hand, sings and tries to force
her to dance.*)

THE CHEVALIER: Come, mother, let us join in a gavotte.

VALERE (*separating them and pushing* the CHEVALIER *out*):
Don't push her any further. Go away.
(*To* MME GROGNAC)
Madam, I beg you also not to stay.
You're too upset. It isn't any wonder.

MME GROGNAC (*leaving*): Oh! Oh! It's past endurance!

LISETTE (*to* VALERE):   What a blunder!
The Chevalier had almost gotten past her
In his disguise as an Italian master
When you arrived . . .

VALERE: Forgive my error, friends!
I'll set to work at once to make amends.
I'll go rejoin her and at least endeavor
To calm her down. She's touchier than ever! (*Goes.*)

LISETTE: She's too annoyed. He doesn't have a chance.

ISABELLE: Yes, but didn't you laugh to see her dance?

LISETTE: What folly! You can dare find humor in it
When thunderbolts may strike us any minute?

ISABELLE: Why not wait here until she's spent her wrath?
Leander's coming. We are in his path.
We don't dare leave, so let's observe his actions.
At least we'll be amused by his distractions.
I'm sure we'll find him in his usual plight.

LISETTE: Let's stay then, but come on, out of his sight.
Listen! (*They withdraw upstage.*)

LEANDER (*entering, speaking angrily to* CARLIN):
Where were you? Why haven't you heeded
My calls? You're never near me when you're needed!

CARLIN: God strike me dead if I've relaxed at all!
Fifteen minutes ago, don't you recall
You gave me ten commissions to fulfill?
I've seen your lawyer, paid your tailor's bill,
Picked up the watch I had repaired for you . . .
Just see how well it runs!

LEANDER (*taking the watch*):   As good as new!

CARLIN: I also had to bring you an example
Of good Spanish tobacco. Try this sample.

LEANDER: Let's see. (*He takes a bit of tobacco.*)

CARLIN: You'll never get a better tin
Than this one. It's been freshly smuggled in.

LEANDER (*tries to inhale the watch, then throws it away*):
You're poisoning me! That tobacco's rotten!

CARLIN: Monsieur! Think what you're doing! I've just gotten
               That watch repaired! You're under some illusion.

LEANDER: Tobacco! Watches! What's all this confusion?

CARLIN: You've done it now. I'll bet that watch is in
               The shop six months before it runs again.

LEANDER: Enough! Go find Clarice, express my wishes
               To see her, if the moment is propitious.
               Describe my love, my agony awaiting
               The marriage that we're both anticipating.
               Quick! On your way!

CARLIN (*holding the watch to his ear*):This watch is badly broken.
               Why not give it to me, sir, as a token
               Of your largesse . . .

LEANDER: What's that? Why do you stand
               About so? Run!

CARLIN: I am at your command. (*Leaves.*)

ISABELLE: Let us approach.

LEANDER (*not seeing the girls, and thinking he is still speaking
               to* CARLIN):   Be careful not to tell
               Clarice too much concerning Isabelle.
               Tell her my heart remains untouched and pure;
               The tender bonds between us are secure.
               Isabelle's pretty, but she scarcely can
               Expect the love of any prudent man.
               Look past her simple pose and you will see
               She's a coquette.

LISETTE: (*to* ISABELLE):   Your curiosity
               Earned that. Eavesdropping's dangerous, you'll find.

LEANDER (*still thinking he is speaking to* CARLIN):

Is that accursed watch still on your mind?
Forget about it. Try to make her see
That Isabelle could gain no hold on me.
My uncle works in vain for an alliance.
There's not the slightest chance of my compliance.

ISABELLE: He doesn't love me much, Lisette.

LEANDER (*still thinking he is speaking to* CARLIN): It's true
Lisette has been a bad influence too.
A constant talker and a constant plotter,
In town she'd be just like a fish in water.

LISETTE (*to* ISABELLE):
Now that you know how you and I appear,
May I at last announce that we are here?

LEANDER: Of course you may. But hurry! How I yearn
To hear what she will tell you in return.
What fools men are to poison all their lives
With those cruel agonies that love contrives.
We savor poison, knowing it destroys.

LISETTE: I've had enough of this. Let's make some noise.
Take the initiative!
(*To* LEANDER) Monsieur, by chance
Could you grant us the favor of glance?

LEANDER (*not seeing them*): Life could be an inestimable treasure
Without that passion poisoning all pleasure.

LISETTE: Welcome back, sir. Allow me to express
My wishes that your trip was a success.

LEANDER (*not seeing them*):
When love exerts his power, there's no resistance.

LISETTE: Monsieur, have charity . . .

LEANDER: Ask heaven's assistance.

LISETTE: We've had his scorn, now here's his pity too.
                (*To* ISABELLE)
                And half of all he said applied to you.
                (*To* LEANDER) Come, turn your eyes this way.

LEANDER: Why, it's Lisette!

LISETTE: Also my mistress.

LEANDER: Ah, that's better yet!
                (*To* ISABELLE)
                No lovelier sight has ever blessed my eyes;
                Wherever you go, there cupid's arrow flies.
                The power of your glances who could measure?
                What joy is his whose presence gives you pleasure!

ISABELLE: Good! Yet your heart remains untouched and pure;
                The tender bonds which hold you are secure.
                I may be pretty, but I scarcely can
                Expect the love of any prudent man.
                Look past my simple pose and you will see
                I'm a coquette.

LEANDER: What an absurdity!
                Lisette, don't you feel any obligation
                To contradict this cruel self-estimation?
                She heeds your words.

LISETTE: True. But I understood
                My influence on her has not been good.
                A constant talker and a constant plotter,
                I'd be in town just like a fish in water.
                Both of us found your little portraits charming;
                Your lack of flattery was most disarming.

LEANDER (*aside*): Carlin, you rascal, you'll soon be repaid
                For all the confidences you've betrayed.

LISETTE: Someone is coming. It's Madame Grognac!
             What evil circumstance has brought her back?

ISABELLE: What did you say, Lisette?

LISETTE: Your mother's here!

ISABELLE: I'm trembling from head to foot in fear!
             I feel the storm already taking shape.
             I beg of you, Monsieur, help me escape!

LEANDER: Slip into my apartment. You can hide
             In perfect safety. She won't look inside.

ISABELLE: Gladly, if you are sure no one will see
             Us while we're there.

LEANDER: Madam, rely on me.

MME GROGNAC (*entering*):
             Where is she, sir? I'm sure you know quite well.

LEANDER: Who, madam?

MME GROGNAC: My girl.

LEANDER: And that's . . .

MME GROGNAC: Isabelle!
             If I can catch that wench I'll box her ears;
             I haven't been so furious in years!
             In the meantime, I've other things to do;
             I also came to have a word with you.
             In brief, I want today to mark the end
             Of your relations with your lady friend.
             You know your uncle's plans, you'd best decide
             That you will take my daughter . . .

LEANDER: As my bride?

MME GROGNAC: Of course! What else? And it is my persuasion
　　　　　　Today is none to soon for the occasion.
　　　　　　The notary is on his way. Please spare
　　　　　　Me any more delays in this affair.
　　　　　　My mind is made up, sir. I'm tired of waiting.
　　　　　　Guarding her is just too debilitating. (*She goes.*)

LEANDER: That fortune has me trapped. My mind's a blank.

(*Enter* CARLIN *and* CLARICE.)

CARLIN: Here is Clarice, and you have me to thank
　　　　　　For telling her your mind.

LEANDER: Madame, I lack
　　　　　　The words to show my joy. What brought you back?

CLARICE: To say that though the forfeit must be paid,
　　　　　　My uncle is prepared to give us aid.
　　　　　　That cheers my heart, but I still fear for you.
　　　　　　What guarantee have I that you'll be true?

LEANDER: These doubts do me great wrong, Clarice. I swear
　　　　　　My heart is yours. You have no rival there.

A LACKEY (*entering, to* CLARICE):
　　　　　　This is a note for you my master writ. (*He goes.*)

CARLIN: (*to the* LACKEY *as he goes*):
　　　　　　I see you are a gentleman of wit.

CLARICE (*reading the note*):
　　　　　　It's from that witness that you wanted me
　　　　　　To gain for you — here is his guarantee.
　　　　　　He wants an answer; I'll write one upstairs,
　　　　　　Then we can get back to our own affairs.

LEANDER (*stopping her*):
　　　　　　Why go upstairs? In my room you can find

> Whatever you need for writing.

CLARICE: You won't mind?

LEANDER: Not in the slightest. Tell me that you'll stay.

CLARICE: I'd be delighted, if you feel that way.
I want to thank him for his interest in you,
And hope his trust and friendship will continue.
I'll only be a minute. (*She enters the apartment.*)

CARLIN: There's no doubt
That all your troubles now are working out.
It seems you can rely on heaven's grace.

LISETTE (*in the apartment*):
Come quickly, madam. Leave this dreadful place!

CARLIN: Monsieur, what does that frightful racket mean
In your apartment? Could Clarice have seen
A ghost?

LEANDER: No, something worse I am afraid.
Carlin, I'm lost. What a mistake I've made!
I told Clarice that she should step inside,
Forgetting I told Isabelle to hide
In the same place.

CARLIN: I'm horrified. Have you
Any idea what carnage may ensue?
Have you gone mad?

(*Enter* ISABELLE, CLARICE *and* LISETTE.)

CARLIN: Ah, what prosperity!
We sent in one, and she turns into three!

ISABELLE (*to* CLARICE): No, madam, I insist. It would be better
If I retire, so you can write your letter.

CLARICE: No, I insist. I'm leaving him with you;
             I'd never interrupt a rendez-vous.

LEANDER: Ladies! Blame chance, not me! I never planned
             For you to meet; I'm sure you understand.
             (*To* ISABELLE) Just now your mother . . .

ISABELLE: I am in despair.

LEANDER (*to* CLARICE): Madam, you know . . .

CLARICE: I neither know nor care.

LEANDER (*to* ISABELLE): I never realized . . .

ISABELLE (*leaving*):   You are a traitor.

LEANDER (*to* CLARICE): It was mere chance . . .

CLARICE (*leaving*):   Don't try to find me later.

LISETTE (*to* CARLIN): A nice trick, Monsieur Carlin, and I pray
             You'll get the beating you have earned today.
             (*She leaves.*)

CARLIN: I'm crushed.

LEANDER: And I. What trials fate has sent!
             Let's follow them and urge them to relent! (*Goes.*)

CARLIN: Yes, and at once! Neither of them were fooling.
             I wouldn't be surprised to find them dueling!

ACT IV

(*Enter* VALERE *and* CLARICE.)

CLARICE: Your willingness to help us is most kind
             But since I spoke to you, I've changed my mind.

VALERE: What's that?

CLARICE: No wedding plans for me.

VALERE: Oh, no?
             You felt quite differently not long ago.

CLARICE: I started thinking seriously of things —
             The almost certain sorrows that marriage brings;
             Loss of that freedom I'm so jealous of;
             How often marriage is the tomb of love.
             I don't want family life yet. I'm afraid
             I have no choice but to remain a maid.

VALERE: Marriage can be distasteful, I agree,
             But no more so than any state might be.
             You asked me for my help in this, I think.

CLARICE: Yes, but as one gets closer to the brink
             The dangers that one runs become more clear.
             Leander's heart is not all mine, I fear.
             And he won't change his heart at your request.

VALERE: Why not leave that to me? Don't be distressed.
             I'll answer for Leander. It is clear
             The love he offers to you is sincere.
             Without that love, indeed, he'd lack the talents
             To keep those shifting wits of his in balance.

THE CHEVALIER (*entering*):

I'm glad I found you, uncle. Since you rate
A thorough dressing-down, I'll tell you straight . . .

VALERE: A nice beginning.

THE CHEVALIER: How have you preserved
                A name for wisdom that's so undeserved?
                If I'd behaved as you did, doubtless you
                Would have called me a fool. Isn't that true?

VALERE: I was in error, but . . .

THE CHEVALIER: But! But!

CLARICE: Why fight?

THE CHEVALIER: Isabelle, whom I love with all my might,
                And who loves me still more, had tricked her mother,
                Who hates me, into thinking me another.
                Just then monsieur arrived, and calling out
                My name, put all our strategems to rout.
                Isn't that so?

VALERE: It is, I must admit.
                But I have promised to atone for it.

THE CHEVALIER: It's odd, upon my soul, when youth must give
                Instruction to the old on how to live;
                When grey-haired men behave as foolishly
                As the most empty-headed young marquis.
                In times like these, it's best to sell your goods,
                Shun man entirely, and take to the woods.

VALERE: You should be married, and your sister too.

THE CHEVALIER: What? Not my sister!

VALERE: Why? What's that to you?

THE CHEVALIER: What an injustice! Would you pillage me?
        Isn't a girl in our society
        Told to renounce the world if that's the way
        To make her brother rich?

CLARICE: Whatever you say
        I know your heart is good. You feel you need
        The money I might get?

THE CHEVALIER: I do indeed.

VALERE: She'll get five thousand crowns. You have my oath
        The rest is yours. That's quite enough for both.
        Let's get this business finished up today. (*He goes.*)

THE CHEVALIER: Let me explain my feelings. If I may
        Speak frankly, as I've always done before,
        Marriage I think you'd find a dreadful bore.
        Your shape is lovely, not an ounce of fat.
        Just think of what a child will do to that!
        Believe me, marriage is a poor career.

CLARICE: And yet you're getting married, brother dear.

THE CHEVALIER: A thousand cares will occupy your mind.
        You hope for roses, but its thorns you'll find.
        Marriage's joys are few, its pains severe.

CLARICE: And yet you're getting married, brother dear.

THE CHEVALIER: Let us speak frankly, and admit our flaws;
        We're both flirtatious souls, doubtless because
        Our mother always was. People suspect
        It runs in families. Now, it's no defect,
        But if you're married and some handsome lad
        Catches your eye, then it's considered bad.

CLARICE: And yet . . .

THE CHEVALIER: Don't bother. Your response is clear —
                "And yet you're getting married, brother dear."
                Sister, your answers always are the same.

CLARICE: Brother, so is your counsel. Who's to blame?

LISETTE (*entering*): Thanks to your joking, sir, Madame Grognac
                Is like a dragon ready to attack.
                I came to warn you if she gets her way
                She'll tie Leander down this very day.
                She has commissioned me just now to get
                A notary.

THE CHEVALIER: Good, good. We'll thwart her yet.

LISETTE (*seeing* CLARICE):
                Ah, you here, madame? Would you mind confiding
                In whose apartment you will next be hiding?
                Whose jealousy are you defying here
                In secret meeting with the Chevalier?

THE CHEVALIER: In secret meeting? What does that imply?
                This is my sister!

LISETTE: What a nasty lie!

CLARICE: Let me explain. Leander said I might
                Use his room for a note I had to write;
                Inside was Isabelle. I thought I'd die.

THE CHEVALIER: Isabelle!

CLARICE: And Lisette.

THE CHEVALIER: The rogue! She's sly,
                But little tricks like this should make me wary
                Of what I must expect the day we marry.

LISETTE: If she were tricking you, then you could fret,

But there's no need for you to get upset.
Don't you recall how Madame Grognac fell
On us and our "Italian master?"

THE CHEVALIER: Well?

LISETTE: Well, fearing she'd return with even more
Vituperation than we got before,
We rushed into Leander's room in fright.
Just after that, Clarice came in to write
A letter. There's no mystery, you see.

THE CHEVALIER: One wants to write, the other wants to flee,
And a young man's apartment suits them both —
An excellent asylum, on my oath!

CLARICE: Lisette, what you have said is very cheering;
I find all my suspicions disappearing.
Such trust may well be foolish on my part,
But once again Leander has my heart.

THE CHEVALIER: Sister, hear me.

CLARICE: Brother, what should I do?

THE CHEVALIER: A convent is what I'd advise for you.

CLARICE: That's good advice, I'm sure, since you're so clever.
It's not quite worth five thousand crowns, however.
(*She departs.*)

THE CHEVALIER: Your empty-headedness caused this dissent!
A woman's tongue's a cursed instrument!
Why cure her jealousy? Could it have hurt you?

LISETTE: What? Shouldn't I defend my mistress's virtue?
Someone is coming. I'll be on my way.
(*She leaves as LEANDER enters.*)

THE CHEVALIER (*aside*): Leander. Good! I have a word to say
        To him. (*To* LEANDER)
                Monsieur, good fortune brings you here.

LEANDER (*to* CARLIN): Let's wait a bit. Perhaps she'll reappear.

THE CHEVALIER: My would-be brother-in-law! I understand,
        Of course, why you desire my sister's hand.
        She's rich in virtues; that must be allowed.
        With money, though, she's not so well endowed.
        Our father left us just enough to pay
        His debts, and live in our accustomed way —
        Little enough, I swear, to make one glad.

LEANDER: Was he the only father that you had?

THE CHEVALIER: What?

LEANDER: I meant sister. I was just confused.

CARLIN (*to* CHEVALIER): A natural error. Don't be so amused.

THE CHEVALIER: Your birth is good, so is your reputation;
        On both those counts I'd have no hesitation.
        One failing, though, betrays you all the time;
        A minor thing, it's certainly no crime,
        And yet I'd like to see you let it go.
        You tend to get distracted, as you know,
        And many feel that lapses of this kind
        Are evidence of an unstable mind.

LEANDER: Monsieur, much as I'd like to earn your praise,
        All men are fools, although in different ways.
        Chacun à sa folie — and I'm content
        That I have no worse folly to repent.

THE CHEVALIER: I only mention it in friendship's name.
        Myself, I don't see anything to blame.
        You're wise enough for me, but you should know

That other people do not find you so.

LEANDER: Gossiping's pleasant, but no one relies
Upon its accuracy, if he's wise.
All men are misers when it comes to praise;
If virtue's present, they avert their gaze,
But see how diligent they are to mention
The slightest fault that comes to their attention.
I'm certain I've dismissed as quite untrue
A hundred things I've heard concerning you.

THE CHEVALIER: What sort of thing, monsieur, just or unjust?
No one looked down upon my birth, I trust?

LEANDER: Oh, no.

THE CHEVALIER: I'll wager no one dared suggest
My courage wasn't up to any test.

LEANDER: No.

THE CHEVALIER: Was I charged with insolence, conceit,
Ingratitude, duplicity, deceit?

LEANDER (*taking his snuff-box, he upsets it; then takes his
gloves for his handkerchief*):
I've never met a person who suspected
That you had any vice that you've suggested.
Still, you could have a better reputation.
It's said (unjustly, in my estimation)
Your willingness to curb your tongue is weak,
That no one's safe from slander when you speak.
It's said your tongue won't give your mind a chance,
That all you're fit to do is sing and dance,
That, wishing to be thought a man of fashion
Made desperate by customary passion,
You passed whole winter nights by Iris's door,
Although she'd never seen your face before.
I've heard it claimed champagne delights you so

That you must always have a friend in tow
To point you homeward when your wits have fled,
Or even now and then put you to bed.
But what's all that? I'm sure I have received
A hundred tales that I have not believed.
A man, if he is prudent, always fears
To trust too much the bad reports he hears.

THE CHEVALIER: Farewell. (*He goes.*)

CARLIN (*after him*):   Monsieur musician, we implore
You, sing to us of Bacchus just once more.

CARLIN: I'm glad to see you put him in his place.
For him to censure you is a disgrace.
If anything, I think you were too kind.

LEANDER: Another worry occupies my mind.
Clarice, remember, is enraged with me,
And giving up herself to jealousy,
Calls me a rogue, committed to betraying.
And Isabelle, what do you think she's saying?

CARLIN: It's your own fault for letting your distraction
So often lead you to some foolish action.
Your wit and grace are worthy of the stage,
Sometimes you reason like a Grecian sage,
But other times the things you do and say
Are quite enough to get you locked away.

LEANDER: Rascal, are you aware comments like these
Could lead to your dismissal?

CARLIN: Master, please!
I never dreamed of asking you to change.

LEANDER: Nor would I. Though my manner may seem strange,
In these days when men often fear to show
Their face or heart to anyone they know

The flaw that bothers you, lack of attention,
Just proves the honesty of my intention.
Look in my heart, you'll find I don't prepare
Unworthy lies to trap my neighbors there.
My thoughts are always open to inspection;
Whatever I do, I do without reflexion.
I follow nature — if from time to time
I seem a bit distracted, it's no crime.

CARLIN: A bagatelle! The greatest wits no doubt
Don't know what conversations are about,
Dream in a chair, respond with some inanity,
Consider odd and foreign all humanity —
This is your little flaw, you can't deny it,
And not your only one.

LEANDER: Rascal, be quiet!
(absent-mindedly removing his valet's cravat)
The shallow thinker finds one thought sufficient;
In conversation, therefore, he's proficient,
But those involved in deeper meditation
May be exempted from that obligation.

CARLIN (*putting his cravat back on*):
I understand, sir, but with your permission,
I'd like to keep my necktie in position.
It's really rather early to retire.

LEANDER (*unbuttoning his valet's jerkin*):
What lesser fault could anyone require?
And after all, it's not our obligation
To join with fools in foolish conversation.
My thoughts are worth a hundred of their speeches;
Why then turn my attention to these leeches?
That callow youth who interrupts my thinking
With boring tales of women and of drinking;
The jester whose poor jibes assault my ears
And move me not to laughter but to tears;
The bore without a trace of wit among

His anecdotes, who will not hold his tongue . . .

CARLIN (*buttoning his jerkin back up*):
              Master, my coat! What are you thinking of?

LEANDER: I fear some alteration in my love,
              The charming creature's angry, and I fear
              To face her, though my conscience is quite clear.

CARLIN: In such a case there is a course of action
              I've used myself with utmost satisfaction.
              Your next encounter with her may go better
              If it's preceded by a stylish letter
              Apologizing, saying you were seized
              By your distraction.

LEANDER: I'd be very pleased
              If this gained the results that you expect.

CARLIN: A letter always has a good effect;
              A few scrawled words will usually suffice
              To patch up lovers' quarrels in a trice.

LEANDER: Carlin, this once I'll trust in what you say.
              Go fetch a pen and paper right away.

CARLIN: Wait here, monsieur, I won't be very long. (*He goes.*)

LEANDER (*alone*): I must show her her jealousy is wrong,
              Correct her error. Ah, charming Clarice,
              My unaffected heart will never cease
              To burn for you as it is burning now,
              And my hand's ready to confirm this vow.

CARLIN (*returns, giving* LEANDER *a book*): Here, master.

LEANDER: Are you drunk? You go to look
              For pen and paper and bring back a book!

CARLIN: You're right. Now I've contracted your disease.
                He who lies down with dogs gets up with fleas.
                Your absent-mindedness, you can't deny it,
                Spreads very easily.

LEANDER: Will you be quiet?
                I'm tired of your unfruitful conversation.
                Valets are contrary by inclination.

CARLIN (*bringing in a table and inkwell*):
                Enough! I brought all this here for your use!

LEANDER (*sitting down to write*): Let's have it.

CARLIN: Now what prose can you produce?
                Or ask Apollo's aid; you could do worse
                Than to conduct your whole campaign in verse.
                Elegies, sonnets, ballads — never fear it,
                Women love poetry.

LEANDER: Some evil spirit
                Is in these pens; not one of them will write.

CARLIN: If you would use the inkwell, sir, they might.
                The sand you're using now won't leave a trace.

LEANDER: Well then I'll follow fashion in this case.

CARLIN (*aside*): For lovers, writing is a useful art.
                It brings together those that are apart;
                Betrothals, pleading, assignations, fighting,
                All of love's business is involved with writing.
                If all the lovers' notes were forced to share
                The taxes that official papers bear,
                This new taxation doubtless would yield more
                Income in one year than the old in four.

LEANDER (*shaking the inkwell over his letter instead of the sand*):
                My letter's finished.

CARLIN: Master, stop and think!
            You've covered everything you've done with ink!
            What sort of painting did you have in mind?

LEANDER: I'm often too impetuous, I find.

CARLIN (*holding up the letter*):
            If you want peace, this hardly will promote it.
            — A note which looks as if some devil wrote it.
            Not even a writing expert could get through
            This indecipherable billet-doux.

LEANDER (*starting to write again*):
            Then I'll start over. I don't count as lost
            Whatever time I take. It's worth the cost.

CARLIN: Poor Isabelle. She has my sympathy.

LEANDER: Isabelle?

CARLIN: Yes.

LEANDER: Don't mention her to me.

CARLIN: All right, but if you want to be productive
            A note to bearer may prove more seductive
            Than all the twaddle one in vain employs.
            Why not try sending that?

LEANDER: Stop all that noise!

CARLIN (*aside*): A lady who receives a little note
            Folded into a letter that you wrote
            Before she reads the letter will decide,
            Like all of us, to look at what's inside.
            Her glance falls on the note. What does it say?
            (LEANDER *absent-mindedly writes what* CARLIN
            is saying.) "Monsieur, for value given me please pay

To mademoiselle who bears this, the amount
In case, two thousand crowns from my account."
God knows the value! Next to such a suit,
Cicero's art and eloquence are mute!

LEANDER (*writing*): For servile souls it may be that is how
    One buys or sells a heart.

CARLIN: But ladies now
    Dabble in commerce.

LEANDER (*finishes the letter*):   There. I've had my say.
    Please get it stamped and send it on its way.

CARLIN: Heaven be praised. The crisis then is passed?
    You've conquered your distractedness at last?
    I didn't really think you could avoid
    The sort of folly you've always enjoyed.

LEANDER: You're insolent.

CARLIN: It's friendship makes me so.

LEANDER: Here. Take this letter where it ought to do.
    My love is in your hands. Make no delay.
    I'd like to have her answer back today.

CARLIN: I'd borrow the wings of Mercury, dear master,
    If that would bring your answer any faster.
    (LEANDER *goes, leaving* CARLIN *alone*.)
    Uniting lovers, that's a task most dear
    To my own heart — but what's this written here?
    "To Isabelle." My vision can't be right;
    Some dark cloud has perhaps obscured my sight.
    No, heaven be thanked, I still have two good eyes.
    Sir! Sir! He's disappeared; that's no surprise.
    I'm absolutely sure, whatever he wrote
    That he meant for Clarice to get this note.
    But on the outside is the other name.

If I could only guess what was his game —
Perhaps he's telling Isabelle his heart
Is pledged elsewhere, and that they have to part.
This note, I'm sure, gives her that information;
My heart assures me that's the situation.
Ah, happy is the master who can find
A valet with a light and facile mind;
With him, there never needs to be a doubt,
The vaguest orders will be carried out! (*He goes.*)

ACT V

*(Enter ISABELLE, LISETTE and CARLIN, ISABELLE holding
an open letter.)*

ISABELLE: He must have thought my heart an easy prey
     If he could try to capture it this way!

CARLIN *(to* ISABELLE): I never said that.

LISETTE *(to* CARLIN):   Does he hope to win
     Our admiration for his lovely skin?
     Or what is worse, for yours?

CARLIN: Mine's not so rough.

ISABELLE: As if he hadn't injured me enough,
     He now sends love notes for Clarice to me.

CARLIN *(aside)*: That's what the traitor did, it's plain to see.

ISABELLE: My answer to this insult should be clear.

CARLIN: Madam, please listen.

ISABELLE: I don't wish to hear.

CARLIN: Grant me a single word.

ISABELLE: Scoundrel, depart!
     Conduct your plots with someone else's heart!

CARLIN: You shouldn't treat a messenger this way.

LISETTE: Farewell.

CARLIN: You know . . .

LISETTE: Get out! What's the delay?

CARLIN: I'm an envoy. At least respect my station.

LISETTE: For lackeys, we have no consideration.

(CARLIN *departs*.)

LISETTE: So much for him and all he had to say.
             Here comes the Chevalier the other way.

THE CHEVALIER (*entering, to* ISABELLE):
             What state is your tormenting mother in?
             Can we avoid arousing her again?

ISABELLE: You know we can't. I'm trembling with fear
             That she'll return and find me with you here.

THE CHEVALIER: Don't waste another thought in that direction.
             While you are here, you're under my protection.
             Aren't you my wife? There's no need for delay.
             I drew our marriage contract up today.
             My uncle has it.

LISETTE: That's progress indeed.
             The contract all drawn up! You only need
             One minor thing, Madame Grognac's permission.

ISABELLE: It won't be easy changing her position.

THE CHEVALIER: All right, then. I'll postpone the celebration
             And try once more to win her approbation.
             I'll grovel at her feet, assault her ears
             With groans and weeping; I'm quite good at tears.
             Lisette will help. Despite Madame's disgust
             We'll flatter her so winningly she must
             At last give me the prize my love deserves.

LISETTE: Your flattery may just get on her nerves.
              You won't reduce her stubbornness, I fear.
              But look, here comes your sister, Chevalier.

THE CHEVALIER (*to* CLARICE, *as she enters*):
              Well, sister, tell us, are you still pursuing
              The same goal as before? How are you doing?

CLARICE: I hope at last Leander's fate and mine
              Will be united by our uncle.

ISABELLE: Fine!
              Since that's the way you and Leander feel,
              Friendship and reason force me to reveal
              A love-letter he wrote me. Here, you see?

CLARICE: He wrote this?

ISABELLE: Yes.

THE CHEVALIER: Then where does that put me?
              What odious rival's pleadings have you heard?

ISABELLE (*to* THE CHEVALIER):
              I'll tell you everything that has occurred.
              Just come along with me. Don't make a fuss.
              (*To* CLARICE) Here is the note. It's valueless to us.

THE CHEVALIER (*to* CLARICE): Good evening, sister.
              (*To* ISABELLE)   Madam, now you must
              Clear up this matter to regain my trust.

(THE CHEVALIER *and* ISABELLE *depart, leaving* CLARICE
              alone.)

CLARICE: What have I heard? Can I believe my sight?
              I need more evidence. What did he write?
              "To Isabelle." Heavens, I am betrayed!
              His perfidy is openly displayed.

Here comes his man. (CARLIN *enters*.)
You bearer of disaster,
Impudent servant of an evil master,
Who is this letter for? Not Isabelle?

CARLIN: It's for her, but it's not for her as well.

CLARICE: Your foolish words aren't leading me astray
Stay where you are. Don't try to get away
(*She reads.*)
"I am in despair, mademoiselle, that the adventure in
my study has given you some suspicion of my
fidelity."
What of that, rascal? Speak!
(*She takes him by the cravat.*)

CARLIN: Upon my life,
That letter is a constant source of strife!
Oof, I give up! You're cutting off my wind!
You could at least read through it to the end!

CLARICE: Read more, you scoundrel? Why should I endure
More shame when his guilt is already sure?

CARLIN: We servants merely follow where we're led.
Here comes my master. Strangle him instead.

(LEANDER *enters, plunged in reverie*)

CLARICE (*aside*): I'd hardly blame myself if I attacked him!

CARLIN (*low to* CLARICE):
Don't speak too loud; you're likely to distract him!

CLARICE: Ah, here you are, monsieur. You hoped, no doubt,
To find my rival still somewhere about?

LEANDER (*coming out of his reverie*):
Ah, madam, have you read the note I sent?

CLARICE: Yes, traitor, if it's Isabelle's you meant!
My rival spurned it without hesitation;
At least my vengeance has that consulation.

LEANDER: What? Carlin gave your note to Isabelle?
The rascal! I will see he's beaten well
For this confusion. Every day he tries
My patience with his trickery and lies.
I see him! Traitor, tell me, on your life,
What did you hope to gain from all this strife?
I'll kill you with these hands!

CARLIN: Let me be spared,
I pray you, master, till my will's prepared.
(*Aside*) I never saw a piece of writing lead
To such an uproar!

LEANDER: Then confess your deed!
You sent my note astray. What was your reason?
What evil spirit led you to such treason?

CARLIN: Treason? No, sir! I've always served you well.
I gave it carefully to Isabelle.

LEANDER (*drawing his sword*):
Your own words seal your doom. Prepare to die.

CARLIN: Master, why kill me?

LEANDER: What? You don't know why?

CARLIN: You may be justified — how can I tell?

LEANDER: I sent it Clarice, not Isabelle!

CARLIN: Master, may I be hanged if I recall
Your mentioning Clarice's name at all.

LEANDER: That's no excuse. Her name was on the note.

Whatever I said, "Clarice" was what I wrote.
(*To* CLARICE) Look at the letter. It's a silent witness
Of how I've been betrayed by his unfitness!

CARLIN (*aside*): Good! My turn now!

LEANDER (*To* CARLIN):   Come, wretch, or I'll compel
You to read it with me! Read! "To Isabelle."

CARLIN: Master, I must admit I've never seen
Another person with a wit so keen:
"Read with me, wretch . . ."

LEANDER: Ah, Madam, please don't make
My heart the sufferer for my hand's mistake.
My love for you sometimes affects my brain.

CLARICE: Your pleas, inconstant wretch, are quite in vain.
So gross a lie is not to be endured.

CARLIN: He means no evil, madam, be assured.
If he weren't mad — distracted I should say
He'd be a perfect soul in every way.

LEANDER: If you'd just read my letter, see what's in it,
Your cruel suspicions wouldn't last a minute.

CLARICE: My curiosity's quite satisfied.
I've read enough.

CARLIN: Heavens! Just look inside.
Change the address, you change the contents too.
Your arm is strong, see what your wits can do.

CLARICE (*reads*): "I am in despair, mademoiselle, that the
adventure in my study has given you some suspicion
of my fidelity. Your rival will serve only to make
your triumph more complete. Monsieur, please pay
to mademoiselle who bears this for value given me.

God knows the value."

CARLIN: Fie, madam! Are you making fun of me?
               That's not what's written there.

CLARICE: Just look and see.

CARLIN (*To* LEANDER): I find it strangely tactless, I must say,
               To mix your love and business in this way.
               Did you think such a note would solve the matter?

LEANDER: While I was writing, rogue, your idle chatter
               Confused my thoughts and altered my design.

CARLIN: It's hard to keep from quoting wit like mine.

CLARICE (*continuing to read*): "Yes, lovely Clarice, I adore only
               you and will find my sole happiness in loving you
               for the rest of my life."

CARLIN (*to* CLARICE):
               There are some sentiments more to your taste.
               Your strangling, you see, was quite misplaced.

CLARICE: I breathe again, Carlin. What a delight
               It is to find your lover in the right,
               When those suspicions you've been guilty of
               Change effortlessly to transports of love.

LEANDER: Whatever faults distraction leads me to
               There's room for no one in my heart but you.

CARLIN (*to* CLARICE):
               It's true; he finds the sight of you so pleasant
               He can't believe you even when you're present.
               Here comes your uncle to confirm your vow.

VALERE (*entering, to* LEANDER):
               I came in haste to tell you sir that now

I'll have the pleasure at long last it seems
To see fulfilled your two hearts' fondest dreams.

LEANDER: Can we rely upon your help, Valere?

VALERE: I've vowed to disentangle this affair.
The forfeit still remains, we've got to clear
That up and marry off the Chevalier.
We won't do either of them easily.

CARLIN: A little strategem occurs to me. (*To* LEANDER)
In the old lady's eyes you have no merit
Aside from all the money you'll inherit.

LEANDER: That's so.

CARLIN: Then I've an idea for a plot
To show her something's true that's really not.

VALERE: I have a contract in my pocket.

CARLIN: Good.
She's never even seen me yet. I could
Without the slightest trouble carry through
The idea I've conceived to rescue you.

VALERE: But do you think . . .

CARLIN: Trust me! I'll be right back!

VALERE: Someone is coming. It's Madame Grognac.

CARLIN: The stage is set. We've everything we need.
Watch what I'm doing. Follow up my lead.

(*Enter* MADAME GROGNAC, THE CHEVALIER, ISABELLE,
and LISETTE.)

THE CHEVALIER: My mind's made up. I won't let you retire

Until I get the answer I desire.
I'll marry Isabelle whatever you say.
There's no one better for her, and you may
Rage all you like. You haven't any choice.

MME GROGNAC: You must be joking. Haven't I a voice
In where my daughter turns her inclinations?
I don't want any fools for my relations!

THE CHEVALIER: Come, madam . . .

MME GROGNAC: Quiet!

ISABELLE: Mother . . .

MME GROGNAC: You be silent!

THE CHEVALIER: Give in to nature.

MME GROGNAC: No!

VALERE: Come, you're too violent.

MME GROGNAC: And you're impertinent! Sir, you've provided
Enough loose talk. The matter is decided.
Monsieur will wed my daughter, and to spare
Us all from any more of this affair,
I've even summoned up a notary.

THE CHEVALIER: He won't get any signature from me.

MME GROGNAC: Where are we then?
(*To* LEANDER) I take it, sir, the most
That you can do is stand there like a post.

VALERE: He doesn't seem too eager to assent.

MME GROGNAC (*to* VALERE) :
Don't get your hopes up. It's not my intent,

Whichever way Leander may decide,
To let my daughter be your nephew's bride.
He is a fool, his conduct crude and low.

VALERE: He dances the gavotte sometimes, I know.

MME GROGNAC: A libertine, in debt to everyone,
                    A scatter-brain . . .

THE CHEVALIER: Pray, madam, when you're done,
                    Pass on to why we shouldn't be united.

LISETTE: Here comes a messenger. He seems excited.

CARLIN (*entering, in disguise*):
                    Monsieur! At last I've found you! How distressed
                    You'll be! Your uncle sends — Oof, let me rest —
                    A message — Wait —

CLARICE (*to* CARLIN):   Wait? What else can we do?

LEANDER: Perhaps he sent a letter on with you?

CARLIN: No. Since he died his writing's fallen off.

THE CHEVALIER (*laughing*): It's Carlin.

CARLIN (*to* THE CHEVALIER): Monsieur, you do wrong to scoff.
                    Rather prepare to give yourself to tears
                    When the cruel news I bring assaults your ears.
                    In eons still to come, the thought of this
                    Will keep all heirs from any hopes of bliss.

CLARICE: Tell us, then, what's the frightful news you bring?

CARLIN: The will of man is such a fickle thing!
                    No sooner had you left your uncle's bed
                    Than he called in his notary and said
                    Since you'd been so unwilling to abide

The girl that he'd selected for your bride,
And since he'd been informed you loved Clarice,
He had decided, out of pure caprice,
To change his will, in spite of all my prayers,
And give his wealth away to other heirs.
For you, the miser didn't even leave
Enough to buy an armband for your sleeve.

MME GROGNAC: Heavens! Can this be true?

LEANDER: What a disgrace!
            I'm doomed forever to my humble place.

MME GROGNAC: I must applaud. You would have been at least
            As well chastised if I'd been the deceased.

CARLIN: Alas, what's to be done?

MME GROGNAC (*to* CARLIN):   Don't bother me.
            (*To* LEANDER)
            Monsieur, go elsewhere with your poverty;
            Our plans are off. I'm sure you understand
            A man of means deserves my daughter's hand.

VALERE: You need not fear a similar disgrace
            If my nephew should take Leander's place.
            If you will just accept the Chevalier,
            He'll have my fortune guaranteed and clear.

MME GROGNAC: He is a fool.

THE CHEVALIER: And has been so from birth,
            And will continue so. Whatever I'm worth
            Is based on that, and on my humorous turns.

MME GROGNAC: The memory of that gavotte still burns.

VALERE: Here is the contract. Get a pen, Lisette.

LISETTE (*bringing a pen*): Here's all that's necessary.

MME GROGNAC (*signing*):   There. It's set.
        I'll sign provided that you guarantee
        His folly will be checked, to some degree.

VALERE (*signing*): Agreed.
        (*To* LEANDER)
        And for the love which you have shown,
        Be happy, sir. Clarice is now your own.

MME GROGNAC (*to* VALERE):
        Are you a man, monsieur? Can you
        Give her a man who doesn't have a sou?

VALERE (*to* MME GROGNAC):
        There's no need to continue your confusion,
        Madam. Leander's loss was an illusion,
        A trick here servant Carlin played, designed
        To stimulate in you a change of mind.

MME GROGNAC (*to* CARLIN): Come here, sir!

CARLIN (*aside*):   Here's the denouement, I'm sure!

MME GROGNAC: The uncle, so you said, could not endure
        Leander's choice, so he was disinherited?

CARLIN: It seems that my assumption was unmerited.
        Thanks be to God for that!

MME GROGNAC: I'm devastated!

LISETTE: What right have you to be so aggravated?
        You showed us all the proper way to marry
        The day you let your noble husband carry
        You off and never raised the least objection.
        Your daughter's clearly nearer to perfection.

MME GROGNAC (*to* ISABELLE): Wretch!

ISABELLE: Hear me!

MME GROGNAC: Quiet! You'll enrage me yet!

THE CHEVALIER (*to* MME GROGNAC):
                 Stop growling, or we'll have a minuet!

CARLIN (*to* MME GROGNAC): You'll pay the forfeit now.

VALERE: Let's be resigned
              With a good grace, since everything is signed.
              To calm your spirits for the trick we've played
              On you, I'll see myself the forfeit's paid,
              And I will give my niece the same amount.

MME GROGNAC: I'm in despair. I hope that you don't count
              On me to bless your tricks.
              (*To* VALERE)   You'll never see
              A single sou of dowry come from me.
              The marriage costs will all revert to you;
              You started this, and you can carry through;
              And I'll attempt, while you join heart to heart,
              To keep them and their property apart! (*She goes.*)

VALERE: Now, all inside. Let's start the celebrations.

THE CHEVALIER: First, girls, embrace, since you are now relations,
              And in the future, please be sure that you
              Don't find yourselves both in one rendez-vous.

ISABELLE: I'll be much more discreet in my affairs.

CLARICE: Next time I won't be taken unawares.

(*All leave but* LEANDER *and* CARLIN.)

LEANDER: Now, Carlin, get my luggage packed today.

I want to see my uncle right away!

CARLIN: Forget your uncle! He will be all right.
            You've got another trip to make tonight.
            You're married now! The contract has been signed!

LEANDER: You're right, of course! How did it slip my mind?
            (*He goes.*)

CARLIN: His wife forgotten on her wedding day!
            But he's not to be blamed--it's just his way.
            Tomorrow we'll see--And some of you I'll bet
            Wish you had wives that easy to forget!

END

The Conceited Count

by

Philippe Néricault Destouches

Preface by the author

This comedy has recently been so favorably received by the public that I would feel unworthy of the applause with which I have been honored if I did not feel obliged to offer my gratitude for it. This gratitude is as sincere as it is deep. I am unable to find words to express it, but in order to demonstrate it in the most comprehensible manner, I assure that same public, to whom I am so deeply indebted, that in seeking new entertainment for them I have spared neither pains nor effort to merit the continuation of their indulgence. Although comic characters might seem exhausted, I still have a number of them to present. Not that I am at all unaware of the difficulties and perils of such an undertaking, since the easiest and most striking characters have already been seen on the stage. But success has redoubled my zeal, and perhaps strengthened my forces, and the general approval that my project has stimulated seems to me at least to augur well. It is known that I always keep in mind that great principle stated by Horace:

Omne tulit punctum, qui miscuit utile dulci.

[One will always strike the mark by mixing the useful with the sweet.]

And I believe that dramatic art is to be valued only to the extent that it aims to instruct while pleasing. It has always been my incontestable maxim that however amusing a comedy might be, it is an imperfect and even dangerous work if the author does not seek in it to correct manners, to expose the ridiculous, to condemn vice, and to present virtue in so positive a light that it commands public veneration and esteem. All my audiences have unanimously informed me, and, if I may be permitted to say so, in terms most flattering for me, that they accept with pleasure so reasonable a goal. I do not hesitate even to add that in honoring me with their applause they do honor to themselves. For in the end, what could bring greater glory to our nation, so renowned abroad for so many qualities that have spread its fame everywhere, than when one finds comedies, traditionally thought to have no object beyond that of pleasing and diverting, and even being capable of doing that only briefly, instead fulfilling not only that innocent and allowable goal, but also contributing to instruction and the correcting of manners? It is therefore my responsibility, while giving the public the thanks it deserves for its recognition of my work, to congratulate it on the good taste that it continues to show in supporting works that purify the stage, that purge it of frivolous entertainment, of debauchery, of imitation jewels, of crude puns and stale witticisms, of those base and vicious situations which have often infected it, and rather to render it worthy of the esteem and attendance of honest folk. It is easy to see in all my works, though filled to overflowing with an infinity of flaws, that it is only the spectators of that sort that I have always striven to please. Only a lack of the talent required has prevented me from more fully attaining so legitimate a goal. The sole accomplishment I can boast of is to have taken an approach that seemed original, although after the incomparable Molière, it seems that there is no secret to causing pleasure other than to follow in his footsteps. Yet how bold one must be to follow a model that the wisest and most judicious authors have always considered inimitable! He has left us in despair of equaling him. Rather we must be satisfied if by some new approach we can make ourselves supportable after him! I restricted myself to that in my dramatic work, and the favorable reception that I have received was without doubt due to this essential precaution.

I am no less indebted to the art of my actors, who have employed all their skills and the finesse, particularly in this most recent comedy, to demonstrate their zeal and their friendship for me. I owe this acknowledgment to all of them, without exception, and I offer it to them with as much pleasure as the public credited them by their applause. M. Quinault the elder, in the role of Lycandre, demonstrated that he knew how to change himself into all sorts of characters which, however different they may be from one another, all offer equally to him brilliant occasions to stimulate admiration for his talent and intelligence. He can give to each the proper tone: rendering the gravity, the internal feelings of a father as accurately as he does the sallies, the liveliness, and the grace of a young man, when that is what he must represent. What veneration, what love he has inspired for the unhappy father of the Count of Tufière and Lisette.

I must extend the same praise to his brother, M. Dufresnes, who had the skill to establish the character of the Conceited Count before saying a word simply by the way he comported himself on the stage. What nobility in his bearing! What grandeur in his airs!

What pride in his gait! What art, what grace, what truth in the entire course of the role, and what finesse, what variety in every one of his theatrical turns!

Never was a character more difficult to represent than Lisette, who is both a woman of quality and a serving-maid. To be too comic would be to deny her birth. To be too serious would risk making the piece cold and the character tedious. A perfect balance must be found between the sallies and spirit of a maid and the noble bearing of a young woman of position. This is just what was accomplished with great success by the excellent actress Mlle Quinault, who was responsible for the role of Lisette.

May I be allowed to recall to the public the air of confidence, of joy, of naivete, and the amusing brusque manner of Lisimon, or rather of the judicious and natural actor, M. Duchemin, who appeared under the name of this bourgeois moving into the aristocracy? The great pleasure that he gave to the spectators removed any doubt about his major contribution to the success of my work.

It would be a most agreeable task to eulogize here my other actors, but the fear of annoying my reader by too long a discussion forces me, reluctantly, to set a bound to my expressions of gratitude.

After my pen has offered this justified tribute, I must take this suitable occasion to devote a few lines of censure to the author of a short comedy, or rather a work that has usurped that title, which appeared for several days at the Théâtre Italien [*Polichinelle, Comte de Ponfier*, a parody of *Le Glorieux*, presented in March, 1732 – translator's note]. But although it less becomes me than it might others who could do so to scorn my fellow authors, since I recognize among them talents superior to my own, I think I can keep silent in respect to the author in question here. I will not even condescend to name him and thus draw him from his obscurity. I leave him to operate freely in the theatre which is his only outlet and which is appropriate to his talents, a theatre which exists only by drawing parasitically upon better works, and whose principle merit is in subjecting them to ridicule and subjecting them to envy and bad taste. It is enough for me that the public had the goodness to support my comedy. In approving it, they undertake its defense at the same time that they give their approval. All that remains for me to say now is that I will always be found quite ready to correct my errors upon the advice of impartial and judicious people, as well as to scorn the censure of minor repressed authors who attempt to ease their situation by attacking excessively and indiscriminately everything that the public considers not unworthy of its commendation.

THE CONCEITED COUNT

by

Philippe Néricault Destouches

Premiered at the Comédie-Française
January 18, 1732

CAST OF CHARACTERS

LISIMON, a well-to-do bourgeois

ISABELLE, his daughter

VALERE, his son

THE COUNT OF TUFIÈRE, lover of ISABELLE

PHILINTE, another lover of ISABELLE

LYCANDRE, an old man

M. JOSSE, a notary

LISETTE, ISABELLE's maid

PASQUIN, THE COUNT's valet

LAFLEUR, a lackey of THE COUNT

A LACKEY of LYCANDRE

Other LACKIES of THE COUNT

ACT I

PASQUIN: Lisette will never come; it's all too clear
The rascal only said she'd meet me here
To see if this poor fool would fall
For it. But wait. She's coming after all.

LISETTE: My dear Monsieur Pasquin, consider me
Your servant.

PASQUIN: And I beg to be
The humble servant of the lovely maid
Who serves a lovely mistress.

LISETTE: I'm afraid
I lack a speech sufficiently refined
To answer your sweet compliments in kind.
Accept instead this gesture of respect.
(*She gives him an elaborate curtsey.*)
Have you been waiting long?

PASQUIN: If it's direct
Address you want, my queen, I have to state
You've come to our appointment rather late.

LISETTE: I'm sorry if I was a bit delayed.

PASQUIN: When I was younger, I was quite dismayed
When someone kept me waiting. Age has since
Brought to my youthful spirits temperance.

LISETTE: Maturity is then why you became
More prudent?

PASQUIN: I admit it, to my shame.

LISETTE: Ashamed of being reasonable?

PASQUIN: Yes,
            At least with you, because your eyes confess
            That with more prudence I would please you less.

LISETTE: Indeed? Were you less prudent, I would disappear.

PASQUIN: I understand. You've made it all too clear.
            You'd find a younger lover much too active,
            An honest husband seeming more attractive.
            I'd patiently accept that appellation
            If you'd accept my service in that station.

LISETTE: I must inform you sir, that you have erred.
            My husband or my lover, both absurd!

PASQUIN: Why are we meeting then? What's all the fuss?

LISETTE: We have important matters to discuss.

PASQUIN: What matters?

LISETTE: Ones that have to be resolved.
            Your master and my mistress are involved.
            We need to have the frankest conversation,
            Since, brighter than most others of our station,
            I think we can address the situation.

PASQUIN: I'd love to help.

LISETTE: Just what I want to hear.
            The count your master's distant and severe.
            He's lived three months near us and I would bet
            He hasn't spoken fifteen minutes yet.
            Between ourselves, what sort of man is he?
            I think my mistress favors him, but she
            May not do so much longer, she is witty,
            Charming, intelligent, well-mannered, pretty,
            But one gift that she lacks, as she'll admit
            Is constancy in love. She won't commit

Herself to anyone with any mystery,
Love having such a long deceptive history.
Isabelle's love affairs are quickly started
But don't assume that makes her tender-hearted
In looking past the slightest imperfection
Indeed, she's eagle-eyed in their detection.
Ashamed then of her weakness, she retires,
Her coldness now as great as were her fires.
She breaks off wedding plans without a tear.

PASQUIN: A pleasant character you serve, my dear!
A tender and loving heart, a lively wit
Until she becomes prudent and tired of it.
Above all, a coquette.

LISETTE: No, you're mistaken.
She's no coquette, not fickle, she's not taken
With artifice. Her love is quite sincere
Except it doesn't last. But now let's hear
About your master. Once you have portrayed him
I'll better understand how I can aid him.
I'm taken with him. Why, I hardly know,
But you will see today that it is so.
If he has flaws, we must conspire to hide them
Knowing that Isabelle cannot abide them.
So tell me frankly, what must we suppress
To make his courting of her a success?

PASQUIN: I understand completely, and I'll show
You every trait he has from head to toe.
His better qualities I'll cover first
Then, hiding nothing, I'll reveal the worst.
The good I'll cover quickly so I can
Concentrate on the other. First, the man
Is really, as he claims a count. His bearing
Is not some clever mask that he is wearing.
There is no question of his noble birth.

LISETTE: Mere chance. Go on.

PASQUIN: His military worth
         All France admits, while men at arms admire
         His valor and his courage under fire.
         He's made his mark, that's certain. He's imbued
         With honor, righteousness, and rectitude.
         Excitable, but with a noble heart.
         That is the good side.

LISETTE: Now the other part.

(*Enter* LAFLEUR.)

PASQUIN: Ah, wait, here comes Lafleur. Where did you leave
         The count?

LAFLEUR: At cards, and winning, I believe.
         He's cleaning out some rude provincial who
         Bemoans the loss of each departing sou.
         Our master, all this having hardly heard
         Pockets his cash and never says a word.

PASQUIN: Why did you leave?

LAFLEUR: To bring a proposition
         To you.

PASQUIN: Which is?

LAFLEUR: Resigning my position.

PASQUIN: And why to me?

LAFLEUR: Because I'm well aware
         You have our master's business in your care,
         And fearing I'd enrage him if I said
         I'm leaving him, I came to you instead.

PASQUIN: Lafleur, I am amazed at your suggestion.
         Our master is a model, without question.

How could you think of leaving? It's absurd.

LAFLEUR: Because you talk too much, he not a word.

LISETTE: This is the strangest thing I ever heard.

LAFLEUR: Young lady, I'm no fool. What has occurred
Defies belief. Three months have passed and he
Has not addressed a single word to me.

PASQUIN: Why all this fuss?

LAFLEUR: What's that? Why all this fuss?
Do you approve of treating people thus?
When I can be with him the whole day long
And only get a growl, isn't that wrong?
To think I left a mistress for his sake
Who loved to talk, and talked without a break.
Never a boring moment. She would mention
Every mistake that came to her attention.
I loved —

PASQUIN: To be the subject of attack?

LAFLEUR: I didn't mind, if I could answer back.
To answer is to speak. My master now
The simplest yes or no will not allow.
He's like a tomb, one never hears him speak.
Why, I would rather serve an Arab sheik.
I'm drying up. My limit is exceeded.
What a relief to speak. I really needed
To open up . . . You're laughing!

LISETTE (*laughing*):   Pray, continue.

LAFLEUR: You'll burst if you hold down such things within you.

LISETTE: He's a delight, straightforward, if uncouth.

LAFLEUR: I swear I'm speaking nothing but the truth.

PASQUIN: It's true our master likes his servants quiet,
But no one can complain we suffer by it;
Well fed, well clothed, and certainly well paid —

LAFLEUR: All that won't buy contentment, I'm afraid.
A former master I most sorely miss
(He being dead) I far preferred to this.
Life in his house was totally ascetic.
The food was bad, the wages were pathetic.
For any trifle I would have to beg,
Exposed to winter naked as an egg.
And yet I loved him. Why? Because his chatter
Amused me, and the rest just didn't matter.
He called me chum and pet, my situation
Was like a bosom friend of equal station.
As for the count, one can't get close to him
He's wrapped up in himself; he's always grim.
Proud and disdainful, colder than a Scot,
In simple words, he's everything I'm not!
The highest recompense could never make me
Serve such a master, may the devil take me!

PASQUIN: Have patience! You will catch his eye some day
And find he has a word or two to say.
Await the proper hour. Don't be nervous.
Remember, I've been ten years in his service
And still dare speak but now and then a word.

LISETTE: The suffering of this poor lad has stirred
My heart. Surely you can request
A few words for him.

PASQUIN: Well, I'll do my best.

LAFLEUR: No compromise! Either I'm spoken to
Or else I'm on my way. Bid me adieu.
That's my last word, and I can guarantee

That I'll speak it if no one speaks to me. (*He leaves.*)

PASQUIN: I pity poor Lafleur.

LISETTE: But can it be
The count is prey to such severity?

PASQUIN: That is my second point: it's his observance
Of coldest condescension toward his servants.
Addressing a valet he feels debased
And if one speaks to him, he's soon replaced.
To sum it up, I think he must be rated
The vainest creature nature has created.
He treats his underlings with cold disdain
And even equals look on him as vain.
Proud of his social rank and of his birth,
He thinks there's no one else like him on earth.
Completely sure of his superiority,
He speaks on any matter with authority.
Convinced that his opinion is the best.
He flaunts himself, while scorning all the rest.
In short, he is a monument of pride,
The vainest man, the most self-satisfied.

LISETTE: How funny!

PASQUIN: What?

LISETTE: Your master's disposition,
His vanity's in perfect opposition
To how his humble rival acts. He will
Refuse to speak, for fear of speaking ill.
Although he is a man of wealth and breeding,
He blushes when you meet him, clearly needing
Assurance. He's so fearful of offending
That his civility is never-ending.
His lowest servants speak in awe of how
He never speaks to them without a bow.

PASQUIN: Good Lord, a perfect contrast! This should be
              A most amusing tournament to see.
              This gentle rival is Philinte, no doubt.
              A single glance and he'll be put to rout!

LISETTE: And your proud count is wealthy too, I guess.
              At least he seems so.

PASQUIN: Wealthy? I confess
              He's not, which makes his vanity more grand.
              All of his income, as I understand,
              Comes from his pension and his army pay.
              But he's a clever gambler; that's the way
              That he can live in such magnificence.

LISETTE: And you?

PASQUIN: I can survive, by diligence.
              Sometimes he drops his guard a bit with me.
              I sulk, he smiles, the opportunity
              I seize, then coldly, play him like a fish,
              My brusque demeanor leads him where I wish.
              He tosses me some coins to pacify me,
              And since my heart is good, I let him buy me.

LISETTE: I understand. Now let me take the lead
              Your count is headed for defeat indeed
              In Isabelle's esteem if he but mentions
              His inclination for these vain pretensions.
              She's rather on the easy-going side;
              But one vice she can't tolerate is pride.
              Whatever rank and fame he may expect,
              His speech and manner should be circumspect,
              Modest, straightforward, full of warmth and charity.

PASQUIN: One hardly can imagine more disparity.

LISETTE: He must restrain himself, or she'll reject him.
              Advise him so.

PASQUIN: You hardly can expect him . . .

LISETTE (*interrupting him*):
        Wait! Someone's coming. It's old Lisimon!
        I beg of you, don't leave me here alone!

PASQUIN: Isabelle's father? What on earth's the matter?

LISETTE: He may be fifty-five, but that old satyr
        Still plays the fool, leaving his son Valere
        To be the chaste, mature one of the pair.

LISIMON (*running to* LISETTE *and trying to embrace her*):
        My dearest child. Come here. Give me a kiss
        What's wrong?

LISETTE: I hardly want to share that bliss
        With madame —

LISIMON: Fie! You surely can't be serious.
        I've just returned from traveling, delirious
        At seeing you . . . but who is this young swain
        In tête-à-tête with you? I must complain!
        You're warm enough with him, but cold with us!

LISETTE: My Lord, we only met here to discuss
        Count Tufière, his master.

LISIMON: What! The very
        Man my daughter may decide to marry?

PASQUIN: Yes, he's the one.

LISIMON: Based on the information
        I have received, he has my approbation.
        His reputation's good; I'm told that he
        Is favored with the highest probity.
        But that is not enough, I would prefer
        A fellow like myself to marry her,

A bon vivant, a man of charm and wit.

PASQUIN: Sir, that's my master. It's a perfect fit.

LISIMON: Good! Does he love the bottle and the table?

PASQUIN: None in the regiment is half as able.
The Germans love him, and the Swiss as well!

LISIMON: He is my man! Philinte can go to hell!

LISETTE: His rival?

LISIMON: Yes, he's no man for my daughter.
I understand he cuts his wine with water.
He is so deferential, so discreet
I get the colic every time we meet.
Even if he's a prince, you'll never see
A water-drinker in my family.
I hear Philinte is favored by my spouse
But she'll find out who's master of the house.
My word is law, and madam must defer
To me. Is someone coming?

LISETTE: Yes, it's her.

LISIMON: Inform my dear companion by tonight
I want her in the country, out of sight.

LISETTE: Why in the country?

LISIMON: Why? Because I'm here
Of course. So she must leave.

LISETTE: But sir . . .

LISIMON: It's clear
Our house must be remodeled so that we
Won't have to move in such proximity.

We need a more commodious design,
So her apartments won't be close to mine.
The same roof can protect us from the weather
So long as we don't have to live together.

LISETTE (*attempting to leave*): I really must attend my mistress.

LISIMON: No,
I need to speak to you.
(*To* PASQUIN)   Sir, you may go.
Seek out your master, tell him that I greet him
And much anticipate the chance to meet him.

LISETTE: His master's coming back.

PASQUIN: Then I'll abide
Right here.

LISIMON (*Pushing him out*): Get moving! Wait for him outside!
(PASQUIN *leaves.*)
Alone at last, thank God! And now, my dear . . .
Where are you going?

LISETTE: Out. I'm sure I hear
My mistress calling. Don't you hear her voice?

LISIMON: I do not.

LISETTE: I must run. I have no choice.

LISIMON: Ignore her.

LISETTE: I'll be scolded if I do.

LISIMON: No one would dare. I want them all to view
You as my mistress. Wife and family
Should give you that respect they owe to me.

LISETTE: Do you think so?

LISIMON: My little queen, I do.
              My heart, my goods, all will be ruled by you.

LISETTE: I don't quite understand what you're suggesting.

LISIMON: Let me explain. I'm planning on investing
              In happiness for you, to place your charms
              Beyond the reach of this rude world's alarms.
              I'll find for us an elegant retreat
              Where in the evenings we can safely meet.
              The costliest of furnishings I'll buy you,
              Fine clothes, and everything to satisfy you,
              Attentive men and maids whose only task
              Will be providing anything you ask.
              You understand me now?

LISETTE: It's crystal clear.

LISIMON: And my discourse, I hope, has charmed your ear?
              What do you say, my dear, to these conditions?

LISETTE: I really can't accept your propositions,
              Monsieur, without receiving the advice
              Of one I trust.

LISIMON: Who?

LISETTE: Madame would be nice.

LISIMON: Madame! My wife? What? Have you lost your mind?

LISETTE: Yes, Madame, sir, if you would be so kind.
              She's interested in all that may concern me
              And doubtless a proposal that would earn me
              Such clear advantages, such luxury
              Will please her just the way it pleases me.

LISIMON: You mock me?

LISETTE: Sir, my mistress, I believe,
And your son should be told. They will receive
This news with joy. I'm sure I'm not mistaken.
They'll be delighted with the care you've taken
For a poor orphan, giving up your treasure
So she can lead a life of ease and pleasure,
That you'd deprive your family of their wealth
For some poor servant's economic health.

LISIMON: You dare to take this tone?

LISETTE: Yes, sir, I do.
You should know better whom you're speaking to.
I have a heart which scorns all high ambitions
If they are purchased by such base conditions.
(*She attempts to leave.*)

LISIMON: Since love and wealth alike fail to persuade,
I'm left with force.
(*He attempts to stop her. She flees, calling out.*)

LISETTE: Help, someone! To my aid!

LISIMON: What! Hussy! Do you dare oppose my will?

VALERE (*entering, to his father*): Father! What's wrong?

LISIMON: Why, nothing.

VALERE: Are you ill?

LISIMON: I am in perfect health. Why are you here?

VALERE: Someone was calling help, and full of fear,
I came in haste . . .

LISIMON: And now you're out of place.
I only need Lisette.

VALERE: But, sir . . .

LISIMON: Your face
            Offends me. Out!

VALERE: What? Leave you in this state?
            Lisette, my father needs me. Please don't wait.
            Go find my mother, tell her to make haste
            To join us.

LISIMON: Your attention is misplaced.
            I'm going crazy.

LISETTE: I'm just going.

LISIMON: Stay
            Right here. And you, monsieur, be on your way.

VALERE: Lisette can stay, if that will satisfy you.
            But you should also have your family by you.
            You're quite disturbed. Your face is flushed. Draw back
            A bit. Sit down. You'll suffer some attack.
            Your trip, I see, has tested your resources.
            At your age, one must save one's fading forces.
            Shall I send for the doctor?

LISIMON: Let me be,
            Traitor! You'll pay for this! (*He leaves.*)

LISETTE: There! Do you see?

VALERE: I do indeed. The old man's a disgrace,
            A public scandal wife and son must face.
            No wonder that her health has suffered by it.
            She's left society to seek the quiet
            Of her own lodgings, where my father's folly
            Reduces her to constant melancholy.

LISETTE: I must depart.

VALERE: No, No! Don't be upset.
              My father really isn't any threat.

LISETTE: I know that, but I still wish to depart.

VALERE: You know how much those words distress my heart.
              I'll die of sorrow if you go away.
              You know my plan.

LISETTE: Of course, and I would stay
              Most happily if there were half a chance,
              But we are so constrained by circumstance
              The formal wedding I anticipated
              Never occurs. You've promised and I've waited;
              Each passing day erodes my innocence.
              Your family is strong, their wealth immense.
              You can't expect that they would tolerate
              A match so out of place with their estate.

VALERE: Love conquers all. To have you as my wife
              Would guarantee my happiness for life.

LISETTE: Consider. I have neither wealth nor station.

VALERE: Your grace and beauty are your commendation,
              Your assets.

LISETTE: Will your family decide
              Such assets are sufficient for your bride?

VALERE: We don't need their approval; we can wed
              In secret.

LISETTE: No, I cannot. I have said
              A formal marriage is my sole condition,
              And I have lost all hope of that fruition.

VALERE: I fear I cannot run that risk. I'm speaking
             In confidence . . . What's that strange fellow seeking?

LISETTE: I know him, he's a man of humble birth
             Who's one of the few friends I have on earth.
             For some years now, this virtuous old man
             Knowing my needs, has done whatever he can
             To ease my burdens. I've come to depend
             On him both as advisor and as friend.
             I must speak with him.

VALERE: Fine, but we'll continue
             This at my sister's house. I know I'll win you.
             (*He leaves as* LYCANDRE *enters.*)

LYCANDRE: Lisette! With what surprise and happiness
             I meet you once again!

LISETTE: Sir, I confess
             I feel more shame than joy.

LYCANDRE: Why are you here?

LISETTE: I do the best I can not to appear
             In public.

LYCANDRE: Why?

LISETTE: I'm serving as a maid.

LYCANDRE: (*aside*) Great heavens!
             (*To* LISETTE) So it was to ply this trade
             You left the convent, giving me no warning.

LISETTE: You used to visit almost every morning,
             But then you stopped, and I was left alone,
             My mother dead, no other kinsman known.
             I bitterly bewept the cruel fate
             Condemning me to this deserted state.

But in the convent I had one close friend
Whose service there was coming to an end.
Knowing my situation, she proposed
That I leave too, my background undisclosed,
Pretending that I served her. I was willing
And that's the role today that I am filling.
I've shed some tears, of course, as who would not.
But I've become accustomed to my lot.

LYCANDRE (*aside*): Cruel fate!
        (*To* LISETTE) And do you get consideration
        From those you serve?

LISETTE: Yes.

LYCANDRE: That's some consolation
        In this sad business, which had been prevented
        Had not my plans for you been circumvented
        By illness. For six months I scarcely moved,
        Then found you missing once I had improved.
        But you are happy now?

LISETTE: I must make do
        With what a servant is entitled to.

LYCANDRE: Alas, poor girl!

LISETTE: You sigh? Please be assured,
        Whatever were the trials I have endured,
        Some hope remains that keeps my spirits high.

LYCANDRE: Your hope is not misguided. Just rely
        On me. Your fortune is about to turn.
        Joy lies ahead. But first, please let me learn
        Who that young man was you were speaking to.

LISETTE: He is the son and heir, and if you knew
        His virtues, he would gain your admiration.

LYCANDRE: As he has yours? (*She reddens.*) You blush?

LISETTE: My estimation
Of him is not a crime.

LYCANDRE: No, not at all.
He's handsome, young and rich, and does he call
Upon you often?

LISETTE: We are hardly strangers.

LYCANDRE: You're young, naive, and lovely. These are dangers.

LISETTE: Monsieur, my heart is much above my station.
My principles control the situation.

LYCANDRE: I hope so. Tell me, what were you discussing?

LISETTE: He's named Valere.

LYCANDRE: Good lord, let's not be fussing
About such things. I didn't ask his name
But what he said to you before I came.

LISETTE: He spoke of love.

LYCANDRE: That's all?

LISETTE: That's all, I swear.

LYCANDRE: You're hiding something else.

LISETTE: I cannot bear
Your lack of trust. There isn't much to hide.
He asked if I'd agree to be his bride
In secret.

LYCANDRE: That arouses my suspicions.

LISETTE: Wait! Far from giving in to those conditions,
            I said my heart was his, but not my hand
            Unless his parents came to understand
            And bless our love, but they will not, I know.
            I beg you, sir, help me avoid this blow.
            I hope to go away this very night
            And take myself forever from his sight.

LYCANDRE: What you request provides clear evidence
            Both of your virtue and your innocence.
            My dear girl, you deserve a happier fate,
            And you will have it. I anticipate
            That you'll be married soon to your Valere
            And that his happy father will be there.

LISETTE: He will?

LYCANDRE: I'll say no more, but I will show you
            That he will bless you when he comes to know you.
            When I've revealed to him your rightful station
            He'll gladly welcome you as his relation.

LISETTE: You mock me, sir. My mother never said
            A word about all this. Now she is dead.
            Who is my father?

LYCANDRE: Someone who will mend
            Your fortunes, bring your sorrows to an end.

LISETTE: But why did he desert me in such pain?

LYCANDRE: He had his reasons, which he will explain.
            For now, keep silent. He will soon relieve
            Your doubts.

LISETTE: A nobleman? I can't believe
            What you have told me, if you have no plan
            To tell me all.

LYCANDRE: I've told you all I can.
                  Your father must explain the whole affair.
                  Now I must find the Count of Tufière.
                  Does he live here?

LISETTE: He's on a lengthy stay.

LYCANDRE: I must see him.

LISETTE: Sir, I'm not sure you may.
                  He won't accept those humble clothes you're wearing;
                  I'm told he's so imperious in his bearing . . .

LYCANDRE: I'll tame his vanity.

LISETTE: You must expect him
                  To scorn you.

LYCANDRE: I've the power to correct him.
                  Goodbye for now. An honest heart is worth
                  More to the world than is a noble birth.
                  Trust in true virtue never is mistaken,
                  And though your worldly goods cruel fate has taken
                  From you, it's left you with a greater treasure,
                  Your virtue, which gives riches beyond measure.
                  (*He leaves.*)

ACT II

LISETTE (*alone*): What's going on? It all seems like a dream.
　　　　　　　Lycandre's news buoys up my self-esteem,
　　　　　　　And yet, appearances can be deceiving.
　　　　　　　There's really little reason for believing
　　　　　　　His story. He's my friend. Why should I doubt him?
　　　　　　　And yet there's something not quite right about him.
　　　　　　　But, wait, I think I can perceive his plan.
　　　　　　　He wants to make me proud so that I can
　　　　　　　Look down upon Valere, and use this pride
　　　　　　　To kill a love that can't be satisfied.
　　　　　　　Yes, that must be the trick that he employed!
　　　　　　　How brief a time my grandeur was enjoyed!
　　　　　　　I am again Lisette, a serving-maid,
　　　　　　　Whose brief reign is concluded, I'm afraid.
　　　　　　　I slept, I dreamed, but now I am awake
　　　　　　　And find my sad condition no mistake.

VALERE (*entering*): I'm waiting for you still. Why are you here
　　　　　　　Alone?

LISETTE:　　　　　　　I'm dreaming.

VALERE:　　　　　　　　　　　　What? Lisette, I fear
　　　　　　　That old man brought you some disturbing news.

LISETTE:　　No, on the contrary.

VALERE:　　　　　　　　　　　But, then, why choose
　　　　　　　To dream?

LISETTE:　　　　　　　Because his news, which should delight me,
　　　　　　　In fact has served more truly to affright me.

VALERE:　　This is the most surprising combination.

LISETTE: You'll think I've lost my mind. The situation
                Is so peculiar. But my mind is clear.
                Indeed, that's why my pain is so severe.

VALERE: I'm totally at sea. Can't you explain?

LISETTE: I'm not supposed to, but I can't refrain
                From speaking. Though my silence was demanded,
                With you I can't be anything but candid.
                My burden's heavy. I can scarcely bear it.

VALERE: You know it will be lighter if you share it.

LISETTE: I know it would relieve me, but I fear
                You'll laugh at my confusion when you hear.

VALERE: I wouldn't.

LISETTE: Swear then, that whatever I say,
                You won't make fun.

VALERE: I swear.

LISETTE: My open way
                Or, if you like, my natural indiscretion
                Requires that I be cautious in confession,
                But I am hoping you can calm the fears
                Tormenting me. So listen.

VALERE: I'm all ears.

LISETTE (*after a short pause*):
                That good man told me . . . promise me, Valere
                That you won't laugh at me.

VALERE: I won't, I swear.

LISETTE: First I must ask a question and expect
                An answer that is honest and direct.

VALERE: Then ask.

LISETTE: Do you find any intimation
            In me of noble birth or education?
            Does anything I say, or think, or do
            Suggest a noble parentage to you?

VALERE: A lover's views may not be taken seriously,
            But you've inspired respect in me mysteriously,
            It deeply pains me one I venerate
            Should have been so unlucky in her fate.
            But that unlucky fate you overcame
            Regardless of what parents you may claim,
            Whoever meets you cannot help but see
            An unmistakable nobility.
            I can assure you this is what I hear.

LISETTE: Your speech is flattering. Is it sincere
            As well?

VALERE: I swear it is, upon my oath!

LISETTE: Then I have news delightful for us both.
            For certain reasons, still to be revealed
            To me, my family history has been concealed.
            Unless I am the victim of some prank,
            I come from people of the noblest rank.

VALERE: Lisette, I'm certain that it must be true.
            I'd swear to it.

LISETTE: What joy!

VALERE: I beg of you,
            Charming Lisette, you now may be above me
            In rank, but if you still can love me,
            Don't hesitate. Accept this revelation.
            Acknowledge to yourself your rightful station
            And grant your jealous lover the permission

To be the first to honor your position.
(*He throws himself at her feet.*)

LISETTE: This is embarrassing. Get up, Valere!

VALERE: You, servant to my sister! How unfair!
I must run to inform her that I love you,
And others must alter their opinion of you.
My father first of all, and I suspect
My mother needs to show you more respect.
I must make sure the family understands . . .
(*He starts to go.*)

LISETTE (*interrupting and restraining him*):
Wait! I have placed my secret in your hands,
But I have been forbidden to reveal it.
If you don't aid my efforts to conceal it,
Far from supporting me . . .

VALERE: I understand.
Mum is the word. Your wish is my command.
Fear nothing.

LISETTE: Quiet, then. Here's Isabelle.

VALERE (*running to her*): Sister, I have exciting news to tell.

LISETTE (*holding him back*): What did you promise?

VALERE: I cannot contain
My joy. Sister, farewell. I will explain
My conduct later.

ISABELLE: Brother, why farewell?
You're joking. What great news have you to tell?

VALERE: It's nothing, really.

ISABELLE: This must be some jest.

VALERE: By no means. When you hear . . .

LISETTE (*interrupting him*):   It would be best
                 To leave.

VALERE (*taking several steps out, then coming back*):
                 Dear sister, when you're speaking to
                 Lisette . . . (*He hesitates*)

ISABELLE: Well, what?

VALERE: Speak kindly when you do.
                 Show more respect for her.

ISABELLE: What! Why respect?

VALERE: Because she's quite entitled to expect
                 It from us. We should honor mademoiselle—
                 What am I saying—I mean Isabelle.
                 I think we should commit ourselves to showing
                 Her more consideration. Now I'm going.
                 (*He leaves abruptly.*)

ISABELLE: I find these vague allusions mystifying.
                 Can you say what my brother is implying,
                 Lisette?

LISETTE: Oh, just some fancy, I expect.

ISABELLE: Why would he speak of showing you respect?
                 It's such an odd request. Wait! Could it be—

LISETTE: Be what?

ISABELLE: Your blushes make it clear. I see
                 It all now. You've attracted my dear brother!

LISETTE: Is it a crime for us to love each other?

ISABELLE: No, but—

LISETTE: He always showers me with praise,
             But I'm suspicious.

ISABELLE: Why?

LISETTE: These are the ways
             Of all young gentlemen. Their words are sweet
             But given freely to each girl they meet.

ISABELLE: No, no, my brother's not the fickle sort
             Who flits from flower to flower paying court.
             He's not some insincere, deceiving youth,
             And if he says he loves you, it's the truth.

LISETTE (*with joy*): You're sure of that?

ISABELLE: I'm sure. There is no doubt.
             You don't seem much distressed to find this out.
             Dear friend!

LISETTE: What is it?

ISABELLE: Now I see it clearly.

LISETTE: What do you see?

ISABELLE: My brother loves you dearly,
             And since he does, and since he's so discerning,
             Your heart and soul are surely worth the earning.

LISETTE: He holds me, he has said, in such esteem
             That, were I someone other than I seem—
             (*She hesitates.*)

ISABELLE: Well, then?

LISETTE: He'd love to claim me as his bride.

ISABELLE (*seeing her embarrassment*):
        And then? What next? Tell me what you replied.
        (*Lisette hesitates.*) Lisette, I've always spoken honestly
        To you. I beg you. Do the same to me.

LISETTE: I answered him, since you insist I speak . . .

ISABELLE: Go on!

LISETTE: No greater happiness I'd seek
        Than to be suitable for such a wedding.

ISABELLE: I trust you, but I fear where you are heading.
        You both may have much suffering in store.

LISETTE: Our ideas may be different on that score.

ISABELLE: How so?

LISETTE: Before long you will be enlightened.
        As for your brother, please do not be frightened.
        Don't be upset by anything I've said,
        And let's consider your affairs instead.

ISABELLE: Most willingly.

LISETTE: You know my heart and mind,
        But what of yours? I know that you're inclined
        To sudden passions, moods quite unexpected.
        How are you faring?

ISABELLE: Badly.

LISETTE: I suspected
        As much. So your heart too is taken?
        You're sure?

ISABELLE: Lisette, I couldn't be mistaken.
        I swear this time it's real.

LISETTE: Best not to swear.

ISABELLE: I'll take an oath—

LISETTE: Madam, it's your affair,
But heaven help you!

ISABELLE: Why?

LISETTE: Madam, I know
You have a heart that's eager to bestow
Your love, and yet you never do, because
Sooner or later, thinking gives you pause.
The Count appears a most attractive catch
If we assume his looks and merit match.
But it's not long that he has been your guest.
You ought to know him better. I suggest
Another week at least, which may reveal
Some defect he has managed to conceal.

ISABELLE: That cannot be. He is a man apart,
Full of perfections that have charmed my heart.
Though, as you say, I'm cautious as a rule,
If he has any flaw, he's somewhat cool.
I rarely see him . . .

LISETTE: That suggests he's clever.
Absence makes hearts grow fonder. One should never
Grow too familiar. That way boredom lies.

ISABELLE: I thought you liked him. Tell me, in your eyes
Does he have any faults?

LISETTE: I know of none.

ISABELLE: That's well.

LISETTE: And if he had a single one,
It wouldn't long evade your circumspection.

>You're so opposed to forming a connection
>With any man possessed of any flaw,
>Seeking some being outside Nature's law.
>If your heart says the Count is this rare creature,
>Trust in that oracle as your best teacher.
>Your feelings, not your wit, should be your guide.
>Then, if you err, it's on the better side.
>A little blindness may not be amiss,
>And little errors lead to greater bliss.

ISABELLE: I'll follow your advice, my faithful friend.

LISETTE: And you will thank me for it, in the end.
But what will then become of poor Philinte?
You once found him attractive and you can't
Just drop him.

ISABELLE: Why? I'm bored to death beside him.
I honor him, but I cannot abide him.
I cannot bear it. Every time we meet
He's practically falling at my feet,
Stammering nonsense, when he speaks at all,
Why have a fool who's at my beck and call?

LISETTE: He's coming.

ISABELLE: And what for?

LISETTE: Perhaps he seeks
To give you further grounds for your critiques.

PHILINTE (*to* ISABELLE, *upstage, after making several bows*):
Madame, I fear I cause you irritation.

ISABELLE (*low, to* LISETTE):
At least he has some gift for devination.
(*Aloud, to* PHILINTE) A man like you . . .

PHILINTE (*interrupting her, still bowing*):

> Ah, Madam, I implore you,
> Punish my boldness, saying I adore you.

ISABELLE (*bowing in return*): Sir . . .

PHILINTE (*interrupting*):   Honor me by showing me the door.

ISABELLE: Sir, you mistake me, what are manners for?

PHILINTE (*bowing*): Madam, in truth . . .

ISABELLE (*interrupting him and returning his bow*):
> Sir, you can have no doubt
> Of my esteem.
> (*Aside to* LISETTE) For God's sake, help me out!

LISETTE (*to* PHILINTE, *after several bows, offering him a chair*):
> Please have a seat.

PHILINTE: Do not insult me, please.
> Before Madame, I should be on my knees.

LISETTE: As you wish, sir
> (*Low, to* ISABELLE) Give him some stimulation!

ISABELLE (*low, to* LISETTE): I'm at a loss!

LISETTE: Ah, fine! This conversation
> Is really sparkling now!
> (*To* PHILINTE)   Monsieur, I see
> It's difficult to talk in front of me,
> So I'll be gone.

PHILINTE (*holding her back*): There's no need to retire.
> I'll only stand in silence and admire.

LISETTE: And let your eyes do all the talking for you?

PHILINTE: That will suffice.

LISETTE: I'm going. I implore you,
                Speak freely.

ISABELLE (*low, to* LISETTE): My good will is wearing thin.

LISETTE (*low, to* ISABELLE): I'm sure he will respond if you begin.

ISABELLE (*low, to* LISETTE):
                Please get us started. Pose some question to him.

LISETTE (*low, to* ISABELLE):
                Why me? You are the mistress. You should cue him.

ISABELLE (*to* PHILINTE, *after some thought*):
                How is the weather, sir?

LISETTE (*aside*):   How stimulating!

PHILINTE: Madame, in truth, it's quite invigorating!

ISABELLE: Monsieur, in truth, that's very nice to know.

LISETTE (*to* PHILINTE): And I, in truth, have also found it so.
                (*To* ISABELLE)
                Since your initiatives have both expired,
                Clearly my intervention is required.
                (*To* PHILINTE) What is the news in town?
                (*To* ISABELLE) Give him a shove!

ISABELLE (*to* PHILINTE): Is the new opera much spoken of?

PHILINTE: It's bad, I hear.

LISETTE (*aside*):   Well, that was pretty terse.

PHILINTE: I don't know much of music or of verse,
                And yet I must admit I often go
                To works of little merit. One must show
                Support, I think, and condemnation never

For any sort of artistic endeavor.

LISETTE: Some say that criticism helps the art.

PHILINTE: The critic has by far the easier part.
That is why critics commonly abound
While artists most infrequently are found.
(*To* ISABELLE, *who is paying no attention*)
You seem distracted, Madam.

ISABELLE: It's my head.

PHILINTE: Oh, dear!

ISABELLE: A migraine. I should be in bed.

PHILINTE: I'll leave you.

ISABELLE: No, remain.

PHILINTE: You are too kind.

ISABELLE: It's I who should depart. I fear you'll find
My suffering too disturbing. So, adieu.

PHILINTE: I'm in despair! I'll come along with you!
(*He hastily puts on his gloves.*)
Give me your hand. I'll help you to your suite!

ISABELLE: I'm too tired now. Tomorrow we may meet.

PHILINTE: What time tomorrow? When will you allow . . .?

ISABELLE: Whenever you like. Just don't pursue me now!
(*She goes.*)

PHILINTE (*to* LISETTE):
Mam'selle, if I may have a word with you . . .

LISETTE: Monsieur, in truth, I have a migraine too.
              Don't think me impolite, but as you know,
              Servants must follow where their masters go.
              (*She goes.*)

(PHILINTE *conducts her out, then returns.*)

PHILINTE: These migraines came so suddenly, I fear
              That it was I who caused them to appear.
              My cursed timidity I've tried in vain
              To conquer, conquered me again.
              How much I suffer, when I always see
              Young men of no more wit or rank than me
              So much at ease. They never seem to share
              The cruel rebuffs that are my daily fare.

(*A badly dressed* LACKEY *enters with a letter.*)

LACKEY: Here is a letter for you, sir.

PHILINTE: Let's see.
              (*He reads the cover.*)
              "The Count of Tufière." That isn't me,
              But he is staying here.

LACKEY: Excuse me, sir.

PHILINTE (*bowing*): Of course.
              (*Aside*) The Count's the one she would prefer
              No doubt, and yet her mother is opposed
              I'll speak to him before the case is closed. (*He leaves.*)

LACKEY (*calling out*): Friend, do you serve the Count of Tufière?

PASQUIN (*entering, in an arrogant tone*): Who wants to know?

LACKEY (*aside*):   Not much politeness there!

PASQUIN: Speak up!

LACKEY: Are you the man whose named Pasquin?

PASQUIN: I am, you rogue, but I assume you can
              Employ the term Monsieur, if there is need.

LACKEY: Monsieur, forgive me. I'm confused indeed.
              I didn't know the right way to address you
              And certainly had no wish to distress you.

PASQUIN (*in a condescending tone*): Enough apologies.

LACKEY: Monsieur, I bear
              A letter for the Count of Tufière.

PASQUIN (*taking it*): I'll take it. Can you say from whom it came?

LACKEY: A gentleman who didn't give a name.
              Adieu, Monsieur Pasquin, my ignorance
              May have, Monsieur, occasioned some offence.
              I will in future be more circumspect
              And offer you, Monsieur, sincere respect. (*He goes.*)

PASQUIN: The rascal's mocking me, and to be fair,
              He has some reason. This affected air
              Is rather foolish and unjustified.
              Why should a servant give himself to pride?
              My treatment of this fellow makes me see,
              My master's traits are gaining hold on me.
              The curse of vanity I must forestall!
              I hear a noise. It's the original
              Of all these affectations, it's the fount
              Of self-aggrandizement itself, the Count!

(THE COUNT *enters, walking with large strides and head elevated. Five
    lackeys accompany him and line up at the rear of the stage with a
    deferential attitude. PASQUIN stands a bit in front of them.*)

THE COUNT: A rogue!

PASQUIN (*offering the letter to* THE COUNT): Monsieur . . .

THE COUNT (*pacing about, not noticing him*):   A fool!

PASQUIN: Monsieur . . .

THE COUNT (*interrupting him*):   No noise!
    (*To himself*) A duke, yet he a common tone employs
    With me, in some disgusting suit he's seeking!

PASQUIN: He's wrong, of course.

THE COUNT: What's that? Is someone speaking?

PASQUIN: He's wrong, I said.

THE COUNT: Are you one of my minions?
    I have no interest in your opinions.
    Hold this (*He gives him a purse*).

PASQUIN: Good Heavens! It must weigh a ton!
    Whatever his attitude, my heart is won!
    (*He opens the purse and takes out several coins.*)

THE COUNT (*surprising him*): What are you doing?

PASQUIN: Checking on your gold.

THE COUNT: It's safe enough! (*He gestures to the other servants. Two
    bring him a table, two others an armchair, a fifth brings a
    writing desk and pens, and a sixth paper. THE COUNT
    sits at the table and begins to write.*)

PASQUIN (*again offering the letter to him*): Sir, may I be so bold
    As to pass on to you, with all respect,
    This letter.

THE COUNT (*taking the letter without looking at it, while
    continuing to write*): More entreaties! I expect

It's from the duke.

PASQUIN: No, the man who came . . .

THE COUNT (*interrupting him*): Was from the princess?

PASQUIN (*continuing*):   . . . Didn't leave the name
             Of him who sent it.

THE COUNT: And who was this man?

PASQUIN: A lackey, poorly dressed.

THE COUNT (*throwing the letter at him*): Enough! Whoever can
             Be bothered, read this. Later, at my leisure,
             Tell me what's in it.

PASQUIN (*picking it up*):   It will be my pleasure.

THE COUNT (*still writing*): Monsieur Pasquin!

PASQUIN: Sir?

THE COUNT: Clear away this crowd!

PASQUIN (*to the* LACKEYS, *with a superior air*):
             Get out! (*They leave.*) Monsieur?

THE COUNT: What?

PASQUIN: May I be allowed . . .

THE COUNT (*aside*): He wishes my attention, I believe.
             (*Noticing* LAFLEUR, *who has just entered*)
             Who is that fellow? Bid him take his leave!

PASQUIN (*to* LAFLEUR):
             I warned you! It's quite hopeless to defy him.
             Remove yourself. I'll try to pacify him.

(LAFLEUR *goes*.)

(THE COUNT *reads silently what he has written, while* PASQUIN *also reads silently the letter.*)

THE COUNT (*aside, having finished his reading*):
>You still persist, but no one of my station
>Could lower himself to your consideration.
>It would dishonor me, you can be sure,
>Even to write your name with a "Monsieur."
>No, humble sir, you lack the dignity
>To gain such an advantage over me.
>I'd be delighted if I could conclude
>"Your humble servant," but that might be viewed . . .
>(*He tears up the letter, to* PASQUIN)
>Remove this table! Have you read the letter?

PASQUIN: I have, Monsieur. Perhaps it would be better
>If I destroyed it.

THE COUNT: What! What does it say?

PASQUIN: Since I am ordered . . .

THE COUNT: Read! Enough delay!

PASQUIN (*reading*): "The one who writes to you . . ."

THE COUNT (*interrupting him*):   "The one . . ." The style
>Is too familiar!

PASQUIN (*aside*):   He will choke with bile!
>" . . . Who writes to you . . .," sir, if I may continue,
>" . . . Is one who takes a special interest in you,
>And begs to tell you that his patience wears
>Quite thin with you and your inflated airs."

THE COUNT (*leaping up*): If I could only lay my hands upon
>The rogue who dared to write . . .

PASQUIN: Shall I go on?

THE COUNT: Yes, finish up. Let's hear the end of it.

PASQUIN (*reading again*): "You're not devoid of merit, I admit . . ."

THE COUNT (*interrupting him*):
        What! Not devoid! It's pure audacity
        To use such language to a man like me!

PASQUIN (*continuing to read*):
        "Yet far from thinking you someone superior,
        All those who deal with you could not be wearier
        Of your impertinent and tedious air."

THE COUNT (*striking* PASQUIN): Take that, you rascal!

PASQUIN: Master! Would I dare
        Speak thus? Why blame me for another's note?
        The devil take him and whatever he wrote!
        (*He throws the letter down on the table.*)

THE COUNT (*menacingly*): I'll teach you . . .

PASQUIN (*interrupting him*):   What? Why seek to punish me
        For someone else's impropriety?
        So much for reading! That's the last task you
        Impose on me!

THE COUNT (*paying no attention to what* PASQUIN *is saying and
        handing him his purse*): How often must I ask you
        To hold this purse! Here are my keys. Take care.

PASQUIN (*continuing*): I'm through with it!
        (*He notices the purse.*) But wait! Are you aware
        How much this purse contains?

THE COUNT: No, not precisely.

PASQUIN: I'll do it. That commission suits me nicely.
            (*Aside*) This will provide the reparations due me.
            (*He goes.*)

THE COUNT (*alone*): If I can guess the villain who left to me
            This ugly calumny, I'll make him pay!
            Perhaps his handwriting gives him away.
            (*He picks up the letter and reads.*)
            "A friend has sent this useful letter to you
            In hand disguised . . ."
            (*interrupting his reading*)
            Villain! I see right through you!
            "My name withheld, till your excessive pride
            Has been allowed some hours to subside,
            So we can speak without its interference.
            Look to this evening, then, for my appearance
            When your demeanor is less elevated."
            I'm outraged! This cannot be tolerated!
            For such a libel, he will pay most dearly!
            I can't imagine who would dare! It's clearly
            Some rogue . . .

PASQUIN (*returning*): Monsieur, I've tallied your account
            Three hundred eighty's the exact amount.

THE COUNT: But . . .

PASQUIN (*interrupting him*): If you find a single centime more,
            Call me a fool.

THE COUNT: But I am sure before
            Your count, four hundred were inside.

PASQUIN: Either you were mistaken, or I've lied.
            Could your head servant be reduced to stealing?

THE COUNT: Monsieur Pasquin!

PASQUIN: Monsieur?

THE COUNT: I see I'm dealing
            With theft!

PASQUIN: I'm too respectful to deny it,
            But I insist . . .

THE COUNT (*interrupting him*): For Heaven's sake, be quiet!
            Other concerns possess me.

PASQUIN: I can tell
            You're having second thoughts on Isabelle.
            I hear she's been complaining of neglect.

THE COUNT (*surprised*): I said I loved her. What does she expect?

PASQUIN: Her father's just returned.

THE COUNT: Good! Doubtless he
            Will soon appear and offer her to me.

PASQUIN: Monsieur, is it a father's obligation
            To take the lead in such negotiation?

THE COUNT: Perhaps not, but I'm sure he understands
            The extra honors rank like mine demands.

PASQUIN: Perhaps you could be somewhat less disdainful.
            Lisette told me . . .

THE COUNT (*interrupting him*): It's really very painful
            To hear that serving girl's incessant chatter
            On every subject.

PASQUIN: Still, upon this matter
            She has some worthy thoughts.

THE COUNT: And what are those?

PASQUIN: That Isabelle is certain to oppose

A prideful suitor. She regards with scorn
All those who boast of being highly born.
Their grandeur is thus dimmed.

THE COUNT: Where do you get
        Such ideas from?

PASQUIN: They're not mine. From Lisette.

THE COUNT: Enough! Someone is coming. Go see who
        It is.

PASQUIN (*aside*):   The future father, right on cue.

THE COUNT: I knew that he'd initiate our meeting.

PASQUIN: But shouldn't we at least extend some greeting?

THE COUNT: I know my place, and his. Don't interfere.
        Go, show him in. I will receive him here.

LISIMON (*entering, to* PASQUIN):
        I'm looking for the Count of Tufière,
        Good fellow.

PASQUIN: You're in luck. He's sitting there.

(THE COUNT *rises nonchalantly and steps forward.* LISIMON
    embraces him.)

LISIMON: Dear Count, your servant!

THE COUNT (*low, to* PASQUIN):   Suddenly I'm dear,
        Like some old friend.

LISIMON: What a delight to hear
        We lodge together.

THE COUNT (*coolly*):   Just what I was thinking.

LISIMON: What pleasant hours we can spend in drinking
                  Together. You're a tippler, so I'm told
                  But so am I, if I may be so bold.
                  I eagerly anticipate the nights we'll fill
                  In mutual toasts . . . What's this? You're looking ill.
                  Your face is drawn. You've a distracted air.

THE COUNT (*to* PASQUIN): Ask him to sit. No, offer him a chair.
                  He will refuse of course, but . . .

LISIMON: Normally,
                  I'd stand, but since you've asked me, let there be
                  No such formality between us. Claim
                  Me as your bosom friend. I'll do the same.
                  What do you say, old boy? May I suggest
                  You come tonight to dinner as our guest.

THE COUNT: Are you addressing me, sir?

LISIMON: Who else, pray?
                  Your servant?

THE COUNT: I believed so.

LISIMON: You display,
                  It seems to me, a touch of vanity.

THE COUNT: It's just I find your manners rather free.

LISIMON: Free up your own then. I'm afraid you must.
                  At my age, they're much harder to adjust.

THE COUNT: Still you could make the effort if you would.

LISIMON: In my own house? I don't see why I should.
                  I'm speaking frankly.

THE COUNT: I prefer discretion.

LISIMON: That's not for me. I think it's a confession
               That one cannot speak honestly one's mind.
               I hate it, and avoid those men who find
               It comfortable, using formal speech
               To keep themselves out of each other's reach.
               It's my opinion that good friends should be
               Above the dictates of formality.

THE COUNT: Friendship also has rules one must obey.

LISIMON: I've never thought of friendship in that way.

THE COUNT: Men of my rank are proud of their positions
               And only enter friendships with conditions.

LISIMON: Indeed. Count, in your circles that may be
               The custom, but it's not at all for me.
               My daughter, I am told, appeals to you.
               She's witty, beautiful, and well-to-do.
               She likes you too, and I'm inclined to bless
               Your hoped-for union, partly, I confess
               Because my wife resists it. She prefers
               A fawning young discovery of hers
               Who drives me crazy with his self-effacing.
               But if you want my blessing, try embracing
               A humbler manner. Otherwise, we're through!

THE COUNT (*aside to* PASQUIN, *and abruptly rising*):
               I'll humor him. There's nothing else to do!

PASQUIN (*low, to* THE COUNT):
               Yes, pride is a small sacrifice to make
               When marriage and a fortune is at stake.

THE COUNT (*low, to* PASQUIN): But still . . .

LISIMON: I'm off. It's growing late, I find.
               Join us for dinner if you're so inclined.
               We can discuss at leisure what you think

Of what I said, but first we'll have a drink.
Drink well, eat well, and don't be concerned
With social niceties, that's what I've learned.
At my house everybody is at ease.
We only have one law — do what you please.
Come on, then. You'll enjoy it all the more
If pomp and pride are left outside the door.
(*He leaves, with* THE COUNT *following.*)

PASQUIN (*alone*): How is the mighty fallen! It is true
Such a corrective was long overdue,
And if he's not converted by this mission,
His pride is an incurable condition.

ACT III

(*Enter* PASQUIN *and* THE COUNT.)

THE COUNT: Though as a rule I never condescend
            To speak to my valets, I will unbend
            A bit, in private, to confide in you.
            I know you're interested in what I do.
            I hope I can rely on you as well
            Concerning this affair of Isabelle.

PASQUIN: You've started well, by wooing her relations.

THE COUNT: Her father loves me now.

PASQUIN: Congratulations!

THE COUNT: I must move cautiously, but I expect
            His love for me will grow into respect.

PASQUIN: In any case, you've made a brilliant start.
            As drinking partner you have played your part
            With such enthusiasm and conviction
            The old man never dreamed it was a fiction.

THE COUNT: He's sworn to have me in his family.
            His daughter lets me understand that she
            Completely shares his feelings. I admit
            I'm quite well pleased with how I've managed it.

PASQUIN: How happily the matter has turned out!

THE COUNT: The father's in my camp, without a doubt.
            And as he comes to know me, he is moving
            Toward more respect. His manners are improving.
            No longer does he treat me as an equal.

PASQUIN: He may come to respect you, but the sequel
            Will probably not follow as you plan.

THE COUNT: Why not?

PASQUIN: Because he's old and he's a man
            Set in his ways. He's not at all impressed
            With rank, for him great wealth is best.

THE COUNT: Doubtless that's what he wishes to believe,
            But I am not so easy to deceive.
            Despite his wealth, I sense his true desires,
            And it's to higher rank that he aspires.
            These nouveaux riches are really all the same
            Advancement is at first their only game,
            But once they have the money in the bank
            They shift their sights to family and rank.
            Old Lisimon was lucky to inherit
            A family fortune quite beyond his merit.
            Now, quite devoid of wit or of ability,
            He seeks to wed himself to the nobility.
            His daughter doubtless shares his vanity,
            And that attracts them to a man like me.
            I can afford to play their little game
            Because my rank will trump them all the same.
            Sooner or later I'll expect submission
            To my no doubt superior position.
            My father was no merchant, but a prince
            Unequaled in his pride before or since.
            It won't require much effort to persuade them
            How an aristocratic match can aid them.

PASQUIN: Such aid may really not be worth the bother.
            I've talked with an old servant of your father
            Who vaguely spoke of certain cruel events
            That overtook him.

THE COUNT: No one of any sense
            Pursues such rumors. Many years have passed

Since those dark days. Though our estates were vast,
They're far from here. No enemy in Paris
Has any information to embarrass
My suit, if you keep quiet.

PASQUIN: Master, I seek . . .

THE COUNT (*interrupting him*):
No fancy speeches. Let your actions speak.

PASQUIN: You know I'm at your service. Any task you
Assign, I'll do it.

THE COUNT: First, they're sure to ask you
Of my possessions. Lay to rest all fears.
Give them no details, but suggest my worth
Must surely be impressive as my birth.
Take special care in dealing with Lisette,
Since she's the strongest ally we could get.
The entire household trusts in her opinion.

PASQUIN: Ask her yourself. You needn't send some minion.
She's on your side already, you will find.

THE COUNT: Me! Speak with a servant! Have you lost your mind?
Such baseness is beyond consideration!
Go, seek her out, engage in conversation,
But give no hint that I am speaking through you.
Encourage her to comment frankly to you . . .
Someone is coming. Go, do what you can!

PASQUIN: When lying is involved, I am your man! (*He goes.*)

(ISABELLE *and* LISETTE *enter.*)

ISABELLE: My father, sir, insists our situation
Requires we have a serious conversation.
He speaks to me as if the case is closed.

THE COUNT: I dare assume that you are not opposed.
     It's true, I seek your hand, all I need now
     Is to receive from you a lover's vow.
     Will you provide the happiness I seek,
     And say those words I long to hear you speak?

LISETTE: I know her thoughts, Monsieur, and can provide
     Assurances to leave you satisfied.

THE COUNT (*to* ISABELLE, *after having given* LISETTE *a
    disdainful look*): Do me the honor of direct address.

LISETTE: Proper young ladies, sir, do not confess
     Their love. Their silence takes the place of speaking,
     And hers should give the answer you are seeking.

THE COUNT (*to* ISABELLE):
     And do you never speak but through a servant?

ISABELLE: She is my friend, both trusted and observant . . .

THE COUNT (*interrupting*): Your friend?

ISABELLE: Why, yes!

THE COUNT: She serves you, I believe.

ISABELLE: She does, but all the same, I can't conceive
     Of having a companion, always present,
     Whose comradeship would make my life more pleasant

THE COUNT: I can't imagine you would condescend
     To call a maid companion, comrade, friend!

ISABELLE: Why not, Monsieur?

THE COUNT: Well, in your own domain,
     Do as you please, but as for me, it's plain . . .

LISETTE (*aside*): He's as conceited as he's said to be!

ISABELLE (*to* THE COUNT):
> Her heart is good, or good enough for me.
> She's witty, she's sincere, she's dedicated.
> The good she's brought me can't be over-rated.
> In short . . .

THE COUNT (*interrupting her*): Your father, has he fixed the date
> When you receive the prize for which you wait,
> My heart?

ISABELLE: You're moving rather quickly, sir.
> Surely that is a stage we should defer
> Until we're more acquainted with the views
> That each one holds, rather than blindly choose.
> People are often other than they seem;
> True love requires both knowledge and esteem,
> And . . .

THE COUNT (*interrupting her*): Speaking frankly, madam, I expect
> From you less caution and much more respect.
> Your father's wishes ought to rule your heart,
> Inspiring sincere ardor on your part.
> The chance to marry someone of my station
> Is not a choice that merits hesitation.

ISABELLE: I hope, Monsieur, that I can make you see
> Your self-assurance hardly honors me.
> If in your passion you were less secure
> And your assumption of my love less sure,
> If you were less assured in your position
> You'd free me from a troubling suspicion.

THE COUNT: And what suspicion's that?

ISABELLE: I must suspect
> Such self-assurance masks some deep defect.

VALERE (*entering*): Sister, can I believe what I've just heard?

ISABELLE: What's that?

VALERE: That you have given the Count your word
               To marry him?

THE COUNT: Monsieur, I dare to flatter
               Myself to think it is a settled matter.

VALERE: I thought . . .

THE COUNT (*interrupting him*): And I'm delighted to accept
               Your brotherly best wishes. You have kept
               To proper protocol. Now don't think me rude.
               Your sire and I have business to conclude.
               (*He starts to go.*)

VALERE (*holding him back*): You may run into difficulty there.

THE COUNT: What, I?

VALERE: I fear so.

THE COUNT: Nonsense. Who would dare
               Oppose my inclinations?

VALERE: Sir, I fear
               Our mother would.

THE COUNT: Your mother! Do I hear
               Correctly? I can't help but laugh! Your mother!

ISABELLE (*low, to* LISETTE):
               What an insulting way to treat my brother!

THE COUNT (*to* VALERE): I take it that she doesn't understand
               That I love Isabelle and that my hand
               Was offered by a common friend.

VALERE: Excuse me.

THE COUNT: Astonishing! She wouldn't dare refuse me.
     I'm certain that my rank and my position
     Should guarantee her gratified submission.
     The many other virtues Heaven has sent me
     I'd mention, did not modesty prevent me.
     Inform your mother that the stand she's taken . . .
     But wait! It may be I have been mistaken.
     (*With irony*) Perhaps my virtues I have over-rated
     To hide some flaw no one anticipated,
     And, far from taking umbrage at your gall,
     I should be pleased you speak to me at all!

VALERE: Our gall, Monsieur? Not so! We know full well
     The honor you confer on Isabelle.

THE COUNT (*ironically, with a disdainful smile*):
     Dear heaven! No honor at all!

VALERE: I much regret
     The situation, but my mother has set
     Her heart, long since, upon this man Philinte.
     She's made arrangements with him which she can't
     Easily break, based on a long affection.

THE COUNT (*in a bantering tone*):
     Doubtless the man's a model of perfection!

VALERE: No, not at all. He's getting on in years,
     Though he's more lively than at first appears,
     Rich without pride, quite charming in his way.

THE COUNT: I am alarmed by everything you say.
     It now appears that I was far too bold
     Confronting such a rival. I was told
     He was a mere eccentric. Clearly not.
     My eyes are opened. Everything I thought
     To my advantage—age and wit and bearing

> Apparently cannot withstand comparing
> With such a paragon, with worth so great.
> You do him wrong to even hesitate!

LISETTE (*to* ISABELLE):
> A modest speech, but could his heart be in it?

ISABELLE (*to* LISETTE): I really don't believe it for a minute.
> This modest manner is but hidden pride.

THE COUNT (*ironically*):
> Madame, in vain I sought you as my bride.
> My ardor was too great, too indiscreet,
> And I respect my rival in defeat.

ISABELLE (*smiling*): On such respect Philinte is not depending.

THE COUNT (*with a bow*): He does me honor.

VALERE: Sir, without offending,
> He has a hundred charming qualities
> But he's embarrassed when we speak of these.
> He can't abide discussion of his virtue.

THE COUNT: He's very wise. Conceit can only hurt you.

VALERE: He's a true gentleman.

THE COUNT: So it appears.

VALERE: His actions prove it.

THE COUNT: Sir, I have some fears
> He does protest too much. People like me
> Accept our rank with full security.
> We have our pride, but it is not conceit
> Because it's never shadowed by deceit.
> If this Philinte were truly so secure
> And if his rank and status were so sure

He wouldn't really need your commendation,
Since everyone would know his reputation.
But since his name is totally unknown
His family's fortunes must be newly grown.

VALERE: No one has said so.

THE COUNT: But you understand,
That's from politeness. On the other hand
Before we ever met you knew my name.

VALERE: I swear I didn't.

THE COUNT: Then that's to your shame.
The name of Tufière is not connected
To some obscure estate, but is respected
Throughout the land, a hundred histories
Recount my family's exploits. Look through these
You'll find my ancestors ensconced in castles
And under them innumerable vassals
More noble than Philinte.

VALERE: Sir, I've no doubt . . .

THE COUNT: All men of quality will bear me out.
Consult them. Modesty prevents my speaking.

VALERE: More honor to you. Pride . . .

THE COUNT: . . . and all self-seeking
I hold in horror. Great men all agree
The highest virtue is humility.
(*Seeing that* VALERE *is moving away.*)
You're leaving.

VALERE: Yes, but I will long recall
Your modesty, example to us all.

THE COUNT (*touching his hand*): Then are we friends?

VALERE: Monsieur, you honor me.

THE COUNT: Bosh! I'm your humble servant. If you see
             Philinte, do me the favor to implore him
             To recognize that I should rank before him.
             He would do better to renounce his suit,
             Give up your sister, cease this vain pursuit.
             Tell him I'm sure that he's a prudent man
             Who will avoid my anger if he can.
             Perhaps he'll take this good advice from you,
             But if he won't, he'll see what I can do.

VALERE: To such suggestions I have no reply.
             I'll pass them on to him, and so good-bye. (*He leaves.*)

ISABELLE: Why is your humble rival so despised?

THE COUNT: No one, it seems to me, should be surprised.
             I'm not a proud man, but I'm deeply shocked
             To find my way by such a man is blocked.
             Philinte's no one at all, so how can he
             Disturb the projects of a man like me?

ISABELLE: A man like me? Sir, I'm astonished you
             Would speak that way.

THE COUNT: It's in the point of view.
             Such words, for most, would smack somewhat of pride,
             But in my case, they're surely justified.

ISABELLE: Have you the right, simply because of birth,
             To lord it over everyone on earth?

THE COUNT: You're speaking for my rival, it is clear.

ISABELLE: I'm not, but since my brother is not here,
             Let me speak freely. Don't become defensive,
             But sir, I find your manner most offensive.

THE COUNT: I can't imagine what would make you feel
That way, since love for you inspired my zeal.

ISABELLE: Love for yourself, you mean. Don't try to hide
Your motive. It's not love you feel, but pride.

THE COUNT: Both are involved, it's pride that has supported
My spirit, when my love for you was thwarted.
It's pride that won't allow my love's survival
By tolerating an unworthy rival.
If you consider pride as a defect,
Then what of honor, and of self-respect?
Honor, of course, insists upon its due,
But it's also magnanimous, when true,
Generous when sincere, the driving force
Behind the other virtues, and their source.

ISABELLE: I'll grant to honor all the goods you claim
But many a sin's committed in its name.
True honor's not so quick to take offense,
Not so preoccupied with self-defense.
It doesn't praise itself, but waits for praise.
Vanity, though, works in quite different ways.
Proud of itself, impatient to be lauded,
It haughtily demands to be applauded.

THE COUNT: A nice distinction! Just what does it show?

ISABELLE: I hoped, it seems in vain, that you would know.
I'm just a bit embarrassed to explain
A difference I would have thought was plain
Between true merit and its pale reflection.
One truly shines, the other, on inspection,
Just seems to shine, to place itself on view,
One is superb but vain, the other true
One seeks renown, the other can't abide it.
One lives to flaunt its glory, one to hide it.
Nay, I'll go further. Those of noblest birth
In affability display their worth.

They're never cruel, nor critical, I find,
But flexible, considerate, and kind.
Conceited snobs are hated everywhere;
The man of fortune with a modest air
Is greater far in everyone's esteem
Than those who make much noise and always seem
Obsessed with rank and name, treating with scorn
Any they judge to be less highly born,
Considering those multitudes who fall
Below their rank to have to rank at all.

THE COUNT: A lovely speech, but what is its intent?

ISABELLE: Lisette, I'm sure, can tell you what I meant.
I see that I've already caused you pain,
So it is best I leave her to explain.

THE COUNT: No, no, I beg you, spare me the disgrace
Of speaking with a servant in your place.
Don't force me . . .

ISABELLE: You must come to realize
Some merits in the people you despise.
I will respect you more if I can see
You honor her as you would honor me.
She may be your best help, if you will let her,
To win my heart, since no one knows it better.
(*She goes.*)

THE COUNT: Are you still here?

LISETTE: Yes. Pardon my temerity,
And hear me out. Extend a bit of charity.
I'm ordered to converse with you and I
Desire it too, although the Lord knows why.

THE COUNT: I cannot cope with your familiar tone.

LISETTE: You're always thinking of yourself alone,

But since her words I'm asked to explicate,
You're looking small by seeking to seem great.

THE COUNT: You dare . . .

LISETTE: I do indeed, and I am in
                 A quandary, since I want to see you win
                 And you are losing, sir.

THE COUNT: What? I am losing?

ISABELLE: You are. Your pride, your grand airs are abusing
                 Everyone's patience. They are compromising
                 The virtues that you should be emphasizing.
                 Conceit will be your downfall. Isabelle
                 Has drawn your portrait for you, all too well.
                 Forgive my frankness. What I would advise,
                 A change of character, is, I realize,
                 Out of the question. Nature's always sure
                 To fortify whatever we abjure.
                 So I do not insist you change your spots
                 But, when with Isabelle, conceal your thoughts
                 Agree with all she says and sacrifice
                 Pride to self-interest. That is my advice.
                 Your family's image Isabelle can burnish
                 By that substantial fortune she can furnish.
                 These are my thoughts, and I have done my part.
                 Heed them or not, they're spoken from the heart.
                 (*Seeing that* THE COUNT *is listening to her with
                 some irritation.*)
                 Doubtless your pride has been somewhat offended,
                 But be assured that all was well intended. (*She goes.*)

THE COUNT (*alone*): So is it now considered a disgrace
                 To have self-confidence, to know one's place?
                 Must I accept this petit bourgeois scorn
                 For anyone who's not ignobly born?
                 If I believed—no, I must play their game;
                 Love and self-interest both urge the same.

When I'm with Isabelle I'll hold my tongue
But that unworthy rival who's been sprung
On me had better not pursue his plan
Or he'll discover who's the better man.
I hope I'll meet him soon; he'll quickly see
How hopeless competition is with me.

PHILINTE (*entering, while making several bows*):
Forgive me, sir, for daring to intrude
Upon your thoughts. Please do not think me rude,
But I have so looked forward to our meeting
I hope you'll overlook this sudden greeting.

THE COUNT: I'm much obliged, but do I know your name?

PHILINTE: I'm sure you don't, Monsieur, but all the same
I would be honored if you'd come to know me.

THE COUNT: What do you want?

PHILINTE: The honor that you show me
By asking, overwhelms me. Know then, Sir,
I'm called Philinte.

THE COUNT: Indeed. I guessed you were.
Your deferential airs gave you away.

PHILINTE (*in a very humble tone*):
Monsieur, I cannot find the words to say
How much I honor you.

THE COUNT: And rightly so.
But what is it you want? Am I to know?

PHILINTE: Valere's my friend, as you may be aware.

THE COUNT: And so?

PHILINTE: He says just now, while he was standing there,

If his report is true, and I suspect
It's not, you spoke of me with disrespect.

THE COUNT: Others were heaping praises. I extended
My contrary opinion. You're offended?

PHILINTE (*bowing*): By no means, Sir. I heartily agree
And honor you the more for honesty.
But there was more I hardly dare repeat,
That Isabelle and I should cease to meet.

THE COUNT: Those were my very words, I won't deny.

PHILINTE: I thought I must have been mistaken. Why?
I can't accept, indeed, can't understand
The cruel sacrifice that you demand.

THE COUNT: You doubt me, sir?

PHILINTE: No, but the love I feel
For Isabelle is past my power to heal.

THE COUNT: I'll cure you, sir.

PHILINTE: Monsieur, I doubt you will.
She and her mother both support me still.

THE COUNT (*picking up his hat*):
And you presume to say this to my face?

PHILINTE: I'm much embarrassed, sir, but that's the case.
Nature has been my tyrant, not my nurse.
I've suffered, but the outcome could be worse.
It's made me weak, but stubborn and resistant
Whenever those against me are persistent.

THE COUNT: You can't rely on stubbornness alone.
I warn you, sir.

PHILINTE: A poor thing, but my own.
                    When I'm attacked, it rallies to my side,
                    And it is never taken in by pride.

THE COUNT: It staggers me that one in your capacity
                    Would dare to speak to me with such audacity.

PHILINTE: In fact, Monsieur, I come to ask a favor.

THE COUNT: Ah! What!

PHILINTE: I wonder if you'd care to savor
                    A glass of wine with me.

THE COUNT: You're bold, I see.
                    That is no favor, it's a liberty!
                    You may well be my rival but the sequel
                    That doesn't follow is that you're my equal.

PHILINTE (*in a light manner, putting on his gloves*):
                    I thank you for your praise, though indirect.
                    It warms my heart to garner your respect.

THE COUNT: Pox on your compliments! You'll quickly see
                    The risks you run in standing up to me!
                    (*Both draw their swords.*)

LISIMON (*running in*):
                    What's all this uproar in my house? Good Lord!
                    Blades drawn! The first . . .

PHILINTE (*sheathing his sword*): I'm putting up my sword
                    Out of respect.

LISIMON: So gentle sir, you show
                    Some fangs.

PHILINTE: Occasionally.

THE COUNT: Still, you know
    He is not dangerous.

PHILINTE: That's to be seen.
    At least I can assure you that between
    Us two, I plan to win the prize.

LISIMON: Don't be too sure.

PHILINTE: Monsieur, I realize . . .

LISIMON (*interrupting him*):
    Within his own house I assume you view
    The father as the master.

PHILINTE: Sir, I do.

LISIMON: And that's the role I claim in these, my quarters
    Despite my forward wife and her supporters.
    The Count admires my daughter; he's my choice.
    Why should I hear from any other voice
    Except my daughter's, and she's not inclined
    To challenge my decisions, as you'll find.
    So, since your situation now is clear,
    You have no reason for remaining here.

PHILINTE: I beg to differ, sir, respectfully.
    Your wife has spoken differently to me.

LISIMON: My wife has spoken? I have given my word.
    She wouldn't dare oppose me! It's absurd!
    I have the power, if she attempts such capers,
    To give both you and her your walking papers!

PHILINTE: I love your daughter, and her mother's vow
    Leads me to hope that I'll prevail somehow.
    Until those two dismiss me, I'll remain.
    I have my rights, and these I will maintain. (*He goes.*)

LISIMON: How stubborn!

THE COUNT: This is what Valere has done.
                And he would suffer were he not your son!

LISIMON: I'll deal with him myself! He'll feel my cane!
                After this trick, I'm damned if he'll remain
                Under my roof. I cannot tolerate it.

THE COUNT: His cocky self-assurance! How I hate it!

LISIMON: The lad's a silly fool, just like his mother,
                So naturally they reinforce each other.
                His mother has an air benign and toothless,
                But she's a demon, iron-willed and ruthless.
                Just now, cold-bloodedly, in level tones,
                But full of enmity, she made no bones
                About declaring, in my daughter's face,
                That she would leave me were I to embrace
                Your suit. I told her I was quite resigned
                To this great loss provided that she signed
                The contract. Once she's given her consent
                I wouldn't care whether she stayed or went.
                Swooning and tears of course were her reply.
                Lisette and Isabelle were standing by,
                And joined in all the shrieks and cries with brio,
                As if they had rehearsed this little trio.
                One would start crying, then a second top her
                And then the third, I powerless to stop her.

THE COUNT: Are these the obstacles we have before us?

LISIMON: Don't worry. I will terminate this chorus.
                As you have risen in my estimation,
                My high regard fuels my determination.
                Old chum, your father, as I understand,
                Cut quite a noble figure in the land.

THE COUNT (*clapping him on the shoulder*):

I'm glad to see the consciousness is gaining
Of what a son-in-law you are obtaining,
Not an "old chum," but a revered relation.

LISIMON: Sorry. I spoke without consideration.
I'm sure I'll get the hang of it in time.

THE COUNT: You promise?

LISIMON: Yes, but surely it's no crime
For us, old chum, to use a lighter tone.

THE COUNT: Your promise!

LISIMON: Right! But can we leave alone
Such niceties for now, and try to find
Some way to change my wife and daughter's mind?

THE COUNT: I urge you, give no opportunity
For them to say a word concerning me.
Assert your power — you are master here —
And all these grievances will disappear.

LISIMON: If you support me . . .

THE COUNT (*interrupting*):   No, it's your affair.
When you have settled it, then I'll be there. (*He goes.*)

LISIMON (*alone*): Some demon must possess me, in the way
I've got entangled with this popinjay.
This is the price I pay for my ambition.
His name and rank got me in this position,
And now I can't reject him, that would be
A fatal blow to my authority.
My son and wife would carry off the day,
And then expect to always get their way.
That is a precedent I cannot set!
No! No! I'm not defeated yet.
Honor compels me and I will defend

Count Tufière unto the bitter end! (*He goes.*)

ACT IV

(LISETTE *and* PASQUIN *enter on opposite sides of the stage,*
    PASQUIN *first. He crosses quickly, not seeing* LISETTE *at first.*)

LISETTE: Am I to be passed by unheard, unseen?

PASQUIN: I swear I didn't see you there, my queen!
              Ask what you will. I'll try to satisfy you.

LISETTE: I badly need to be instructed by you.

PASQUIN: Is that your wish?

LISETTE: It is.

PASQUIN: Then have no fear.
              I'm at your service.

LISETTE: It may cost you dear.

PASQUIN: Whatever the cost, just tell me. I would treasure
              A chance to show my zeal and give you pleasure.
              Inform me, what's this Herculean task?

LISETTE: To answer truthfully whatever I ask.

PASQUIN: An easy job!

LISETTE: We'll see. I want to know
              If you have visited the Count's chateau?

PASQUIN: A hundred times! (*Aside*) Already forced to lie!

LISETTE: Is it impressive?

PASQUIN: That I can't deny.
                From all the region people come to gape.
                The building is pentagonal in shape . . .

LISETTE: Pentagonal? Good lord!   I'm quite at sea.

PASQUIN: It's an art term.

LISETTE: Well then, explain to me
                Just what it means.

PASQUIN: I would that I could show
                You every bit of that superb chateau,
                So your own eyes could judge the many ways
                The thing itself exceeds my humble praise.
                First, seven towers raised on three small hills,
                A crenellated battlement which fills
                The space between. Within, a massive keep,
                Surrounding all, a moat, both wide and deep
                A bastion within a barbican
                And forming as a whole — a pentagon!

LISETTE: It seems the Count has nothing but the best.

PASQUIN: I guarantee that you would be impressed.

LISETTE: And this is where the house of Tufière
                Holds court?

PASQUIN: It is indeed, and gathered there,
                Around the father of the Count, my queen,
                Magnificence as you have never seen —
                Horses and carriages, cellars full of wine,
                Abundant tables when you wish to dine,
                Numberless pages, still more numerous rooms,
                One can't conceive the wealth all this consumes.

LISETTE: The house's resources must be immense!

PASQUIN: Their splendor gives you ample evidence.

LISETTE: Perhaps it does, and yet I must advise
            That you should be consistent in your lies.

PASQUIN: Consistent?

LISETTE: Liars who can't recall
            Their previous lies are headed for a fall.
            The Count's extremely wealthy, now you say.
            But that's not what you told me yesterday.

PASQUIN: Frankly, I must admit your accusation,
            But it's a complicated situation.
            About the facts themselves I never lied,
            But only in the timing I implied.

LISETTE: Explain this riddle.

PASQUIN: Gladly. You must know
            The family's wealth was sound two weeks ago,
            But now, alas, the fickleness of fate
            Has quite reversed my master's former state.
            But though he's fallen now into obscurity,
            The poor man's pride remains in all its purity.
            He hopes his pompous airs will compensate
            For loss of fortune, prospects, and estate.
            That is his secret. Can it stay between us?

LISETTE: You have my word, since I have pledged to Venus
            To help your master, I'll keep under wraps
            All rumors of these troubling mishaps.
            Valere's unwavering in opposition
            But I have hopes of changing his position.
            I see him coming now, most apropos.

PASQUIN: It's you he's looking for, I'm sure. I'll go. (*He leaves.*)

LISETTE (*disdainfully*): Ah, so it's you, Monsieur. What a delight!

VALERE: Your tone says otherwise.

LISETTE: As well it might!

VALERE: Well, what is wrong?

LISETTE: You let me understand
My slightest wish you'd take as your command.

VALERE: That's so.

LISETTE: But when the Count made his appearance
You wouldn't tolerate my interference.
Against my wishes you embraced with zeal
The rival suitor. How should that make me feel?

VALERE: I merely told a friend of an attack
Against his honor, made behind his back
And nothing more. Since honor was involved
The matter really had to be resolved.

LISETTE: This constant talk of honor. I can't bear it.

VALERE: What bothers you? Philinte's a man of merit.

LISETTE: Let me speak plainly. If I can't rely
On you to work with me to satisfy
The Count and drive this tedious Philinte
Out of the house, I'm warning you, you can't
Expect me, maid or mistress, as God plans,
To put my name upon your marriage banns.
That's my decision. Now yours must be made.

VALERE: But for what reason . . . (*He breaks off.*)
                              Wait, I am afraid
Someone is coming. Quickly, tell me why . . .

LISETTE: Lycandre! I must speak with him. Goodbye
For now.

(She hurries him out as LYCANDRE *enters.)*

LYCANDRE: It seems I'm always seeing
You two together.

LISETTE: Yes, but disagreeing.
So far I've failed in pressuring Valere
To get behind the Count of Tufière.

LYCANDRE: So Tufière's the one that you support?

LISETTE: Yes, against everyone with every sort
Of pressure. He's not easy to defend.
His vanity appears to have no end.
His pleasure in himself is quite unbounded,
The more I see, the more I am astounded.

LYCANDRE: I'm sorely troubled.

LISETTE: What is your concern?

LYCANDRE: Answer me first. What has he done to earn
Your interest? Is it possible that he
Has recognized how helpful you can be?
Does he in fact acknowledge your assistance?

LISETTE: He scarcely even knows of my existence.
It's hard to think what circumstances made him
So cruel, yet I still desire to aid him.

LYCANDRE: Good heavens! What forgiveness on one side,
And on the other, what disgusting pride.
There is no vice to which we are susceptible
That rivals this in being unacceptable.
To feed its own illusion of perfection
It stifles all compassion, all affection.

LISETTE: I feel it.

LYCANDRE: But you have compassion left,
                    I hope, for your poor father, quite bereft
                    Of everything.

LISETTE: You spoke of him before
                    And said he'd come today. Sir, I implore
                    Your pity. Is he going to appear?

LYCANDRE: A little patience. He will soon be here.

LISETTE: Why does he hesitate so long to face me?
                    Doesn't he feel some yearning to embrace me?

LYCANDRE: He fears his presence, though your heart is good,
                    Would trouble you.

LISETTE: You know it never could!

LYCANDRE: Still, he's concerned his obvious misfortune
                    Would lower your affection in proportion.

LISETTE: He little knows me.

LYCANDRE: Still, that's why he chose,
                    Before appearing to you, to disclose
                    His situation, fearing you expected
                    A dashing father, not one beaten and dejected.

LISETTE: He'll be the dearer to me. He will see
                    My heart goes out to him in misery.
                    My tears will indicate that the rejection
                    He feared is turned to fondness and affection.
                    The little that I have I'll gladly share
                    With him. His happiness will be my care.
                    I haven't got much money, heaven knows,
                    But I've been given some expensive clothes,
                    My mother left to me her diamond ring,
                    To help my father, I'll sell everything.
                    I hope to find a thousand ways to show him

How much I love him, and how much I owe him.

LYCANDRE: Stop! Stop! Give me a chance to breathe, I pray.
I'm overcome by everything you say.
Despite his pains, your father's blessed in you!

LISETTE: And our reunion is long overdue.
But say, what evil brought him to this state?

LYCANDRE: What evil?

LISETTE: Yes.

LYCANDRE: I'm sorry to relate,
It was your mother's pride, worst of obsessions,
That ate up all his goods and his possessions.

LISETTE: How so?

LYCANDRE: Your mother claimed she was unable
To give her place to someone else at table.
The ladies quarreled, their feud became ferocious,
Both behaved in a manner quite atrocious.
The lady's husband mounted an attack
Upon your father. They were coming back
From hunting. No one witnessed the assault,
Nor knew that he who fell was most at fault.
Your father's arm was raised but in defense,
And yet his foe's death was the consequence.
The dead man's kin rallied to their relation,
Calling the accident assassination.
Bribed witnesses supported this contention.
In vain your father fought their base invention.
Warrants were issued; he went into hiding
And saved himself from hanging by abiding
In England, where you and your mother came
To share his humble exile and his shame.
Your mother died soon after.

LISETTE: But I thought
          She took me to the convent.

LYCANDRE: That was not
          Your mother, but your nurse, and she was acting
          Under your father's orders, most exacting.
          He told your nurse, your mother being dead,
          To bring you here and raise you in her stead,
          Claiming her role, and keeping dark your history.

LISETTE: But why did he insist on all this mystery?
          What did he fear?

LYCANDRE: He hoped you could avoid
          The ill effects of pride, that had destroyed
          His own life, and to spare you vain regret
          For those advantages you'd never get.
          Whether his plan protected you or not,
          To save you suffering was all he sought.

LISETTE: I long to see him, but I'm filled with fear.
          Unjustly sentenced, how can he appear
          Without great danger?

LYCANDRE: Fortunately, he
          Had faithful friends, who worked unceasingly
          To prove his innocence, and gained a hearing.
          The perjured witnesses recanted, fearing
          Themselves in peril. All was put to right.
          Your father, long sequestered out of sight
          Was brought at last the news so long awaited,
          That his long suffering was terminated.

LISETTE: Let him remain concealed. Do not restore him.
          I fear some subtle trap is waiting for him.
          We must be prudent. Tell him to beware.
          Stay where he's hidden. We will meet him there.
          Let's go, monsieur, I long for his embrace
          And for the bliss of meeting face to face.

LYCANDRE: You needn't move a step to greet your sire.
           Heaven's already granted your desire.
           Yes, your unhappy father stands before you,
           Finally free to claim you and adore you!

LISETTE (*falling at his feet*):
           Father! At last! Goodbye to pain and strife!
           This is the happiest moment of my life!

LYCANDRE: Daughter, arise! I share your happiness,
           And yet I am concerned, I must confess,
           That in this joy your brother may not share.

LISETTE: My brother!

LYCANDRE: Yes, the Count of Tufière!

LISETTE: My head is whirling. Is this some illusion?

LYCANDRE: If you're upset, imagine his confusion
           When he knows who you are.

LISETTE: His sister! I?

LYCANDRE: Indeed you are.

LISETTE: I finally see why
           The first time that we met, I was attracted
           To him, despite the pompous way he acted!
           My heart was not deceived, it recognized
           Our common bond of blood, however disguised.

LYCANDRE: Your heart knew him, but he did not know you.
           I'm now resolved to see this matter through
           And witness what will be his consternation
           To find the one he scorned is his relation.

LISETTE: 'Til then must I avoid him?

LYCANDRE: Yes, you must.
            But I'll confront him soon, and then, I trust,
            Our mutual talk will be a lively one,
            Since I will tell him frankly, as a son,
            Just what a legacy he has inherited
            And how much his presumptions were unmerited.

LISETTE: But will he recognize you?

LYCANDRE: Never fear.
            So go inside and wait for us, my dear.
            Someone is coming. What I have revealed
            Keep confident.

LISETTE (*kissing his hand*):   Father, my lips are sealed.
                (*She goes inside.*)

(PASQUIN *enters and stops, regarding* LYCANDRE.)

LYCANDRE: I'd like to see the Count of Tufière.

PASQUIN: What for?

LYCANDRE: To speak with him.

PASQUIN: The Count can spare
            No time for you.

LYCANDRE: Why not?

PASQUIN: He's occupied
            With his affairs.

LYCANDRE: I think he will decide
            When he knows who I am, to speak with me,
            Whatever his so-called affairs may be.

PASQUIN (*condescendingly*): And who are you?

LYCANDRE: I am . . . someone dismayed
                    At the impertinence you have displayed.

PASQUIN (*aside*): Good lord, he's right. I've got to use discretion.
                    (*To* LYCANDRE)
                    Excuse me, sir, for giving the impression
                    Of arrogance. I'm given to abuse,
                    But be assured, I have a good excuse.

LYCANDRE: And what is that?

PASQUIN: Well, without vanity,
                    And in a word, I'm what I seem to be,
                    A fool.

LYCANDRE: No one's a fool if he admits
                    His folly.

PASQUIN: Sir, my master has such fits
                    Of arrogance, and such a lofty tone,
                    That I, unthinking, take it as my own.
                    Eventually reason and good sense
                    Provide some check to my impertinence,
                    And then I view this vanity with shame.
                    Tell me, monsieur, may I inquire your name?

LYCANDRE: Young man, inform your lord it's my intent
                    To follow up the letter that I sent.
                    He's read it, I assume.

PASQUIN: Yes, and if you're
                    The unknown sender, then you can be sure
                    He wants to see you. (*He touches the cheek* THE
                    COUNT *slapped when he was given the letter.*)
                                         But I ought to say,
                    I got his answer earlier today,
                    And I still feel it.

LYCANDRE (*smiling*):   Do not fear for me.

I think he'll treat me rather differently.

PASQUIN: What! Do you dare . . .?

LYCANDRE: The risk is not so great.

PASQUIN: I fear, monsieur, you underestimate
His anger.

LYCANDRE: You may leave.

PASQUIN: Monsieur, I fear . . .

LYCANDRE (*impatiently*): Go!

PASQUIN: You were warned! I hope I made that clear!
(*He exits into* THE COUNT's *rooms.*)

LYCANDRE (*alone*):
The servant's airs suggest his lord's perspective,
Yet if my son consents to be objective
And own some faults, in time he may decide
To let his reason modify his pride,
And yet I fear . . .

THE COUNT (*entering with* PASQUIN):
Sir, say why I should bother
With your impertinence?
(*Aside, in confusion*) Good lord! My father!

LYCANDRE: A touching welcome. I am much impressed.

PASQUIN (*aside*): I've never seen my master so distressed.

THE COUNT (*recovering himself*):
Our first reactions take us unawares.
Pardon me, sir.

PASQUIN (aside): What happened to his airs?

THE COUNT: I thought . . . (*to* PASQUIN) Get out!

LYCANDRE: It's all right, he can hear . . .

THE COUNT (*to* PASQUIN):
          Get out, I said! Do you no longer fear
          My wrath?

LYCANDRE (*to* PASQUIN, *who is leaving*): Remain!

PASQUIN: No, he's too hot!
          I must do as I'm told. (*He goes.*)

THE COUNT (*shouting after him*):   And I am not
          At home to anyone!

LYCANDRE: Why send him out?

THE COUNT: I have my reasons!

LYCANDRE: What's this all about?

THE COUNT: Should I present my sire to my valet?

LYCANDRE: Say rather, are you willing to display
          My misery? That is the thing you fear,
          And far from being pleased to see me here,
          You blush with shame, your outraged pride concealing
          All traces of your heart's spontaneous feeling.
          Thus we may see, when men grow too conceited,
          Artifice rules, and nature is defeated.
          Clearly in vain I sent to you that letter,
          Thinking mistakenly you'd take it better
          From some unknown who thought you worth the bother
          Instead of your own miserable father.

THE COUNT: What makes you think I scorn your situation?
          I'm quite offended by the accusation!
          You've always had my love and my respect!

LYCANDRE: If asked to prove that, then, you'd not object?

THE COUNT: Demand whatever you like, I'll demonstrate
My claims!

LYCANDRE: All right, then. In my present state,
Go to the others in the house and name me.
If as your absent father you dare claim me,
I will believe you.

THE COUNT: Can you be aware
What it will cost me to accept this dare?

LYCANDRE: The family's honest. This is no disgrace.
Conduct me to them; let me plead your case.

THE COUNT: Don't be so eager. You may be subjected
To different greetings than you have expected.
We may have pride, but it cannot surpass
The arrogance that drives the middle class.
Whatever your background or your birth may be,
Pomp and display is all they want to see.
They only are concerned with outward show;
Indigent virtue they don't wish to know.
Since your disgrace, my bravery and my name
Are all my riches, and my only claim
To prominence. In military action
I gained success, increasing my attraction,
And as I came to grow in estimation,
I took on airs appropriate to my station.
If I am now respected, you can thank
This fine facade, and not my name or rank.

LYCANDRE: I scarcely can believe you. This must be
Simply a cover for your vanity.
I, without pretensions or defenses,
Will be myself, and take the consequences.
(*He starts to leave.*)

THE COUNT (*holding him back*):
>Wait a few days, I beg you on my knees.
>Allow me this, and then do as you please!
>(*He throws himself at* LYCANDRE's *feet.*)

LYCANDRE: I understand. You needn't try concealing
>Your vanity and shame of me by kneeling.
>Your mother's pride brought on my present shame,
>And I'm afraid your character's the same.

THE COUNT: Well, then, have pity, if I have not merited
>The prideful nature that I have inherited.
>Yet be assured that I revere you still;
>My life is yours. Command me as you will.
>All that I ask is that you use discretion,
>And not create too shocking an impression.

LYCANDRE: Your weakness touches me, and I will try,
>Out of concern for you, to modify
>My plans. (THE COUNT *rises.*)
>But watch yourself! I'll be observant!
>If your conceit breaks out . . .

LISIMON (*entering*):   Monsieur, your servant!
>I've come to seek you out, old chum, to say
>It's time to press your suit, without delay.
>My wife's begun to waver.

THE COUNT: Can it be?

LISIMON: She's showing far less animosity
>Toward you. Apparently at last she knows
>The trouble I could cause her if I chose.
>Now you should meet with her, and I expect
>It you treat her with caution and respect,
>All will go well. Remember, she's as proud
>As you are, and if she's allowed . . .

THE COUNT (*interrupting*): I am delighted at her change of heart!

LYCANDRE (*aside to* THE COUNT):
>You'll see, my son, I will support your part.

THE COUNT (*ironically*): Good news!

LISIMON (*taking off his hat*):   I guarantee you can't do better
>Than follow my instructions to the letter.
>It's up to you.

LYCANDRE (*to* THE COUNT): Listen to him and learn.
>This marriage should be your foremost concern.
>Strike quickly, while your star's in the ascendent!

LISIMON (*aside, to* THE COUNT): Who is this fellow?

THE COUNT (*aside, to* LISIMON):   He's . . . He's my attendant.

LISIMON (*aside*): He cuts a sorry figure. It is clear
>Attendance isn't much of a career.

THE COUNT: I trust him, though.

LISIMON: Indeed?

LYCANDRE (*aside*):   I see
>He isn't speaking honestly of me.
>His father's aspect undermines his pride.

THE COUNT: And his appearance . . .

LISIMON: Yes?

LYCANDRE: For now, I'll hide
>My wrath, but soon, when my true self is known,
>My son will rue the disrespect he's shown.
>The strongest means are more than justified
>To cure him of this overweening pride.

THE COUNT (*aside, to* LYCANDRE):

Constrain yourself, I beg you. Do not say
Anything that would give yourself away!

LYCANDRE (*aside, to* THE COUNT) All right.

THE COUNT (*to* LISIMON):   He's rather quiet, but he's reliable.

LISIMON: Enough of that! I said my wife was pliable
Right now. Seize the occasion. She expects
That you will come to pay her your respects.

THE COUNT (*smiling*): Respects?

LISIMON: That's right.

THE COUNT: I'm troubled by that word.

LYCANDRE (*to* THE COUNT):
Your quibbles over language are absurd!

LISIMON (*indicating* LYCANDRE): He's right!

LYCANDRE: You can't be serious in raising
Such problems over some small bit of phrasing.

THE COUNT (*rather haughtily*): But, sir . . .

LYCANDRE (*interrupting him in a commanding tone*):
But, sir, you must heed what I say!
Do what you must do, with no more delay!

THE COUNT (*aside*): He'll martyr both of us!

LISIMON: It seems to me
The old man shows a rather high degree
Of boldness.

THE COUNT: He may give you that impression.
(*Aside to* LYCANDRE)

I beg of you, exercise some discretion!

LYCANDRE (*aside, to* THE COUNT):
Do what he says or I'll drop all pretension!

LISIMON: My wife awaits you. Don't forget to mention
How much it means to you that she'll receive you.

LYCANDRE (*aside, to* THE COUNT): Submit, you hear?

THE COUNT (*aside, to* LYCANDRE):   I will. I do believe you!
(*To himself*) Good God!

LISIMON (*to* LYCANDRE):   Good sir, I hope you sympathize
With this advice.

LYCANDRE: Completely. If he's wise,
He'll follow it exactly and be grateful.
It's quite to his advantage.

THE COUNT (*aside*):   This is hateful!

LISIMON (*to* LYCANDRE):
How long have you been in your master's service?

THE COUNT: Excuse us, we must go! (*Aside*) I'm getting nervous!

LISIMON: One moment more.
(*To* LYCANDRE) What would you estimate
Your master's worth is?

LYCANDRE: I don't know. I'd hate
To guess.

LISIMON: But still . . .

THE COUNT (*aside, to* LYCANDRE): Tell him . . .

LYCANDRE (*aside, to* THE COUNT):   I cannot lie.

(*To* LISIMON)
Sir, I am pressed, and must bid you goodbye.
You'll soon get the assurances you need.
Meanwhile, I urge you, let your plans proceed.
This present turbulence will not endure,
And both of you will be content, I'm sure! (*He goes.*)

LISIMON: How can you leave your servant free to scorn
His proper place?

THE COUNT: Because he saw me born,
He's taken liberties all of my life.

LISIMON: An odd relationship! But now my wife
Awaits us.

THE COUNT: If you wish, then let us go.
What shall I say?

LISIMON: As if you didn't know!
Must I instruct you further?

THE COUNT: Yes, you see
The role that I must play is new to me.
You understand I have no preparation
In begging favors or solicitation.
My rank, my birth, all hinder my compliance
However much I wish for this alliance.
Can't you stand in, say what I ought to say?
That surely will suffice.

LISIMON: Is this the way
You thank me for my pains? What do you need?
My entire family and I to plead
On bended knees, that you deign to select
My daughter? Well, if that's what you expect,
You're much mistaken. You should understand,
Many would like to gain my daughter's hand.
So don't go see my wife, you'd just offend her,

And I'll leave you in solitary splendor! (*He goes.*)

THE COUNT (*alone*): How proud nobodies are! You never find
Any humility among their kind.
To gain their friendship we must sacrifice
Both pride and honor. It's a heavy price!
Ah, cruel fortune, is it your delight,
To witness me reduced to such a plight? (*He goes.*)

ACT V

(*Enter* LISETTE *and* ISABELLE.)

LISETTE: Mademoiselle, between the two of us
             We have important matters to discuss.

ISABELLE: What are they?

LISETTE: It is clear your mother's heading
             Toward dropping opposition to your wedding,
             But far from being pleased, as I expected,
             At this reversal, you seem quite dejected,
             Indeed, you're sad as I have ever seen you.

ISABELLE: It's true.

LISETTE: The Count! Has something come between you?
             He loves you, you can see it in his eyes.
             He's asked your hand, and you must realize
             How hard that was.

ISABELLE: Yes, that's what troubles me.
             He speaks to me with such frigidity!
             His mocking smile, his attitude disdainful,
             His haughty silences I find most painful.
             I don't impress him, it may be I bore him.
             My father must do all his pleading for him,
             While he remains aloof, and at a distance,
             And if it hadn't been for your assistance,
             Asking Valere to help prepare the way,
             I'd have no Count to trouble me today.
             I've done my best to quell my reservation,
             But when I think of his last conversation
             And with what cool disdain he sought to win me
             My tender heart quite shrivels up within me.

LISETTE: And so your former love has lost its fire?

ISABELLE: At least it's greatly cooled.

LISETTE: May I inquire
              If you feel any inconsistency?

ISABELLE: You quite misunderstand!

LISETTE: Oh! Pardon me!
              But if I may speak frankly . . .

ISABELLE: Go ahead.

LISETTE: It seems you're acting out some book you've read
              With you as heroine.

ISABELLE: If you are seeking
              To make some joke . . .

LISETTE: Mademoiselle, I'm speaking
              The sober truth. You know that you're inclined
              To anger when the slightest fault you find.
              You have your own fault; you are too severe,
              And this may cause you suffering, I fear.

ISABELLE: Am I too sensitive? As you can see,
              Far from exchanging tender vows with me,
              The Count insults me every time we meet!

LISETTE: He's not without presumption or conceit,
              But that's expected in his way of life.
              He's proud at present, but become his wife
              And he'll become a sweet, submissive mate.

ISABELLE: Can I dare hope for such a happy fate?
              (*Enter* VALERE, *distracted*.) Brother, you're pensive.

VALERE: I have cause to be.

My dearest friend has been betrayed by me.
I've served his rival, and before you two
I scorn myself for what I had to do.
I'd never have descended to such treason
Except for love, which was my only reason.

LISETTE: Do you repent?

VALERE: No, but if I loved you less,
Indeed I would. But now, won't you confess
What is your motive? Why is it you seem
To hold the Count in such a high esteem?

LISETTE: My motive is as strong as it is pure,
And I'll be praised, not blamed for it, I'm sure.

VALERE: I hope you're right. But can I be so bold
As to ask why?

LISETTE: No. I was only told
Just now myself, and asked not to reveal it.

VALERE: Whatever it is, you surely won't conceal it
From your own lover?

ISABELLE: So, you've really vowed
To win Lisette?

VALERE: Yes, and it does me proud.

ISABELLE: I quite agree with you, but our relations
Will want to know what are her expectations.

LISETTE: But that's just what I cannot speak about.

ISABELLE: Then I'll desist, until we straighten out
My own affairs.

VALERE: But those are settled.

ISABELLE: How?

VALERE: Good Lord, I thought you knew. Our father now
               Is at the lawyer's, putting all to rest.

ISABELLE: Where is my mother? Didn't she protest?

VALERE: She didn't, thanks to me and my persuasion.

LISIMON (*entering, to* ISABELLE):
               Daughter, let's celebrate this great occasion!
               The battle's won; the enemy is routed;
               The field is mine! It's true I briefly doubted,
               But now your mother's opposition's vanished.
               She'll sign the contract. Poor Philinte is banished.
               My friend the Count is now your only votary.
               At any moment I expect the notary.
               A few details remain but I foresee
               No obstacle, my dear. Tonight you'll be
               Madame the Countess!

ISABELLE: What! Tonight!

LISIMON: Why tarry?

ISABELLE: But also why this rush? No one should marry
               Without reflection and a little thought.

LISIMON: Reflection! Mademoiselle, I hope you're not
               Going to have another of your fits!
               You've done this five or six times now and it's
               Not something that the Count will find amusing!
               Think of the joy you run the risk of losing!

VALERE: But after all, my father . . .

LISIMON: After all,
               My son, I can't believe you have the gall
               To give opinions, after I have wrought

Such miracles. Who ever would have thought
Your mother would be reasonable, she
Who never was before and probably
Won't be again. Do you think I'll allow
My headstrong children to defeat me now?
To harm the masterpiece that I've created?
I warn you, I'm becoming irritated!
I swear, and you had better not forget it,
Arouse my anger, and you'll all regret it!

LISETTE: Bravo, Monsieur! I'm glad to hear you speak
             As father of the family, not to seek
             Advice or to reflect on your decision,
             But just to act, with firmness and precision.

ISABELLE: Lisette . . . ?

LISETTE (*interrupting her*): Your father has pronounced your fate.
             Complaint now is too little and too late!
             If it's his will, you and the Count must marry,
             Whatever may be urged to the contrary.

LISIMON (*aside*): The girl is charming!
                         (*To* LISETTE) Yes, my dear Lisette!
             (*More quietly to her*)
             Just watch your tongue, and you'll be perfect yet!

LISETTE: What good advice!

LISIMON (*attempting to embrace her*): And yours is also good.
             Let me embrace you for it, as I should!

LISETTE (*pushing him away*):
             I beg you, leave these tender salutations
             'Til I have fully filled your expectations!

LISIMON: That might be quite a wait. If you'll allow,
             I'd rather show appreciation now.

VALERE (*holding him back*):
>Father, you're getting over-wrought! Take care!

LISIMON (*pushing him off*): Monsieur the doctor, it's not your affair
>How wrought I am. I'll thank you not to be
>Solicitous. Just leave my health to me!
>(*Aside*) The rascal's over-wrought himself! I'll bet
>He's got some understanding with Lisette!
>I'll try to smoke him out.
>(*To* VALERE)   Son, I believe . . .

VALERE: Here is the notary. (*He starts to go.*)

LISIMON: No, no! Don't leave!
>We'll finish our discussion presently.
>(*To* M. JOSSE, *the notary*) Come in, Monsieur!

M. JOSSE (*entering*):   Good morning! Do I see
>Everyone here?

LISIMON: Yes!

M. JOSSE: Then we can proceed.
>(*He takes a contract from his pocket.*)
>I've drawn up all the articles you need.
>(*Indicating* ISABELLE)
>Is this the bride?

LISIMON: Yes.

M. JOSSE (*regarding her through his spectacles*):
>   She appears to be
>Well suited to begin a family.
>And where's the groom?

ISABELLE: Not here.

M. JOSSE: He's kept you waiting?
>That's a bad sign. If he is hesitating . . .

LISIMON: No, here he comes!
             (LISIMON *offers* M. JOSSE *a chair behind
             a small table.*)   If you would be so kind.

(THE COUNT *enters and all sit except* LISETTE.)

M. JOSSE (*putting on his spectacles and reading*): Whereas . . .

LISIMON (*to* ISABELLE, *who is speaking in a low voice to*
             LISETTE):   Be quiet!

M. JOSSE (*continuing*):   We, the undersigned,
             Notaries of his majesty, bear witness . . .

LISIMON (*to* VALERE, *who is speaking quietly but animatedly with*
             LISETTE):
             Be quiet, there! Have you no sense of fitness?
             Valere, come here, and leave the maid alone!

M. JOSSE (*to* THE COUNT):
             Your name, and any titles that you own.

THE COUNT: I will dictate them. Don't forget a one.
             (*Looking at the contract.*)
             You haven't got much space.

M. JOSSE: Once you've begun,
             I'll use the margin if it's necessary.

THE COUNT: Write, then! "The very powerful and very
             Exalted Lord . . .

M. JOSSE (*interrupting him*): Monsieur, that's not the way . . .

THE COUNT (*interrupting in turn*):
             Don't argue with me! Write down what I say!

M. JOSSE (*writing*): . . . Exalted Lord . . .

THE COUNT (*dictating*):   Monseigneur Alexandre
            Cesar Henri Armand Louis Leandre . . .

M. JOSSE (*interrupting*): Lord! What a list! Even the margin won't
            Contain it all! (*To* THE COUNT) And then?

THE COUNT: Of Mont-sur-Mont.
            Baron and knight, Marquis of Tufière.

M. JOSSE: You're a marquis?

THE COUNT: Actually, I'm the heir.
            My father holds the title, but I claim
            It after him, so it's almost the same.

LISIMON (*clapping him on the shoulder*):
            Well done, my boy! What noble pedigrees!
            Just think! My only daughter a marquise!

M. JOSSE (*to* THE COUNT): So, is that all?

THE COUNT: All? We have just begun!
            Lord of . . .

M. JOSSE (*interrupting him and writing*):
                            . . . Et cetera. I'm never one
            To stretch things out.

THE COUNT: Then say "of other places,"
            But put the letters all in upper cases.

ISABELLE (*aside, to* LISETTE): And golden letters?

LISETTE: Quiet!

ISABELLE: No, no! I swear
            Such vanity is more than I can bear!

LISETTE: But it's a common fault with men of rank,

Especially when there's nothing in the bank.

M. JOSSE (*to* LISIMON): And now for you, Monsieur.
(*Looking at his papers.*)   Well, then, let's see.
(*Reading*) "Monsieur Antoine Lisimon."

LISIMON: Yes, yes, that's me.

THE COUNT: "Monsieur Antoine?" Surely that's not your name!

LISIMON: It is. Why not?

THE COUNT: Of course, you're not to blame,
But it's so bourgeois!

LISIMON: Is it? No more so
Than multitudes of others that I know.

THE COUNT (*disdainfully*):
Well, let it pass. It's neither here nor there.
What matters is the titles that you bear.

LISIMON: I don't have any.

THE COUNT: What! How can that be?

LISIMON: Wait! I remember one!
(*To* M. JOSSE)   Write down for me
"Lisimon, Gentleman."

THE COUNT: And is that all?

LISIMON: It is, but if you want to, you can call
Me sovereign — of a hundred gold ecus.

THE COUNT: You're mocking me!

LISIMON: A title, if you choose,
More brilliant, I think, than most of yours.

> And I have notes of credit, sinecures
> Worth more than attics full of ancient deeds
> Fit more for nesting rats than human needs.

M. JOSSE (*aside*): He's right.

THE COUNT: You dare to call tradition trash?

M. JOSSE: We bourgeoisie would rather have the cash.
(*To* LISIMON) There, name the dowry.

LISIMON: For my son, the Count,
Nine hundred thousand francs is the amount.

M. JOSSE (*to* THE COUNT): A handsome title, it must be conceded,
Just the new blood your ancient lineage needed.

THE COUNT (*haughtily*):
Gold, Monsieur Notary, is your profession,
But it is purified in our possession.

M. JOSSE (*writing again*): And what goes to your wife in the event
Of your demise?

THE COUNT: She's guaranteed a rent
Of twenty thousand francs.

LISETTE (*aside*):   I'm quite impressed.
In promises, my brother's at his best.

M. JOSSE: For this amount, have you some guarantee?

THE COUNT: Of course, Montorgueil, our barony.

M. FOSSE (*writes, and then rises*):
That finishes our business. I will need
Everyone's signatures.
(*The others also rise.*) Then we can proceed
To hold the service

(*To* THE COUNT) once your father's here.

THE COUNT: My father! He cannot attend, I fear.
          For six months he has suffered so with gout
          That he can't leave his bed, much less go out.

LISETTE (*aside*): My brother really shows enormous skill
          At lying.

THE COUNT (*to* LISIMON): When we're married, then you will
          Of course go visit him.

LISIMON: I'd be delighted
          To make the trip.

THE COUNT (*looking offstage, aside*):
                      Good lord! I think I've sighted
          The man himself. I'm headed for disaster!

(LYCANDRE *enters*.)

LISIMON (*to* LYCANDRE, *not recognizing him at first*):
          What do you want?
          (*Then, recognizing him as* THE COUNT'*s presumed
          servant*) Oh! Looking for your master?
          He's here.

LYCANDRE: My son! I see it's time I came!

(*All except* LISETTE *are astonished*.)

VALERE and ISABELLE (*to each other*): His son!

THE COUNT (*aside*):   What a disgrace! I'll die of shame!

LISIMON: You have misled us, Count, that much is clear!
          Explain yourself!

THE COUNT (*aside, to* LYCANDRE): How can you dare appear

In such a state?

LYCANDRE (*aside, to* THE COUNT): If my poor garb alarms you,
I think it honors me more than it harms you.
The rights of father clearly supercede
The claims of wealth and fortune, and you need
To honor them.

THE COUNT (*aside, to* LYCANDRE): What! Must I do so now?

LISIMON (*interrupting him*):
Well, Baron de Montorgueil, is this how
You show us it was no exaggeration
When you were bragging of your wealth and station?

LYCANDRE: My son's confusion, which he cannot hide,
Is punishment for his excessive pride.
(*To* THE COUNT)
My misery at least one end has served,
To give you the corrective you deserved.
Now, give me peace. Accept, do not despise me!
Speak! Claim me as your father! Recognize me!

ISABELLE (*to* LISETTE, *whom she sees weeping*):
Lisette! You're crying!

LISETTE: You'll soon know the cause.

LYCANDRE (*to* THE COUNT):
Your pride must be subjected to the laws
Of family feeling. It is time to choose!
Embrace your father, or hold back and lose
His love, and rather take his curse instead!

THE COUNT: My heart is moved by everything you've said.
Since it's your wish, leave me with no illusion.
Enjoy my suffering and my confusion.
Pride is defeated, and the heart has won.
You are my father, and I am your son!

(*He throws himself at* LYCANDRE's *feet.*)
Look tenderly upon my altered state
And grant me, since you know the cost was great,
Your future blessing.

LISIMON: Handsomely expressed!
(*To* LYCANDRE) So you're the missing father!

LYCANDRE: He confessed
As much. His heart won out at last.
I trembled, fearing that he could not cast
His pride away, but nature proved the stronger.
We won't be separated any longer!
(*To* THE COUNT)
So be assured, my son, you've amply paid
For all of the mistakes that you have made.
Our sorrows are over. Heaven has confounded
The enemies by which I was surrounded.
Our noble monarch, hearing of my woes,
Saw through the machinations of my foes.
His justice quelled their menace, evidently.
My honor is restored, and consequently
You have regained a father who possesses
All of the goods and rank that his distresses
Deprived him of. My joy is overflowing.
If anything it has increased by knowing
That I can share it with you.

THE COUNT: Do my ears
Deceive me? Happy fortune, it appears
Favors the virtuous. My goods, my rank
My birth restored! (*To* LYCANDRE)
                                And I have you to thank!

LYCANDRE: Temper your happiness with modesty.

LISIMON: Well said! I am delighted you and he
Have triumphed, though I didn't need this news
To give your son my friendship, nor to choose

Him above others for my son-in-law,
Because despite his arrogance I saw
He was all right at heart. Now all we need
Is your name on this contract.

LYCANDRE: Yes, indeed.
But still you haven't fully been repaid
For all the sacrifices you have made.
With this alliance happily concluded,
I'd like to see another one included!

LISIMON: Another?

LYCANDRE: Yes. I'd love to see your son
United with my daughter!

VALERE (*to* LISETTE):   I'm undone!

LISIMON: My family's honored, and I couldn't be
More gratified! Your daughter! Where is she?
In Paris?

LYCANDRE: Yes, indeed! (*To* LISETTE) Approach, my dear,
And greet your husband!

LISIMON: What is this I hear?
That is our maid, Lisette!

LYCANDRE: No, you're mistaken.
She is Constance. The person you have taken
For chambermaid exceeds you all in rank.
For all of these confusions you can thank
The spin of fortune's wheel. Yet, heaven be praised,
Her virtue is no less than someone raised
At court.

VALERE: I ask for nothing more than this!

ISABELLE (*to* LISETTE):

Heaven be thanked that we can share such bliss!

LISETTE: Embrace me, brother; I will do the same!

THE COUNT: It is an honor that I gladly claim (*They embrace*).

LISIMON (*to* LYCANDRE):
               As for my family, we have good prospects
               To give your daughter more than she expects.
               Money buys influence, and I have got
               My eye upon a handsome marquisat
               To give my future son-in-law his due.
               Now, Monsieur Josse, I leave it up to you.
               Arrange things with the seller so that we
               May hail the Count tomorrow as a marquis!
               (*To* THE COUNT) Are you content?

THE COUNT: I couldn't ask for more!

LISIMON: It seems a double wedding is in store.

ISABELLE (*to* THE COUNT):
               You've won my heart, but I still fear your pride!

THE COUNT: I know love will bring out my better side
               Count on its power, soon you will be shown,
               Your tastes, your feelings have become my own.

LYCANDRE: Despite his pride, my son is good at heart
               Which compensates for all.

LISIMON: And one can start
               Building a character upon that base,
               Where even bits of pride may find a place.

THE COUNT: No, now my goal's becoming master of
               Myself, and nurturing respect and love.
               My eyes are open now; I realize
               The love of others is life's highest prize.

Pride only stirs up hate and indignation.
On trust and love is built true reputation.

END

LA CHAUSSÉE

The Fashionable Prejudice

by

Pierre Nivelle de La Chaussée

Introduction

The author did not provide a preface for this work, but a commentary by the Abbe Prevost, reprinted from his *Pour et Contre* (vol. 5, p. 357) was used as a preface to it in the 1762 edition of the *Oeuvres,* and it is reproduced here.

The Fashionable Prejudice, a Comedy

To set oneself clearly against this work would be a shock to public opinion. Universal approval is rarely in error. I do not know if among the crowds of spectators who have flocked to every performance there is a single one who has not applauded. However, there have been also few among them who have not found something to criticize, and by the same rule it follows that *The Fashionable Prejudice* must have its faults as well as its beauties.

Be that as it may, extraordinary marks of approval have been given to this new play. People have laughed, have cried, have felt all the emotions that it pleased the author to inspire. The style is smooth, noble, elegant. There is a wide and abundant choice of material, eloquence, and admirable strength. The author has dealt with his situations artfully, indeed some of them have no equal in any previous comedy. The scene in the fourth act when Durval declares to his wife that they must part, and the manner in which it is developed and sustained, seems to me one of the most beautiful things in the world. If it has been formed by Art, its depths come from Nature alone, and this draws forth the tears that one sheds in watching it.

What a character Constance is! All the beauties of Art and Nature unite in her! What virtuous suffering! What perfection in both love and forbearance! Sometimes a single speech is worth an entire scene, such as:

"Ah! Once I was respected, and I am no longer."

There are elements throughout the play that show the hand of a Master whose knowledge of the human heart is perfect. Among them is the subtle change in Durval's language when he becomes again the jealous and brutal husband.

After the character of Constance, one cannot praise too highly that of Damon. The author must be honored for the episode of his love for Sophie, and for the skill with which it is related to the main action.

In general, *The Fashionable Prejudice* seems to me to have deserved all the applause that it has received. Virtue, wit, and sentiment have perhaps never been better employed in the theatre.

But even so, some criticism may be justified. Some have expressed regret that the author did not reduce the play to three acts, in order in some places to speed up the action. I must admit that I do not share this opinion. Not that I feel that I can defend the play against this charge, especially in the third act, when interest is sustained almost entirely by theatrical tricks, but could not this be remedied with a little invention? The subject could certainly bear it!

Nothing is so ill-conceived, in my opinion, as the news that comes to the two marquis about a situation so parallel to that of Durval and about the comedy in which they want him to take a role himself. Coincidences this unusual and this apposite are an affront to all verisimilitude. Everything that results from this arouses the same irritation. What, then, might be substituted? That would be for the author to consider, but it is certain that even five acts would not exhaust the potential of so interesting a subject.

Complaints have been made of another flaw in the very first scenes that could have been more easily avoided. Constance's sufferings appear too vividly before the cause of them is known. She is clearly unhappy and one suffers for her and sympathizes with her pains, but one is not well enough informed of the reasons for these sufferings.

The character of Durval is extremely uneven. He begins in a manner so self-assured that he can take the freest tone and even enjoy the embarrassment in which he places his wife, but then he suddenly becomes disturbed, unsure, introspective, he becomes so distracted as to threaten both his rest and his reason. It is not that his love was less strong before, since it led him to leave the Court, and, considering the time that would have been necessary for the artist to complete the portrait, he must have been suffering in secret for more than a month. Is it conceivable that so passionate a man would have been able to leave his wife in agony over his presumed infidelity for so long a time? Even if his misplaced shame prevented him from full expression of his love, he could have at least shown her enough respect and concern to keep her from suffering too much about his situation.

Argant is intolerable. How can a courtier who is the father of Durval be seen in this flat buffoon who deals continually in the sort of crude comedy of traditional farce? The two marquis are insipid characters who would be a disgrace to the Court, even in their lowly roles there.

It is true that these flaws can to some extent be blamed on the actors, since it is clear that with a little discernment they would understand that characters sometimes need to be softened a bit. Durval and Argant are better on the page than on the stage, where the latter is distorted by the burlesque antics of one actor and the former by the studied contortions of another. As for Constance and Damon, it appears that in their actions, as in their role, nothing can be changed without loss. In the tender denouement in particular, when Constance's speech contains more beauties than have ever previously been assembled and which the actress delivers with a thousand beauties more through the superiority of her talent, cursed would be the Muses and the Graces alike if they did not shower their admiration on both author and actress.

THE FASHIONABLE PREJUDICE

by

Pierre Nivelle de La Chaussée

Premiered at the Comédie-Française
February 3, 1735

CAST OF CHARACTERS

DURVAL, an aristocrat

CONSTANCE, his wife

ARGANT, father of CONSTANCE

SOPHIE, niece of ARGANT

DAMON, friend of DURVAL, lover of SOPHIE

CLITANDRE, a marquis

DAMIS, a marquis

FLORINE, CONSTANCE's maid

HENRI, DURVAL's valet

ACT I

Scene: DURVAL's *country retreat. Enter* DURVAL's *wife,*
CONSTANCE, *and his best friend,* DAMON.

DAMON: Ah, Constance, is it your responsibility
              To plan my marriage?

CONSTANCE: So, is my ability
              Called into question? Why do you refuse me
              Your trust?

DAMON: Madam, I beg you to excuse me.
              (*Aside*) A virtuous wife, but she's a victim, too.

CONSTANCE: You will win Sophie, as I've pledged to you.
              You know full well that I'd be pleased no end
              To satisfy my husband's dearest friend.

DAMON: Indeed, he honors me with his respect,
              But Sophie sees our ties as a defect.

CONSTANCE: What, your close friendship . . .

DAMON: She claims to despise!
              Not everyone sees matters through your eyes.

CONSTANCE: That cannot be the Sophie that I know!
              She clearly doesn't hate you, so why show
              You such injustice?

DAMON: That I cannot guess.
              Within her heart, she may dislike me less,
              But her continued stubborn opposition
              Puts my love in a perilous position.
              She sees in certain marriages deep flaws.

> And then makes these exceptions into laws.
> Marriage she sees as human sacrifice
> In which the woman always pays the price.
> I don't know what example or what error
> Inspired in her this strangely baseless terror.
> To speak the truth, she thinks you are abused
> And blames me for the shameful way you're used
> Because she thinks me in your husband's thrall.

CONSTANCE: Monsieur, she's wrong, and she insults us all.

DAMON: She thinks your husband seeks for ways to grieve you.

CONSTANCE: Damon, it's nothing.

DAMON: But can I believe you?

CONSTANCE: No more of this, I pray. Before you leave
           I'll speak with Sophie and you will receive
           Her vows of love.

DAMON: Madam, I trust in you.
           You know you must enlist your father too.

CONSTANCE: I'm waiting for him now. I hope that he
           Can help advance your cause.

DAMON: I'm quite at sea.

CONSTANCE: Go, now. And let me do what I must do,
           Alter his language and his point of view,
           Above all, keep my husband from this strife.

DAMON (*aside, as he leaves*):
           A happy husband, to have such a wife!
           I hope Durval appreciates her merit!

CONSTANCE (*alone*): My situation's cruel, but I must bear it.
           Damon's a friend as faithful as he's wise.

If only he could open Durval's eyes!
Meanwhile my suffering I must conceal,
And feign a happiness I do not feel,
Obeying the unwritten law which states
All women must be happy with their mates!
I must be careful to preserve the peace
For fear my difficulties will increase.
It's hard to bear indifference in a mate,
But better his indifference than his hate!

ARGANT (*entering, somewhat angrily*):
You asked me for a meeting, and I came
Somewhat surprised, since I desired the same.

CONSTANCE: You seem disturbed.

ARGANT: That's no exaggeration!
Sophie and I just had a conversation.
What I was told made it extremely clear
Just why you thought of meeting with me here.
You needn't ask; I'll give you my reply.

CONSTANCE: You know already . . . ?

ARGANT: Daughter, please don't try
To second-guess me. Let me speak my mind.

CONSTANCE: I'm silent.

ARGANT: Good! I know quite well what kind
Of man Durval is since in him I see
Much the same traits that I recall in me.
My youth was rather livelier than his
But when I married, as the custom is,
I settled down, and, had my wife consented
I could have lived eternally contented.
A long time passed, a year I would suppose,
And nothing, at least on my side, arose
To cloud our joy, but on the other side,

Women, of course, are never satisfied,
And when love changes, as of course it will,
To friendship, women always take it ill.
They cannot understand that it's the fashion
To treat one's wife with fondness, not with passion.
She couldn't stand the change, and though she tried,
With some success, a month or two to hide
Her disappointment, soon it came to light.
We started in to quarrel, then to fight.
My wife complained, my father heard her claim.
His own experience was much the same.
He didn't really give me any latitude,
But neither did he try to change my attitude.
Since he won't change, he said, he should remarry.
I quite agreed, and so I did.

CONSTANCE: That's very
          Illuminating, but what do you seek
          To get from me?

ARGANT: Though contradictions pique
          My interest, yours has something odd about it.
          You seem content and happy.

CONSTANCE: Do you doubt it?

ARGANT: No one has ever witnessed you disparage
          Durval.

CONSTANCE: I never have.

ARGANT: You claim that marriage
          Is not invariably a cruel ordeal
          For any woman.

CONSTANCE: That is what I feel.

ARGANT: As Sophie's guardian, then, was I mistaken
          In thinking you, her closest friend, have taken

Some liberties in speaking?

CONSTANCE: Please say clearly
        What troubles you. Both of us love her dearly.

ARGANT: We do, but someone's got her all perturbed.
        Both Damon and your husband are disturbed.
        Who could have filled her heart, so full of trust,
        With this unfounded fear, this strange disgust,
        The marked aversion and the scornful air
        She has toward marriage. Who has put them there?
        From someone of her age one never hears
        Such fancies as she poured into my ears!
        On the contrary, virgin hearts should drift
        Enchanted in those dreams that are the gift
        Of Nature. Thoughts of marriage should inspire
        Them not to fright but rather to desire.
        Yet, far from feeling happy and elated,
        Poor Sophie's totally intimidated,
        And to speak frankly, Madame, I suspect
        Your personal complaints had this effect.
        Thanks to your friendship, she's no longer pure!

CONSTANCE (*aside*): How much more suffering must I endure?
        (*To* ARGANT)
        My thoughts upon this matter, sir, are these:
        Listen to them, and after, as you please,
        Pursue the accusations you are making.
        My marriage was a happy undertaking.
        My fortune has exceeded my deserts.
        But if, some day, I undergo some hurts,
        If my dear husband's previous affection
        Should lessen, I would have the circumspection
        To hide my shame, and not increase my woes
        By talking of my sufferings to those
        Who couldn't help, instead of seeking ways
        To reignite my husband's love and praise.
        If any situation's calculated
        To make a loving wife appreciated,

To throw her qualities into relief,
It's when, without complaint, she bears her grief.
These are my thoughts; now draw your own conclusions

ARGANT: It's hard to free yourself from your illusions.
I don't care what you say, but what you do.
So prove to me your sentiments are true
By working with me to convince my niece
Her groundless negativity should cease,
And she should take Damon . . .

CONSTANCE: You hardly need
To ask. I want the same.

ARGANT: Then we're agreed.

CONSTANCE: I never realized she was opposed.

ARGANT: You thought she loved him?

CONSTANCE: That's what I supposed.
At least I thought so from the way she acted.

ARGANT: But why refuse the man if she's attracted?

CONSTANCE: That's a strong word. Perhaps she'd rather take
A bit more time when there's so much at stake.
She's young and she's still learning, don't forget.
Perhaps she doesn't trust her feelings yet.
Perhaps she's still attempting to discover
The way her heart should open to a lover.

ARGANT: She's coming! Stop this idle speculation.
Let's see what she'll reveal in conversation.
(*Enter* SOPHIE)
Dear niece! Just now we were discussing you!

SOPHIE (*regarding* CONSTANCE): And saying what?

ARGANT: Nothing, I hope, untrue.

SOPHIE: Well, if it was the truth Madame was speaking,
            I trust that means that you're no longer seeking
            To sacrifice me.

ARGANT: What? On the contrary,
            You'll be a happy woman when you marry
            Damon. I know you favor him.

SOPHIE: And who
            Provided such enlightenment to you?

ARGANT (*indicating* CONSTANCE):
            Madam, of course. Like me, she has decided
            That at your age you ought to be provided
            With a good husband.

SOPHIE: Which I'll never find!

ARGANT: Sophie! It's your own good we have in mind!
            My daughter only wishes you to share
            Her happiness!

SOPHIE: Or what she has to bear!
            She's happy, then?

ARGANT: As happy as could be!

SOPHIE: She told you so?

CONSTANCE: I did. I must agree.

SOPHIE: That's a surprise, but my misgivings seem
            Still quite legitimate. I have esteem
            For Damon, as I often have admitted,
            And if some happiness in marriage were permitted
            For my poor sex, so often victimized,
            I might choose him, but I have realized

> That in our circles the display of passion
> In married life is clearly out of fashion.
> We leave such folly to the bourgeoisie,
> While making married life a mockery.
> Husbands today expect to lead their lives
> With no consideration for their wives.
> This cruel prejudice means the rejection
> Of any sort of mutual affection.
> If love exists, the wife will never know it,
> Because her husband is forbid to show it,
> Until at last the man no longer cares
> And wastes his love on casual affairs.

ARGANT: Why think of marriage in so dark a way?

SOPHIE (*indicating* CONSTANCE):
    Because I see examples every day!

ARGANT: Constance is happy.

SOPHIE: I do not believe you.

CONSTANCE: But I am happy. Why would I deceive you?

SOPHIE: No, you are not!

CONSTANCE: I tell you that I am!

SOPHIE: Madam, how can you bear to live this sham?
    (*To* ARGANT)
    When truth is cruel, illusion she prefers.
    She's given you my secret, that is hers.

ARGANT: Is this the truth?

SOPHIE: It is.

ARGANT: I'm quite confused.

CONSTANCE: You know I've never claimed to be abused.

SOPHIE: Yes, and I blame you for it. You have tried
To keep it secret, but you could not hide
The sorrow in your heart, your constant fears.
I've often seen the traces of your tears.
What can I say if it's your choice to be
Silent when faced with such indignity?

ARGANT: One says she's happy, one says she is lying,
And turns her back on marriage, thus defying
All custom. It is like a madhouse here,
But happily the proper course is clear.
(*To* CONSTANCE)
Madam, happy or not, you know my mind
(*To* SOPHIE) And as for you, I'm going now to find
Damon and cheer him up. Ladies, feel free
To find more grounds on which to disagree.
(*He goes.*)

CONSTANCE: What have you done?

SOPHIE (*thoughtfully*):   Damon will think the same.

CONSTANCE: For what you've said, I'll have to bear the blame.

SOPHIE: Did I do wrong then?

CONSTANCE: No, I must confess,
I couldn't help myself, and I have hurt you.
What you have said is true and shows your virtue.
Your rigor and directness I admire,
But when you challenge men you play with fire.
The name of husband gives a man the right
To treat you as his chattel day and night,
To scorn the vows he took to love and cherish,
Letting your happiness decline and perish.
Trampling on your rights, all this because
It always is the men who make the laws.

SOPHIE: Is it too radical of me to crave
                To be a man's companion, not his slave?
                It seems to me your lack of protestation
                Suggests that you accept this situation.

CONSTANCE (*gently*): Do you suspect that's so?

SOPHIE: No, to be fair,
                I know you suffer more than I could bear.
                But don't you understand that some may see
                The motive for your actions differently.
                The happiness you work so hard to feign
                Is read but as indifference to pain,
                And gives your husband license to continue
                His pleasures, while your pleasure dies within you.

CONSTANCE: Ah, Sophie. Spare your victim!

SOPHIE: I could go
                Much further.

CONSTANCE: Don't! My husband, you must know,
                Esteems me!

SOPHIE: That reveals he hardly knows you.
                It's not esteem, but love a husband owes you.
                Love is the feeling that should rule our lives.
                Have husbands different rights than those of wives?
                Would any of them settle for esteem?
                Perfidious as they are, they wouldn't dream
                Of anything but love. But as for me,
                I can't subscribe to such duplicity.
                I couldn't lead the life that you endure;
                I love Damon too much, and I am sure
                I'd grow resentful, then we'd move apart,
                Our love would end, and that would break my heart.

CONSTANCE: Isn't your love for Damon worth your trust?

SOPHIE: All men behave the same. They simply must!

CONSTANCE: What of the qualities that love assures?

SOPHIE: Weren't those same qualities at one time yours?
               What has become of them?   What now is left?
               Only a fatal trap, one quite bereft
               Of all those joys you once were certain of,
               Since marriage never pays the debts of love.

FLORINE (*entering*): Madame, I came to bring you a surprise.

CONSTANCE: What is it?

FLORINE: No, you won't believe your eyes!

CONSTANCE: What's going on? Tell me!

FLORINE: Wait, I'm still trying
               To catch my breath. It's really stupefying!
               Hurry to your apartment; you will see . . .

CONSTANCE (*interrupting her*): My husband?

FLORINE: Surely not! Since when has he
               Dropped by? That would be news indeed! You know
               He stays in his own end of the chateau!

CONSTANCE: Florine! Be more respectful of your master!

FLORINE: I will be silent, but . . .

CONSTANCE (*interrupting*): Now, what disaster
               Has stirred you up?

FLORINE: Madame, you'll never guess!
               You've just received a most delightful dress!

CONSTANCE: What?

FLORINE: It just came, madame, and it's a dream!

CONSTANCE: You are exaggerating.

FLORINE: If I seem
            Excessive, come and see. I wonder, is it
            Designed for hunting? It is quite exquisite!
            Come, try it on at once. Don't waste a minute!
            You'll go from conquest unto conquest in it!

CONSTANCE: Stop weaving fantasies and tell me who
            Sent me this gift.

FLORINE: I haven't got a clue!

CONSTANCE: I never ordered it. There's some mistake.

FLORINE (*after some thought*):
            Ah, now I see! Madame must make
            Her little joke! It's some gallant has sent it.

CONSTANCE: But not to me!

FLORINE: For whom then has he meant it?

CONSTANCE (*after some thought, to* SOPHIE):
            But surely you're the object of this courting!
            Damon, whose suit your father is supporting . . .

SOPHIE (*delighted*): If only he would take such liberties!

CONSTANCE: Should I receive advances such as these?
            Here comes my husband. Should I let him know
            About this gift, or simply let it go?

DURVAL (*aside, as he comes in*):
            Let's see just what results I am obtaining
            For my small gifts. (*To* CONSTANCE)
            Madame, you've been complaining.

I understand, about the life you lead.

CONSTANCE: Monsieur, I'm shocked!

DURVAL: And so am I, indeed
            I never dreamed, despite my worst suspicions
            That you would make such negative admissions.
            I won't forget this soon, you may be sure.

CONSTANCE (*to* SOPHIE): Just as I feared!
            (*To* DURVAL)   I swear to you, Monsieur,
            That I was innocent of this report.
            But clearly you have tried me in your court
            And will allow no plea for innocence.

SOPHIE (*aside*): It's all my fault! I'll come to her defense.
            (*To* Durval)Your cruelty, sir, is beyond compare!
            At first you were unfaithful, now unfair!

DURVAL (*aside*): No longer!

SOPHIE: Ingrate!

CONSTANCE: Sophie, please restrain
            Yourself.

FLORINE: No, no. Don't spare him any pain!
            If I were in your place . . .

SOPHIE (*To* DURVAL):   What right have you
            To haul her into judgement as you do?
            You fill her heart with bitterness and pain
            And then condemn her if she dares complain!
            She should bear everything and finally die
            Without the consolation of a sigh!

CONSTANCE (*to* SOPHIE): You make things worse!

DURVAL (*aside*):   It's time to end this game!

SOPHIE (*to* DURVAL): If you're offended, I'm the one to blame.

DURVAL: What, you?

SOPHIE: Yes, I. I really couldn't bear
                To see my friend Constance in such despair.
                Against her wish, I strongly felt the need
                To name her wrongs!

DURVAL: You are a friend, indeed!

SOPHIE: My dear Monsieur, spare me your irony.

FLORINE (*with spirit*): Were you the husband that you ought to be,
                Blessed with a wife so gentle and so sweet,
                You'd kiss the very ground beneath her feet!
                But you reject her!

CONSTANCE: Florine! Go away!

FLORINE: Me? Go?

DURVAL (*holding her back*): Don't be so cruel. Let her stay!
                She loves you. It is natural. Dear Florine,
                Take this for your advice (*giving her money*).

FLORINE: Well, now I've seen
                Everything.

DURVAL (*to* CONSTANCE): Madame, do not take it ill.
                She's only spirited.

FLORINE: Well, if you're still
                Paying for truth, next time I'll make it worse.
                If that much truth gets coins, I'll take the purse!

SOPHIE: Wit is a great resource!

DURVAL: It is, but now

More pressing matters wait. Do you know how
You're going to spend the day? Doubtless you've made
Some assignations.

FLORINE (*aside*):   Madame is afraid
            Of just that possibility.

DURVAL: Of course, today
            A hunt is scheduled. Then a grand soiree
            And dancing all night long. Madame, we'll go
            Whenever you are ready
            (*looking closely at her*) and I know
            You have new clothing fit for the occasion.

CONSTANCE: Monsieur . . .

DURVAL: Don't tell me that you need persuasion.
            You'll want to be there from the very start.
            Your brand-new horse and carriage will impart
            An air of grandeur to you. If you're lacking
            In anything, you know you have my backing.
            (CONSTANCE *appears troubled.*)
            Madame, you don't seem fully at your ease.
            Feel free to spend whatever amount you please.
            I know that such expense is justified!

FLORINE (*aside*): This husband surely has his better side!

CONSTANCE: What you have told me comes as some surprise,
            But painful as it is, I realize
            I must reveal the cause of my distress.
            I'm most unhappy!

DURVAL: Why, I cannot guess.

CONSTANCE: I really had no reason to foresee
            Someone would take such liberties with me!

DURVAL (*pretending to be astonished*):

You speak of liberties! What do you mean?

CONSTANCE: I don't know who . . . that is . . . I've never seen . . .

DURVAL: Go on, who's stopping you?

CONSTANCE: This dress, this horse . . .
          I've never witnessed either one, of course . . .

DURVAL: They're at your lodgings.

CONSTANCE: But then, who would dare
          Send me such gifts when I was unaware . . .

DURVAL: But you have gotten gifts. That much is clear.

CONSTANCE: And I have no idea who sent them here.

DURVAL: And you've not tried to find who it might be?

FLORINE (*aside*): I would throw out the lot, if it were me.

DURVAL: But who are your suspicions pointed toward?

CONSTANCE: I'd rather leave such questions unexplored.

DURVAL (*aside*): Could I be really this far from her thought?

CONSTANCE: When one receives offensive gifts, one ought
          To just ignore them.

DURVAL (*aside*):   Clearly this will require
          Some stronger measures.
          (*To* CONSTANCE)   Madame, though I admire
          Your scruples, I have reasons of my own
          For clearing matters up and making known
          Who sent those gifts. I cannot overstate
          How much it means to both of us—what great
          Importance it may have. So please pursue it.

Use any means. You cannot overdo it!
Discover if you can who it may be
Who dared to offer you this gallantry.
But, presents quite apart . . . madame, you still . . .
(*Recovering himself*)
Yes, please pursue this matter, if you will. (*He goes.*)

SOPHIE (*to* CONSTANCE):
Isn't it odd, the tolerance he's showing?

FLORINE: Whoever saw a man so easy-going?

CONSTANCE (*after some thought*):
Could it be he who sent me such a present?

FLORINE: No husband ever did a deed so pleasant.
Why would he bother? Madame, on my life,
No husband showers gifts upon his wife.
He gives her less than she anticipates
And anything he gives he over-rates.
Consider what young suitor it might be.
Clitandre, for example, or Damis.
As candidates these are as strong as any.

SOPHIE: Do you have some suspicion?

FLORINE: I have many.

SOPHIE: Durval's indifference seems strange to me.
Husbands are rare with such complacency.

CONSTANCE: Oh, please say nothing to increase my care.
I already have more than I can bear.
I'll shut myself away in my disgrace.
You go enjoy yourself. Attend the chase.

SOPHIE: I will not leave you.

CONSTANCE: No, it's my affair.

I beg you, go! You show me too much care.
Go to the hunt. Enjoy your tender years
And leave me to my sorrow and my tears.
(*She goes.*)

SOPHIE: What misery! Yet I'm supposed to claim
A husband? Say no more! They're all the same!

ACT II

DURVAL (*thoughtfully walking back and forth*):
    Hunting's not always entertaining, is it?

DAMON: It's not. Let us recover with a visit
    To Constance.

DURVAL (*still distracted*): Though I shouldn't be depressed.
    My horse and clothing were among the best.

DAMON: A pity Constance wasn't here today.

DURVAL: I've partly guessed just why she stayed away.

DAMON: Let's speak with her. A visit from her mate
    Is surely something she'd appreciate.

DURVAL: I rarely visit her. When necessary
    I send someone.

DAMON: A cruel choice. Why marry,
    And then ignore her? Surely you could soften
    Your rigor. It is true affections often
    Can change, but if your love for her has shattered,
    You still could treat your wife as if she mattered.

DURVAL (*looking about*):
    The hunting party's gone. There's only us.
    And I have several matters to discuss. (*He sighs.*)
    Dear friend, I must apologize. I've not
    Been frank and open with you as I ought.
    The fear of what you'd say, what you'd advise me
    Has served, I must admit, to paralyze me.
    I'd start, but shame would never let me finish,
    For fear our treasured friendship would diminish.

DAMON: Durval, I have my faults, you may be sure
                But when it comes to friendship, I abjure
                The tyranny of those whose friends must be
                Treated like slaves to serve their vanity.
                A friend for them is nothing but a soul
                Whose conduct they can model and control.
                True friendship suffers no such contradictions,
                It is a liaison without restrictions
                Where hearts and minds and temperaments are willing
                To join in unions mutually fulfilling.
                The ties that bind them never are constraining
                But rather are supporting and sustaining.
                I think that such a friendship we can claim
                Or so I feel, and hope you feel the same.

DURVAL (*with a serious air*):
                I do. That's why I'm willing to reveal
                A secret to you that I would conceal
                From all the rest, to you alone impart
                The deepest inner workings of my heart.
                I love—although that word is far too weak—
                A flame is lit, or rather I should speak
                Of one re-lit, to which I am returning
                Which I know now will be forever burning.

DAMON (*astonished*):
                What! Can a heart like yours one object claim
                Which until now has leapt from flame to flame?
                Those many tender loves that you have sworn,
                Can't any of them also be reborn,
                Or have you really changed your point of view,
                Seeing inconstancy has drawbacks too?

DURVAL: When you know who . . .

DAMON: Don't tell me! For that end,
                Seek an accomplice rather than a friend.

DURVAL: Do not abandon me just when my need

Is greatest. Rather be a friend indeed.

DAMON (*withdrawing*): This confidence I do not wish to hear.

DURVAL (*drawing his back*): I will say nothing to offend your ear.
               She's charmed me so, down to my very core,
               I feel as if I've never loved before.
               This admirable woman, who has stirred
               Such passion in me — Don't think me absurd —
               It is my wife!

DAMON: Constance!

DURVAL: Yes, it is she.

DAMON: Dear friend! I am as happy as can be!
               But are you sure this feeling is sincere,
               Not just some fancy that will disappear?

DURVAL: You and my wife may well have some misgiving,
               Considering the life I have been living.
               More solid evidence, I know, will be required
               To show my wife how much she is admired.
               I've sought for special methods for revealing
               To Constance the emotions I am feeling.
               Thus I invented this mysterious lover,
               Who is myself, hoping that she'll discover
               My stratagem, and realize the passion
               I feel for her, regardless of the fashion!
               While others waste their time in speculating
               About my rival, I'm anticipating
               The life of wedded bliss I am preparing.

DAMON: But have you thought of what your wife is bearing?
               What is she thinking? How will this affect her?

DURVAL: Don't be concerned. Her virtue will protect her.
               I've seen her suffering, without revealing
               Responsibility for what she's feeling.

I feigned indifference, although almost told
Her twenty times . . . I know you'll think me cold.
I love her with a passion, but I lack
The courage to speak out. Shame holds me back.
I'm prisoner to the prejudice in fashion
Holding that marriage can't be blessed with passion.
The ridicule is more than I could bear.

DAMON: You would be ridiculed should you declare
            You loved your wife?

DURVAL: It's difficult to handle.
            I must move cautiously, avoiding scandal.
            Already this affair has complicated
            My life in ways I'd not anticipated.
            I finally gained permission from the court
            To come and spend two weeks in this resort
            Providing me occasion to be next
            To Constance, with your marriage as pretext.
            I thought, were we together and alone
            I'd find some way to make my feelings known,
            To quietly reforge the marriage chain.
            But all my hopes and planning were in vain.
            My rank and my position guarantee
            That I can never hope for privacy.
            Clitandre and Damis, to name but two,
            Are quite aware of everything I do.
            So far they've spared me, but you know that they
            Are ruthless once they seize upon a prey.
            Others would share their scorn. It's a disgrace
            I simply cannot bring myself to face.
            I cannot bear it. I will disappear,
            Perhaps be forced to go in hiding here,
            Seek out some cottage, close the doors behind me,
            And hope none of my friends would ever find me.
            Society's a meaningless convention
            For one who's undivided in attention,
            Whose every thought is focused on his wife.
            He's placed under her tutelage for life.

DAMON (*coldly*): If one should put your theories into practice,
          Only the wives of others should attract us.

DURVAL: You jest! Society does not allow . . .

DAMON: Was there no meaning in your marriage vow?
          Clearly self-interest holds you in its thrall.
          If you'd sworn any other oath at all,
          Once it was given you would not suborn it,
          However humble he to whom you'd sworn it.
          Both law and honor force you to be just.
          A woman lacks these guarantees. She must
          Rely upon her weakness and her tears.
          Such feeble arms should cause no husband fears.
          All power is the husband's. He should use it
          In such a way that he does not abuse it.

DURVAL: I'm desperate, but custom rules us all.
          The wisest man does not escape its thrall.

DAMON: Fashion lays claims upon us, I confess,
          In passing fads of furnishings or dress,
          But virtue is another matter quite.
          Vices are black, fads cannot make them white.
          In moral judgements one's own heart is best
          And social custom can dictate the rest.
          Don't bend to fashion, to yourself be true,
          Do what you should, and not what others do.

DURVAL: There have been times, my friend, when I was set
          To give up everything without regret,
          To simply gather Constance up and flee.

DAMON: That seems a rather desperate course to me.

DURVAL: And yet it was the one that I preferred,
          At least until another thought occurred
          To me. Of course I should have known
          Fleeing created problems of its own.

Once Constance was aware of victory
And recognized her power over me,
How would she use the power she had gained?
What if love lost, and only pride remained?
One sees examples every day when men,
Their power lost, don't get it back again.

DAMON: Examples aren't ever far to seek
For any cause we wish, however weak.
Nothing in Constance justifies your fear.

DURVAL: You don't know women, friend. That's all too clear.
They always want to place themselves above us.
They'd far prefer to dominate than love us.
They love to be loved, seeking out a mate
So they can have a heart to dominate.

DAMON: These charges also could to men be laid.
Why should you be the master, she the maid?
When women wed, experience has shown
We shrink their empire to enlarge our own,
Explaining always, unjust as we are,
How men are their superiors by far.
We can't help loving them, so we decide
To denigrate them just to feed our pride.

DURVAL: I've wronged my wife so often in the past
That she'll be sure my change of heart won't last.
She'll fear a new relapse, a fresh disdain,
Her pardon I can only hope to gain
By full elimination of her fears
Through abject posturing, with sighs and tears.
Yet, the more weakness and more love I show,
The greater her ascendency will grow.
(*He grows pensive.*)
No, it's too much. I must accept my fate.
I am resolved. I will not hesitate . . .

DAMON (*embracing him*):

Dear friend, I much admire you for displaying
Such virtue. Your reward . . .

DURVAL: What are you saying?
You thought that I . . .

DAMON: . . . was ready, I supposed,
To bear what loving bonds your wife imposed.

DURVAL: Quite the contrary!

DAMON: What!

DURVAL   It's my intent
To flee the servitude they represent!
Forget the feelings that I have disclosed,
And do not speak. I know you are opposed.

DAMON: But just consider. What is the effect
Of this decision? What do you expect?
Your poor Constance will waste away in tears
When you could give her happiness for years.
Your cruelty in this could not be greater
If you decided not to love but hate her.

DURVAL (*in a penetrating tone*):
You're right. She must be spared, whatever the cost,
Even if my own self-respect is lost.
No longer will my heart resist love's call.
Come, see us reunited after all.
(*He starts to leave, but* CONSTANCE *enters and he
becomes troubled.*)
Oh heavens! It is she. I am not ready
To meet her yet, before my nerves are steady.
(*He tries to leave, while* DAMON *holds him back.
After some resistance, the two go to meet her.*)

DURVAL (*to* CONSTANCE):
I had to hold Damon and to implore him

To stay, but surely we can speak before him?

CONSTANCE: He's always welcome.

DURVAL: Madame, you did not
        Attend the hunt.

CONSTANCE: I didn't.

DURVAL: It was thought
      That you were ill.

CONSTANCE: I feigned to be, and came
      To tell you why.

DURVAL (*gently*):   I didn't mean to blame.

CONSTANCE: Alas, I felt the need to be alone.
      You know the reason. My unease has grown
      Since we last spoke, and so I have remained
      At home until those gifts can be explained.
      Till I know why and by whom they were sent
      I do not wish to give encouragement.

DURVAL: You can reject the gifts. There is no shame.

CONSTANCE: My reputation suffers all the same.

DURVAL (*embracing her, tenderly*):
      Take comfort. It is I . . . who . . . will protect you.

CONSTANCE: I'll die of shame.

DURVAL: Nonsense. I still respect you.
     (*aside, to* DAMON) I just can't do it!

DAMON (*aside, to* DURVAL):   Why not let me try it?

DURVAL (*aside, with feeling, to* DAMON):

If you say anything, I will deny it!

CONSTANCE (*to them, in astonishment*): What's going on?

DURVAL: Nothing. But I could barely
        Restrain Damon. He wanted, quite unfairly,
        To make you party to a secret plot.
        You hardly will believe the plan he's got—
        It's so embarrassing—and you're involved!

CONSTANCE: What is it?

DURVAL: He's impatient, and resolved
        To speak, but fearful. He's afraid to start,
        And, hoping you could see into his heart . . .

CONSTANCE: Damon's?

DURVAL: Indeed.

DAMON: Madame, don't be misled.
        He is the one who feels the way he said.

DURVAL: No! He begged me to speak—see his distress!
        He's timid and unwilling to confess
        His love or ask you to intercede.

DAMON (*aside, to* DURVAL): You torturer!

CONSTANCE: He knows there is no need
        To gain my aid. He's had it all along!

DURVAL: I guarantee his love is deep and strong.

DAMON (*aside, to* DURVAL): Good Lord! Speak for yourself!

CONSTANCE (*aside*):   A guarantee
        From one himself unfaithful!

DURVAL: But, you see,
          Sophie views marriage with a cold disdain.
          Of course she is mistaken; it is plain
          The two of them would live in perfect bliss.
          There cannot be a happier state than this.
          For those whose joy both love and reason bless,
          Marriage alone completes their happiness.
          Then in untroubled joy they pass their days
          Growing accustomed to each other's ways
          And ministering to each other's need.
          That husband is a happy man indeed
          Who in a single person can discover
          A cherished wife, companion, friend, and lover.
          His fondest hopes and dreams are thus requited;
          His duty and his pleasure here united.

CONSTANCE (*tenderly*):
          Your portrait seems so true I cannot doubt you.

DURVAL (*regarding her, equally tenderly*):
          Madame, there are examples all about you.

CLITANDRE (*speaking to* DAMIS *and* ARGANT, *who enter with
          him*): I can't believe this! It is too absurd!

DURVAL (*to* DAMON, *troubled*):
          Damis! Clitandre! Have they overheard?

CLITANDRE: Come, everyone! Don't even try containing
          Your mirth! The matter's far too entertaining!
          I'm laughing still!

ARGANT: Tell us, and let us share it.

CLITANDRE (*to* DURVAL):
          I'm told . . . . I'm not quite sure that you can bear it!

DURVAL (*coldly*): Then try me.

CLITANDRE: Well, we need no longer fear
          A man who made seduction his career,
          Whose conquests were the envy of us all
          Is toppled. We can triumph in his fall.
          I mean Saintfar.

ARGANT: Indeed, a famous name
          In love affairs; his father was the same,
          Pursuing liaisons with such success
          That I could tell you tales . . . but I digress.
          What have you heard of Saintfar's contretemps?

DAMON: Some angry husband caught him in a romp
          With tragic consequences, I suppose.

ARGANT: Who'd punish him for that?

CLITANDRE: Everyone knows
          Indulgence is expected in such cases.

CONSTANCE: Financial trouble, then, is what he faces?

CLITANDRE: He gambles, but I've always seen him win.

DURVAL: Someone has beat him?

CLITANDRE: Maybe. That's no sin.

DAMON: He's been disgraced, then?

CLITANDRE: Worse!

ARGANT: What! He's not dead?

CLITANDRE: No, worse than that! Our friend has lost his head
          Over a woman.

DURVAL, ARGANT, DAMON: Who?

CLITANDRE: One, it appears,
          You wouldn't think of in a million years!
          You won't believe his boldness!

DAMON: Wait! I'll bet
          He's made alliance with some fresh coquette!

CLITANDRE: What's bold about that?

ARGANT: Could it be that he's
          Succeeded with that difficult marquise
          Who only likes the suitors who ignore her?

CLITANDRE: No, not the marquise.

ARGANT: Others would rank before her
          In my opinion. Could it be some prude?
          I can't believe his taste would be that crude.
          He's done too well to suffer such a lapse!

CLITANDRE: No, that's not it!

ARGANT: An actress, then, perhaps?

CLITANDRE: Certainly not!

CONSTANCE: I wonder, could it be
          His wife?

ARGANT: His wife!

CLITANDRE: Yes, truly. It is she.

ARGANT: Such fairy tales don't happen in real life!

CLITANDRE: I'm sorry . . .

DURVAL (*aside, to* DAMON): Someone else who loves his wife!

DAMIS (*to* CONSTANCE):
>Someone has told you. Such a situation
>Is far beyond my own imagination.

CONSTANCE (*with a touch of pride*):
>Such love affairs seem not as strange to those
>Of sensitivity as you suppose.
>They see a heart that duty has called back
>And placed once more upon the proper track,
>Which found no true fulfillment in its travels
>And now gives little heed to others' cavils.
>I'm sure, however, that my thoughts don't please,
>So I'll leave you to gossip at your ease. (*She goes.*)

CLITANDRE: Constance must take the woman's side, it's clear.

ARGANT: For form's sake only.

DAMIS: She can't be sincere.

ARGANT: I'm sure that she is laughing up her sleeve!
>As for Saintfar, I really can't believe
>He's so in love with women that he's paying
>Attention to his wife!

DURVAL: What are they saying
>About his love?

DAMIS: What do you think, Durval?
>He is, of course, the laughing stock of all!
>His folly is the talk of town and court,
>The subject of lampoons of every sort,
>Till finally, bowing to the storm and strife,
>He packed his baggage and packed up his wife,
>And fled into the provinces to wait
>For time to change this amity to hate.

ARGANT: Like an elopement!

DAMIS: But how unconventional!

ARGANT: Indeed! Elopements ought to be intentional,
               Pursued to gain the world and not to leave it!

DURVAL: Perhaps in their retreat, should they achieve it,
               They'll come to see their happiness completed!

CLITANDRE: I've never seen Saintfar look so defeated!
               He is a slave to his disdainful spouse,
               Merely the first of servants in his house!
               She's clearly using her despotic power
               To punish him each day and every hour
               For his past sins, and with this he must bear
               The tedious exile that they now will share!

DAMIS: She'll treat him like a child, without respect!

ARGANT: It is the custom.

CLITANDRE: What did he expect?
               His wife's become his demon! He's possessed!
               Durval! Why aren't you laughing like the rest?

DURVAL: It's quite amusing!
               (*Aside, to* DAMON) I shall choke with rage!

CLITANDRE: The man is lost! Imagine, at his age!

ARGANT: Disgraced!

CLITANDRE: Dishonored!

DAMIS: Dead!

DURVAL (*aside, to* DAMON):   What an affair!

DAMON (*aside, to* DURVAL):
               So fools are gossiping! Why should you care?

DURVAL: There was a time when I'd have laughed as well.

DAMON: And who finds such things laughable, pray tell?
             Only those specialists in idle chatter
             Who think they are the only ones who matter
             And others merely subjects for their wit.
             But I believe, if you would think a bit,
             You really have more morals than you're claiming,
             And as for those at whom your barbs are aiming,
             What right have you to scorn them as you do
             Because they are more dutiful than you?
             They may not have your wit, but they have virtue,
             So let them practice it. How can that hurt you?

DAMIS (*to* DAMON):
             We know you're full of sentiments like these;
             Save them for courting Sophie, if you please.

DAMON: I speak for those who'll listen. For the rest,
             I'll simply take my leave. I've done my best.

DAMIS: Well said, Damon. But please forgive my choosing
             To laugh at things the whole world finds amusing.
             Saintfar is such a case. His impropriety
             Defies, you know, the rules of our society.
             He's even been depicted on the stage.

ARGANT: A play about him?

DAMIS: Yes. It's all the rage.
             In fact I have a copy, and I aim
             To do a reading of it. Are you game?

ARGANT: I'd love to.

DURVAL (*coldly*):   If you wish.

DAMON (*angrily*):   Not on your life!

DAMIS: It's called "The Loving Husband and His Wife."

ARGANT: Good. Clearly it's a work that merits showing.
                 The situation's rare, but it is growing,
                 And satire makes a powerful impression
                 For keeping husbands from such indiscretion
                 Is there a part for me?

DAMIS: Of course!

ARGANT: What fun!

DAMIS: We'll need some women. Constance can be one.
                 She'll be the wife whose husband scorns the fashion.
                 Durval can play the man who feels such passion.
                 Who'll play the friend? I thought that Damon might.
                 (*To* CLITANDRE) And you the fool.

ARGANT: The casting's a delight!

DAMIS: We also need a servant. Who can do it?
                 (*To* DURVAL)
                 Ah! Your valet Henri! Will you see to it?
                 As for the rest . . .

DAMON: Please do not count on me.

DAMIS: Durval, it's your responsibility . . .

DURVAL: For what?

DAMIS: To get Constance to join our piece.

ARGANT: I'll go encourage her. So will my niece. (*He goes.*)

DAMIS (*to* DURVAL): Work on Damon. I know you won't refuse.
                 Why should you? You have nothing here to lose.
                 (*He goes.*)

DURVAL (*irritably, to* DAMON):
> Well, have you heard enough? I think it's clear
> How little your opinion matters here.
> You nearly caused my ruin. Don't deny it.
> I'll thank you in the future to keep quiet.

DAMON:
> You'll let them play this tasteless farce, and you
> Even accept a role in it?

DURVAL:
>   I do.
> I can speak words of love, if in disguise,
> And see myself reflected in her eyes.
> I run a bit of risk, but since I'm playing,
> No one could guess — alas, what am I saying!
> I should have seen the trap within this fiction!
> I will betray myself by my conviction.
> All of my words and actions will express
> The love I feel. I shouldn't have said yes.

DAMON:
> You cannot pull out now. It's much too late.
> If Constance hears you won't participate
> She'll think your scorn for her has caused your quitting.
> (*Aside*) He must go on!

DURVAL:
>   You're cruel. It's just not fitting
> For me to do this. I can merely say
> I'd love to help, but I've been called away.
> I'll go make my adieux and then depart. (*He leaves.*)

DAMON: What weakness!

DURVAL (*returning*):   Something else, before I start!
> I've secretly commissioned, you should know,
> A portrait of my wife a month ago.
> The painter lives nearby. Could you go see
> If it has been completed? It would be
> A solace to me when I am away.

DAMON: I'll undertake it, but can't you delay

Your setting out?

DURVAL: I leave this very night! (*He goes.*)

DAMON: I need some motive to delay his flight.
What use is virtue? Why should we enjoy it
If fashion won't permit us to employ it?

ACT III

DAMON: Durval's come back; he's given me his word!
                I've shown him that his fears were quite absurd.
                His happy homecoming was all my doing.
                I've crossed one barrier to my own wooing.
                Another may lie ahead with bar still higher.
                Sophie is coming. Do I dare inquire?

SOPHIE (*crossing the stage*):
                Ah, here you are, Monsieur. I'm on my way
                To hear the concert.

DAMON: I'll come, if I may.

SOPHIE: I heard that we had lost you. Is that true?

DAMON: The term's more flattering than is my due.

SOPHIE: Instruct me then.

DAMON: It was Durval who thought
                Of leaving. I convinced him he should not.

SOPHIE: Why did you?

DAMON: Through the same perversity
                That keeps me hoping you will favor me.
                I've kept my distance, as you have decreed,
                Although it has been difficult indeed.
                Pardon my protests, but do not refuse
                The pleadings of the one you would accuse
                Of crimes that other people have committed.
                And for which I am totally unfitted.

SOPHIE: I see that the reports of you are just.
                Perhaps I was too harsh.

DAMON: Why can't you trust
               My vows? Could you be hoping you will find
               A worthier lover?

SOPHIE: That won't change my mind
               Upon this subject.

DAMON: I have your esteem,
               You say, so why is it I can't dream
               Of love as well?

SOPHIE: Since you draw that conclusion,
               I have no wish to shatter your illusion.
               But must I love you simply from respect?

DAMON: I know the sacrifice that I expect.
               You love your error.

SOPHIE: So, can you disprove it?

DAMON: You have one central case. If I remove it?
               What if Durval . . .

SOPHIE: I know that you defend
               His infidelities. He is your friend.

DAMON: But let's suppose that he were . . .

SOPHIE: What he is!

DAMON: I know what you expect from him, but his . . .

SOPHIE (*interrupting him*): Don't lie to me or scoff at my alarm!
               You think that you can conquer me with charm;
               Speaking of everlasting love that I've produced.
               That's just the way poor Constance was seduced!
               Why would you think that I would run such danger?
               You know in her own house she's like a stranger,
               A person scorned, without authority,

As if she were in her minority.
The name that might bring some of what is due her
Is shared by one who is unfaithful to her.
Without a husband's love our lives are vain,
Our title is his heart, he's our domain.

DAMON: But poor Durval, on whom you've passed your sentence,
What would you say if he should show repentance?

SOPHIE: Habits once set can rarely be displaced.

DAMON: But when one errs, one's steps can be retraced.

SOPHIE: He won't retrace his steps, I guarantee.
He's too devoted to inconstancy.
And his example . . . it's a troubling sign . . .

DAMON: Of what?

SOPHIE: No, I am getting out of line.

DAMON: Say what you wish. I am in too much pain
To take offense.

SOPHIE: I won't attempt to feign
Indifference, but state frankly my position.
I know the value of your proposition.
Your character is honest, I am sure.
Your virtue and your love seem strong and pure.
Doubtless I could live happily with you
If husbands had the power to be true.
But after marriage, little love remains.
You're like Durval.

DAMON: But he's resumed his chains!

SOPHIE: Damon, Durval's a bad example for you.
Don't use him as your model, I implore you!

DAMON: Allow me just one hope, that's all I ask.
           I have begun. Let me complete my task.
           And if Durval . . .

SOPHIE: In that case . . . (*she hesitates*)

DAMON: You've begun.
           Please finish.

SOPHIE: I'm embarrassed.

DAMON: Do you run
           Some risk? Not if you know Durval, and he
           Cannot be weaned from infidelity.

SOPHIE: Trusting him to reform I'm sure will raise
           False hopes. Why should he change his ways?

DAMON: I can but hope.

SOPHIE: Then we must wait and see.
           But until then, please do not bother me
           With anything that might be compromising.

DAMON: Such as?

SOPHIE: You know.

DAMON: I do?

SOPHIE: Nothing surprising.
           In short, I wish . . .

DAMON: Speak, and I'll understand.
           You know your every wish is my command.

SOPHIE: I promise nothing.

DAMON: Then my pledge must do

For both.

SOPHIE: Perhaps.

DAMON: I cannot lie to you.

SOPHIE: Please hear me out. I have instructions for you.
            You say you love me.

DAMON: Rather, I adore you.

SOPHIE: All right, then. I forbid your further speaking
            Of love or of the solace you are seeking.
            No sighs, no glances, no seductive airs,
            Which seek to catch a woman unawares.
            Don't put me in an awkward situation.

DAMON: Would you deprive me of all consolation?

SOPHIE: I know the way you feel without display.

DAMON: You may forget, though. How can I obey?

SOPHIE: Damon, if you persist, I must depart.
            (*She starts to leave.*)

DAMON: I will be silent, though it breaks my heart.

SOPHIE: Now, not another word of love to me . . .

DAMON: Until Durval's reform. Yes, I agree.
            Cruel mistress, though my love demands its due,
            I'll temper it, out of respect for you.
            (*He takes her hand.*)
            I promise that I will not compromise
            Your honor with my mouth or with my eyes.
            (*He throws himself at her knees, kissing her hand.*)
            Upon my knees I swear, if I forget . . .
            (*He continues kissing her hand.*)

SOPHIE: Damon! So I must reprehend you yet?

DAMON (*astonished*): Was that excessive?

SOPHIE: Yes, at least for now.
              Another time do not forget your vow. (*She goes.*)

DAMON: A happy future beckons, and the chance
              Of happiness brings pleasure in advance.
              Durval has promised me. I'd better find him.
              It may be necessary to remind him.

DAMIS (*entering*):
              Damon, here is your role. Would you look through it?

DAMON: I beg of you; get someone else to do it. (*He goes.*)

DAMIS: He'll come around.
              (CLITANDRE *enters.*) Clitandre! I was seeking
              You also. Here's your part. Have you been speaking
              With Constance?

CLITANDRE: Not exactly. I was used
              To keep a bevy of her friends amused.

DAMIS: By doing what?

CLITANDRE: I gambled and I lost.

DAMIS: Ah, you're a sly one.

CLITANDRE: What? At such a cost?

DAMIS: You know the way to win the ladies' hearts.
              I wish I were as clever in these arts.

CLITANDRE: Nevertheless, Marquis, you're quite a prize.

DAMIS: But so are you.

CLITANDRE: My friend, I have sharp eyes.
          The lady you've been charming as a guest
          At all her parties — she's your next conquest?

DAMIS: You're more loved there than I could ever be.

CLITANDRE: Would you divert suspicion onto me?

DAMIS: So much discretion seems beyond the rules.

CLITANDRE: I never boast.

DAMIS: No, no one does, but fools.

CLITANDRE: I quite agree.

DAMIS: Indeed, when I discover
        The strategies of some potential lover,
        I strive to thwart them. It is like a game.

CLITANDRE: I must admit I often do the same.
           Speaking of which, are you aware . . .

DAMIS: I'm not.

CLITANDRE: Unconsciously, you . . .

DAMIS: What?

CLITANDRE: Now, let's not plot
        Against each other. We should be allies.
        There's no use our competing for some prize
        Because we don't communicate.

DAMIS: That's true.
        (*Aside*) I'll teach this idiot a thing or two.
        (*To* CLITANDRE)
        We'd have a lot to fear if we were foes.

CLITANDRE: We would, so let us mutually expose
            The galantries that we are proudest of
            Since we're both masters in the game of love.
            We've each made scores of offerings to Venus.

DAMIS: It's true.

CLITANDRE: So let's divide the field between us.

DAMIS: What would your choices be? Mine know no bounds!

CLITANDRE: Don't jest. We all have our appointed rounds.
            Time keeps on rolling and we cannot falter,
            Devoting too much worship to one altar.
            So it's inevitable our inspection
            Will sometime focus in the same direction.
            Choosing between us would be too complex;
            We must have pity on the weaker sex
            For their own greater pleasure. Thus we need
            To keep coordinated.

DAMIS: We're agreed.

CLITANDRE: Good! What is the heart you're now pursuing?

DAMIS: And you? Who is it you're intent on wooing?

CLITANDRE: Mine gives me little hope I'll gain access.

DAMIS: Mine offers little prospect of success.
            (*Mysteriously*) Though I have hope.

CLITANDRE (*the same*):   And I.

DAMIS: That calms my fears.
            If both of us have hope, then it appears
            We're not competing.

CLITANDRE: That's a great relief.

We've fortunately spared each other grief.
We'll each in our own way pursue our quarries,
See how we fare, and then exchange our stories.
(*He goes.*)

DAMIS (*laughing as* CLITANDRE *disappears*):
    Just as I thought! Once more Clitandre's shown
    That he's the greatest fool I've ever known!
    We'll see who profits most from our relation,
    Since love is not my goal, but reputation!
    His object is Constance, that's all too plain.
    I woo her too, but both our suits are vain.
    Still I can win this context, since I know
    That happiness is judged by outward show.
    (*He takes out a portrait.*)
    I have no peer in such manipulation,
    This portrait will provide my inspiration.
    (DURVAL *and* DAMON *enter.*)
    Durval, I have here your and your wife's parts.
    Though Damon has resisted all my arts.
    I leave him to you.

DURVAL: I will do my best.

DAMIS: Now I must find Argant and all the rest. (*He goes.*)

(DURVAL *begins reading the script he is holding.*)

DAMON: Why are you reading? I thought you would never
      Support the foolishness of this endeavor!

DURVAL: I was distracted. All my thoughts are racing
      About this crucial step that I am facing.
      Only one fear remains of all that host,
      But it's the one that worries me the most!
      If you could guarantee, but you cannot,
      That if I once obtain the goal I've sought,
      Will she, the woman that I now recover,
      Still have the virtues that first made me love her?

That quiet deference, that humility,
That deep conviction she was meant for me.
Will I discover that same fire still burning
Within her heart now that I am returning?
That flame a wiser lover would have cherished,
But I did not, and fear it may have perished.
A thousand lapses lie behind this fear;
I've caused her cruel suffering, that's clear.
The kind of pain she's felt could not be hidden,
And sighs and tears must flower forth unbidden.
Yet as a fire in darkness burns the brightest,
Her charms have not diminished in the slightest.

DAMON: Don't be misled. She's learned to play a part,
Hiding the sufferings of her virtuous heart.
She still may love the man who shares her house
Since it may be this estimable spouse
Still cherishes the hope her husband cares
Since he has been discreet in his affairs.
A wife who's sensitive is quite averse
To asking questions that might make things worse.
In any case, her virtue is reliable.

DURVAL: What a slim hope! Is that love really viable
That's only based on duty? Never mind.
Go find your Sophie. Tell her I'm resigned
To reconciliation. Use my state
To help improve your own, my friend. But wait!
Don't speak a word. Let Constance deal with Sophie,
And wish me well. I go to gain my trophy.

DAMON: For one last time I beg you. Don't desert me!

DURVAL: Dear friend, your doubts astonish me and hurt me.
(DAMON *goes*. HENRI *enters*.)
Henri, go quickly and then come back here . . .

HENRI: Go where? Come when? Your orders aren't too clear.

DURVAL: Fly quickly to my house; don't lose a minute!
            Then run back here and tell me who is in it!
            (HENRI *doesn't move*.)
            You're standing like a wall! Why don't you stir?

HENRI: To which apartment, sir, do you refer?

DURVAL: What's that? Didn't you hear me? Pay attention!

HENRI;   What's not been said can bear a second mention.

DURVAL: Go see what company my wife's receiving!

HENRI (*aside*): Concerned about his wife? It's past believing!
            (*He goes.*)

DURVAL: If luck is with me she will be alone
            And without witnesses I can make known
            The secret that has filled my heart . . . but wait!
            He's coming back! I soon will know my fate!

HENRI: I come . . .

DURVAL (*interrupting, impatiently*):
                     From her apartments. Did you see
            Anyone there?

HENRI: Clitandre and Damis.

DURVAL: What a misfortune! I am broken-hearted!

HENRI: Both of those gentlemen, though, have departed.
            I think nobody else was in the room

DURVAL: So she's alone?

HENRI: Alone? So I assume.

DURVAL: You're sure? You saw her?

HENRI: Sir, why should I lie?
            She only had her maid, Florine, nearby.
            (*He withdraws upstage.*)

DURVAL (*to himself*):
            Florine, you say? There's always someone near.
            Eager to listen and to interfere.
            Still, I must go. I really shouldn't care
            If someone else should happen to be there.
            I am obsessed; I can't postpone revealing
            Unto Constance the changes I am feeling.
            Why should it be so difficult to say
            What fills my heart? Why can't I find the way?
            To leap right in would surely be too frightening.
            It can't just strike her like a bolt of lightening!
            I can't embark without consideration
            And Damon isn't here for consultation.
            I can't go on! The risk is far too great!
            My spirit fails! It would be best to wait.
            No doubt . . . it's true . . besides, she is so charming,
            Her tender attributes are so disarming
            That the remorse and love I must display
            Will plunge my senses into disarray!
            Love is a sickness of which there's no healing
            Until one can express what he is feeling.
            (*To* HENRI)
            Come, bring a chair and table. It is better,
            When all is said, to start off with a letter.
            That first step taken, then my path is free.

HENRI: Another love affair! Good news for me!
            Masters in love are rarely too observant—
            A pleasant situation for a servant!
            Once he's embarked on that trajectory
            I can relax; he has no need of me.

DURVAL (*writing*): I never wrote a letter half so sweet!
            It cannot fail to sweep her off her feet!

HENRI (*reading his part*): Now that romance has occupied his mind,
　　　　　　　Let's see what sort of role I've been assigned
　　　　　　　To carry out in this projected play.
　　　　　　　What's this? I can't believe it! A valet!
　　　　　　　An homme de chambre, maybe, or a very
　　　　　　　Trusted adjunct, perhaps a secretary.
　　　　　　　This is an insult that I don't deserve!
　　　　　　　Let's see, however, who I am to serve.
　　　　　　　(*He looks through the papers, reading both sides.*)
　　　　　　　The plot is hopeless, far removed from life.
　　　　　　　I serve a man enamored of his wife.
　　　　　　　What sort of master seeks connubial bliss?
　　　　　　　What kind of whimsical device is this?

DURVAL (*aside*): The rogue disturbs me. It's his part, I'll wager.

HENRI:　　　　Master, I have objections which are major
　　　　　　　To this strange script. It is so full of wit
　　　　　　　That there's no hope of understanding it.
　　　　　　　Listen! I'm speaking: "Ah, well met, Nerine
　　　　　　　You know my Lord plies this bucolic scene
　　　　　　　Because his tender heart with love is festering
　　　　　　　For his own wife, whom he is here sequestering
　　　　　　　While he perambulates in helpless rage,
　　　　　　　A bear locked in a matrimonial cage."
　　　　　　　Lots of big words with very little matter!

DURVAL (*aside, impatiently*):
　　　　　　　The rogue distracts me with his constant chatter!
　　　　　　　(*To* HENRI):
　　　　　　　Haven't you somewhere else that you can go?
　　　　　　　When I need something, I will let you know.
　　　　　　　Keep within call, Henri, but not too near!

HENRI:　　　　Just send a summons and you'll find me here!
　　　　　　　(*He goes.*)

DURVAL (*rising*): Even my servant finds the role I'm playing
　　　　　　　Ridiculous! . . . But still, no more delaying!

(*He sits down again.*)
The rascal's gone. My inspiration too!
But I must finish what I meant to do! (*He writes.*)
This letter bears the hopes of my succeeding.
Henri! Come here! I'll give it one more reading.
(*He reads.*)
"The ingrate who has caused your heart such grief
Regrets his past and promises relief!"
(*He continues to read silently.*)
I'll sign it now and send it on its way (*He signs.*)
If only I could guess what she would say!
(*He takes out a small box.*)
I'll send along these diamonds, though I know
Constance has little interest in such show.
But I enjoy embellishing her beauty.
Henri! Why don't these servants know their duty?

HENRI: Master, I'm ready. What is your request?

DURVAL: Where do you think you're going? You are dressed
              For travel.

HENRI: I assumed I would be hieing
              To Paris. There's a duchess you've been eyeing . . .

DURVAL (*hiding the letter*): You needn't go so far.

HENRI: Sir, I suspect
              The Duchess isn't someone to reject.
              She'll be revenged. Already she's maintaining
              That to pursue a new intrigue you're feigning
              A reconciliation with Madame.
              I don't know what she's up to with this sham,
              But frankly she might do some harm to you,
              She's not like some soubrette I might pursue.

DURVAL (*giving him the letter and box*):
              Deliver these two items and request
              An answer.

HENRI: Diamonds! Now I am impressed!

DURVAL: Enough discussion! Carry out your task
            And try not to be seen. That's all I ask.
            (HENRI *goes*.)
            (*Thoughtfully*) At last my indecision is resolved.
            I've taken action; now I am involved.
            Did I do right? It's dangerous revealing
            A love that I may be ridiculed for feeling.
            Should I have waited? No, I must be steady
            In my decision.
            (HENRI *appears*.) What! You're back already?
            What answer did she give?

HENRI: No answer yet,
            Because the lady's name I didn't get.

DURVAL (*taking back the letter and diamonds*):You fool!

HENRI: Please, Sir, the choices are so wide,
            With lovely ladies here on every side,
            How could I guess which one you have preferred?

DURVAL: I gave you no address?

HENRI: None that I heard.

DURVAL (*aside*): It's better thus. This rascal would have guessed
            My secret if the letter were addressed,
            The diamonds should suffice, and I can set
            Them secretly myself on her toilette.
            Constance will come to plead her innocence
            In the inspiring of this new offense.
            This will prepare her for my explanation
            Without a compromising situation.
            (*He puts the letter in his pocket.*)
            My plan of action's clear now, and I know
            Damon will like it! (*To* HENRI) You are free to go.

(*He leaves.*)

HENRI (*looking after him*): If he conducts his own affairs, I'm lost!
                     I can't begin to estimate the cost!
                     The tip I would have gotten for delivering
                     Those diamonds is enough to set me shivering.
                     Ten, twenty louis, who could guess how many?
                     And now instead I won't receive a penny! (*He goes.*)

ACT IV

CONSTANCE (*entering with* FLORINE. CONSTANCE *has letters
　　　　　　and* DURVAL's *box in her hand.*):
　　　　　　Durval's not here. Go find him and implore him
　　　　　　To join me. Tell him I am waiting for him,
　　　　　　But do not tell him why I'm agitated;
　　　　　　I fear that that would make him irritated,
　　　　　　And he'll disdain to come if he knows why.

FLORINE:　　I doubt if I can bring him, but I'll try. (*She goes.*)

CONSTANCE: From every side I feel cruel fortune's blows,
　　　　　　And every day an increase of my woes.
　　　　　　Whenever some small ray of hope appears,
　　　　　　It's over-ruled at once by threats and fears!
　　　　　　(*She opens the packet of letters.*)
　　　　　　This unsigned letter warns me to beware;
　　　　　　My faithless husband has a new affair!
　　　　　　(*She looks at another.*)
　　　　　　Some cruel rival for my husband's favor
　　　　　　Writes that he now regrets the gifts he gave her
　　　　　　And now pursues a new infatuation!
　　　　　　Is she the one betrayed? My situation,
　　　　　　Already painful, now brings greater pain
　　　　　　(*She opens the box.*)
　　　　　　With these unwanted gifts I can't explain!
　　　　　　(FLORINE *returns.*)
　　　　　　Did you succeed?

FLORINE:　　　　　　　　　　He's nowhere to be found.

CONSTANCE: All things conspire against me.

FLORINE:　　　　　　　　　　　　　　He's around,
　　　　　　I'm sure.

CONSTANCE: I'll wait for him. I must reveal
                    Something of all the suffering I feel.

FLORINE: Speak frankly, Madam, holding nothing back.
                    His love is lost; you might as well attack.

CONSTANCE (*tenderly*): His love is lost.

FLORINE: He has his weak side, too.
                    Give me your leave; I'll see what I can do.

CONSTANCE: No, on my own appeals I must rely.

FLORINE: Your own appeals? Such as?

CONSTANCE: A tear, a sigh.

FLORINE: Oh, good! He'll let you weep and sigh, that's true.
                    Men think that that's what women like to do.
                    They give us pain without a thought or measure
                    Thinking our hearts incapable of pleasure,
                    That women's souls are naturally tormented
                    And that our sex can never be contented.
                    Confront him with those letters that you get
                    From discontented rivals. Make him sweat!
                    I'd give the rascal more than he could handle!

CONSTANCE (*putting the letters in her pocket*):
                    I never would encourage such a scandal!
                    He'll never know that I've been made aware
                    Of every sordid folly and affair.
                    I've spared him pain, no matter what the cost,
                    To keep alive the hope I've never lost,
                    Feigning tranquility and resignation
                    In hopes of future reconciliation.
                    I've given him no reason to abuse me,
                    But if he wishes to, he can excuse me.
                    I'm going to tell him someone has been sending
                    Me gifts, and beg for his advice on ending

This torment. I'll give him these diamonds, too.

FLORINE: Madam, you will regret it if you do.
             Such harmless gallantries, he'll say, one learns
             To tolerate. He'll laugh at your concerns.
             He always does. You'll suffer quite in vain.
             His own dishonor causes him no pain.

CONSTANCE: You think? . . . It's true . . . The trouble in my soul
             That I have so long struggled to control
             Threatens to overwhelm me, bringing more
             Distress and pain than I have felt before.
             My only course is flight; I cannot face
             Still further evidence of my disgrace.
             I cannot see Durval; I will repent it.
             Here, take this gift. (*Giving her the diamonds.*)
                         If you're aware who sent it,
             Tell him I hate him!

FLORINE: Which one do you mean?

CONSTANCE: Which one?

FLORINE: There's two at least to choose between.

CONSTANCE: Give it to either. I don't care a whit.
             It's up to you. Just speak no more of it!
             Just take this hateful object out of sight! (*She goes.*)

FLORINE: But Madam, how can I be sure I'm right
             If I just guess from whom this token came?
             The two marquis are very much the same:
             Frivolous bores with scarcely different habits,
             Full of self-pride and really bland as rabbits,
             Boring by instinct and by inclination,
             Inordinately boastful of their station,
             Hoping always to better their condition
             Through projects never carried to fruition,
             Self-satisfied, impudent, pushy, shrill,

Jealous of good and always seeking ill,
Rascals in love, whose largely false confessions
Do us more harm than any indiscretions.
This foolish duo once a day or more
Tell me of conquests that they have in store.
Doubtless from one of them this gift has come,
But is it Tweedledee or Tweedledum?
One or the other, I'm unsure which way
To lean. But wait! Suppose I just delay?
Pocket the present, put it on the shelf —
Not that I want to keep it for myself —
But til I find by whom this gift was sent,
I'll save my mistress more embarrassment.
This might be misinterpreted, I'm sure,
But what care I, if my intention's pure.
Yet fortune smiles on me; here comes the pair.
I'll soon be disencumbered of this care!
(*Enter* DAMIS *and* CLITANDRE. FLORINE *holds
out the box to them.*)
Take back your gaudy token. You're absolved.
My mistress doesn't want to get involved,
So she returns your gift, but don't regret it.
Some other will be very glad to get it. (*She goes.*)

DAMIS (*handing the box to* CLITANDRE):
Here is your gift, Marquis. My sympathy!

CLITANDRE (*refusing it*):
It's not my gift. It must be yours, Marquis!

DAMIS: Your vanity prevents you from admitting
The truth.

CLITANDRE: The truth depends on where you're sitting.

DAMIS: Your pride . . .

CLITANDRE: Your honor . . .

DAMIS: Take it, all the same.
           I'll keep your secret.

CLITANDRE: I will hide your shame.

DAMIS: You should have told me.

CLITANDRE: Why were you afraid?

DAMIS: Perhaps you'd have succeeded with my aid.
            Let's see how high you rate this new conquest.
            (*He opens the box.*)
            Diamonds! Good Lord! Marquis, I am impressed!

CLITANDRE: She is unique. One really cannot measure
            Her price. I understand. Here is your treasure.

DAMIS: It's yours. The task of pleasing is expensive.

CLITANDRE: For me as well. You needn't be defensive.
            You are disturbed.

DAMIS: I know it was unpleasant
            For you to be turned down while I was present.
            I understand.

CLITANDRE: Can't we cut short these lies?

DAMIS: I find you much more obstinate than wise.

CLITANDRE: Here comes Durval!

DAMIS: Who cares? Just name no name.

CLITANDRE: I see! It might be an amusing game!

DURVAL (*entering, aside*): What's this? My gift!

CLITANDRE: The quarrel you have caught

Us in concerns this object.

DURVAL: So I thought!
        (*Aside*) Constance must have felt one of these her suitor!

DAMIS (*indicating* CLITANDRE): He is the master!

CLITANDRE (*indicating* DAMIS):   He could be my tutor!

DAMIS: Or he be mine!

CLITANDRE: I give you the award!
            Durval, here is the Apple of Discord.
            (*Gives him the box.*)

DURVAL: You couldn't put it into better hands.

DAMIS: But on deposit.

CLITANDRE: Yes, he understands.

DAMIS: Until the proper owner should appear.

DURVAL: Of course.

DAMIS: But now the matter's far from clear.

CLITANDRE: No name can be revealed.

DURVAL: Of course. That's shrewd.

DAMIS: A certain lady, whom we've both pursued,
            Sent back this gift, but just whom she rejected
            She didn't mention.

DURVAL: Just as I suspected.

DAMIS: One of us sent it.

CLITANDRE: That is clearly true.

DAMIS: But both deny it.

DURVAL: Just what I would do!

CLITANDRE: Damis, for vanity, has not confessed.
                He'd rather lose it.

DURVAL: Sirs, I am impressed!
                You're both more honest than I had believed.

DAMIS: So which one sent the gift we've now received?

DURVAL: Monsieurs, I put to you a proposition.
                If one of you, just as a supposition,
                Had sent this gift, what end could be expected,
                Considering that it has been rejected?

DAMIS: No one rejects a token they hold dear.

CLITANDRE: It can't be mine, then. The conclusion's clear.

DAMIS (*striking* DURVAL *on the shoulder*):
                If it were mine, I surely would have kept it!

DURVAL: I see your point, Marquis, and I accept it.
                But he's convincing, too, there's no denying.
                Could it be neither one of you is lying?
                And some third party, whom you'd never guess,
                Has caused all this confusion and distress?
                Another may have seen the charms you savor
                And tried to overtake you in her favor.

DAMIS: Let this mysterious rival show his face
                And I'll be pleased to put him in his place.
                I'm sure that once he's heard that I have spoken,
                He'll hurry elsewhere with his tawdry token.

DURVAL: Clitandre seems unsure.

CLITANDRE: I doubt Damis
                    Can prove his boasts.

DAMIS: It's indiscreet of me,
                    But I have proofs.

CLITANDRE: Then in your own defense,
                    Durval and I would like some evidence.

DAMIS (*to* CLITANDRE): I'll satisfy just you.

DURVAL: Can't I be witness?

DAMIS: Pardon, I have some qualms about the fitness
                    Of sharing with too many my confession.
                    (*To* CLITANDRE, *drawing him to the rear of the
                    stage*)   Remember, I rely on your discretion.
                    (*He shows* CLITANDRE *a portrait.* CLITANDRE *is
                    disturbed.*)   Control yourself.
                    (*To* DURVAL) You see how he is shaken.
                    (*To* CLITANDRE)
                    Is this the lady—could I be mistaken—
                    Who sent the gift back?

CLITANDRE: Ah, unfaithful beauty! (*He goes.*)

DAMIS (*looking after him*):
                    Unfaithful? When she only did her duty?
                    His vanity is hurt. Durval, you must
                    In future learn from this whom you can trust!
                    (*He goes.*)

DURVAL: Is this some evil dream, some foul illusion?
                    Oh, cruel fate, you've plunged me in confusion.
                    You've robbed me of my pride, my goods, my wife,
                    Complete your enmity and take my life!
                    What fearful doubts! What pain! What misery!

Why give their frightful confidence to me?
My Constance! How can I believe my ears?
Is she less virtuous than she appears?
Still, women's hearts are weak and all men must
Remember that or else regret their trust.
My natural suspicions now I see
Were blinded by my own credulity.
I must renounce her! What else can I do?
I cannot live a lie and call it true!
In her false virtue my poor heart believed.
Feeling secure, it was the more deceived!
Could not her weakness have remained concealed?
Instead the frightful truth now stands revealed!
Her strange tranquillity is now explained,
Her calmness, which I often thought was feigned!
She never seemed to have an ugly thought,
Which I believed was prudence. It was not!
Rather the wiles of love, the schemes of reason,
Both pressed into the service of her treason!

DAMON (*entering*): Give me the news at once! Leave nothing out!
　　　　　The diamonds worked like magic, I've no doubt!

DURVAL:　　Indeed they did.

DAMON:　　　　　　　　So they were worth the price!
　　　　　Now aren't you glad you heeded my advice?

DURVAL:　　Constance surprised us both in her demeanor!
　　　　　I'm waiting for her.

DAMON:　　　　　　　　What! You haven't seen her?

DURVAL (*angrily*): I'll see her now!

DAMON:　　　　　　　　You're troubled! May I know
　　　　　The cause of it?

DURVAL:　　　　　　　An unexpected blow!

My friend, you are about to be subjected
To an encounter none of us expected.
I'm desperate!

DAMON: What a fury you are in!
          Could you be jealous?

DURVAL   Never have I been!
          Constance I trusted without hesitation.
          I was too happy with our situation!
          Esteem, love, honor — all are changed to hate!
          Ah, could there be a torture half so great
          As to despise a lover of the past?

DAMON: Suspicion's easy. Don't decide too fast!

DURVAL (*in a rage*): I just observed two happy rivals part!
          One has her portrait and one has her heart!
          They've sworn as much!

DAMON: Don't let their oaths dismay you!
          I'm sure that Constance never would betray you!

DURVAL: Don't waste your time. There's nothing to defend!
          If love is false, why should one trust a friend?

DAMON: Try to control yourself. She is approaching.

DURVAL (*to her, in a somewhat more moderate manner*):
          Madam, I will not waste my time reproaching.
          The bonds that tied us once I hereby sever.
          Go where you wish, but leave my sight forever,
          'Til Heaven grants the wishes of wife,
          A termination of my weary life!
          Keep all your goods; those baubles I despise,
          Except for one, the only one I prize,
          The only one I'm still enamored of,
          Our only child, the first fruit of our love.

CONSTANCE: My fate is in your hands; I won't complain
If anything I've done has caused you pain.
I'll go where I am sent, without a sigh,
There to live out my days, and there to die!

DURVAL: Live, Madam!

CONSTANCE: Live? And what's worth living for?
I'll try to satisfy you. Furthermore,
Keep all the things I have received from you;
I don't wish to deprive you of a sou.
I give up all without a qualm except
My daughter, the one gift I would have kept!
Her mother's fate I pray she doesn't share.
May she be no less faithful, you more fair!

DURVAL (*furious*): I can't imagine such temerity!
Ingrate! How dare you take that tone with me!

CONSTANCE: Ingrate? Is that how I am to be known?

DURVAL: It is!

CONSTANCE: After the tenderness I've shown?
Alas! What has aroused in you such passion,
To treat a former loved one in this fashion?

DURVAL: You have no longer claims upon my love!

CONSTANCE: Why not? What crime have I been guilty of?
What have I done?

DURVAL: This conversation's ended!

CONSTANCE: But can't you tell me how I have offended?
Must I die never knowing how I'm tainted?
I cannot bear it! . . . It's too much . . .
(*She collapses into a chair.*)

DAMON: She's fainted!
            (*As* CONSTANCE *falls, she attempts to pull out her*
            handkerchief and also pulls out the packet of letters,
            which fall to the floor. DAMON *furtively tries to*
            gather them up, but DURVAL, *seeing him,*
            seizes them.)

DURVAL: Give them to me! Do not attempt to shield
            Her crimes! Doubtless these notes will yield
            New evidence of how I've been betrayed!

DAMON: Excuse me! Someone needs to bring her aid!
            (*He goes.*)

DURVAL: No further spinning fancies on the past!
            These letters verify the truth at last!
            To what a sad conclusion I've been carried.
            Forced to expose the woman that I married!

CONSTANCE (*opening her eyes*):
            Those letters! I had hoped to see them burned!

DURVAL: They prove you guilty. That's why you're concerned!
            They're all addressed to you.

CONSTANCE: Please do not heed them!

DURVAL: Your fear convinces me that I must read them!

CONSTANCE: Destroy those sad epistles! Let them be!
            The harm in them concerns no one but me!
            I beg you, listen . . .

DURVAL: I don't wish to hear.

CONSTANCE: Since we're alone now . . .

DURVAL: Let me make this clear!
            It is no longer possible to hide!

> This matter calls for truth on either side!

CONSTANCE: Durval! I beg you at your feet . . .

DURVAL: Don't try
>   To justify yourself.

(DAMON *rushes back in with* FLORINE, *followed by* SOPHIE
>   *and* ARGANT.)

FLORINE: Dear mistress! Why
>   This abject posture?

SOPHIE: Constance on her knees!
>   (*They pick her up and seat her in a chair.*)

DURVAL: I beg you all! Acknowledge, if you please,
>   Which one of us has been the most abused,
>   Considering the wiles my wife has used!
>   (*To* ARGANT)
>   Damon has told you what just happened here?

ARGANT: A part of it. His story's far from clear.

DURVAL: It will be soon. New facts will make it so.

ARGANT: What do you know that Damon didn't know?

DURVAL (*handing out the letters*):
>   The guilty secret's here for all to see!
>   A happy accident gave these to me!

SOPHIE (*taking a letter*): Perhaps they're false.

DURVAL: You fear what they'll reveal.
>   But I will swear that every one is real!

CONSTANCE: I beg you, sir, one final time! Refrain!
>   I'm much distressed by what these notes contain!

ARGANT (*surprised, as he opens a letter*):
> Good Lord! This sheds new light on the affair!
> This letter . . .

DURVAL: What about it?

ARGANT: I could swear
> It's your handwriting!

DURVAL: What!

SOPHIE: Yes, mine is too!

DURVAL: What! My handwriting?

ARGANT: Yes.

DURVAL: That can't be true!

ARGANT: Just look!

DURVAL (*looking at the letter and recognizing his handwriting*):
> Good heavens!

ARGANT: Surely it's your letter!

FLORINE: Is this one yours, sir?

SOPHIE: This is getting better!

ARGANT (*giving his back*): No more of this. It is a fruitless task!

SOPHIE: No, we must read them. That is what he asked!
> (*She reads.*)
> "You do me injury with your alarms.
> It's true that my wife Constance has her charms,
> But they have long since lost their power to win me,
> Unlike the flames that you have kindled in me.
> A spouse is not a rival to prefer.

How can you think that I would favor her?"
The style is pretty.

ARGANT: No sarcasm, please.
Women love situations such as these,
Quite unlike men, where everyone respects
The minor follies of the other sex.

SOPHIE: Well said!

FLORINE: It's my turn now! Wait! No, indeed!
This letter is too strong for me to read!
(*She returns it.*)
Monsieur, your style in writing does you proud!
A pity it cannot be read aloud!
(DAMON *collects the letters.*)

DURVAL (*recovering from his astonishment*):
        And yet the portrait . . . ?

SOPHIE: What proof did you find?

FLORINE: He can't believe the treason's in his mind!

SOPHIE: You wish to add insult to injury?
That is too cruel!

FLORINE: It is clear that he,
Untrue himself, has found the tables turned!

SOPHIE (*to* CONSTANCE): Revenge yourself!
        Give him what he has earned!
        (*They help* CONSTANCE *to her feet.*)

CONSTANCE (*carried along, despite herself*):
        I can't . . . Please let me . . . Am I not to learn . ?

SOPHIE: Come, Madame. It's no longer your concern.

FLORINE: He doesn't even merit your attention!

SOPHIE (*turning back, to* DAMON):
           Now, Damon. What's become of your contention?
           (*She leaves, with* CONSTANCE *and* FLORINE.)

DAMON: Oh, heaven!

ARGANT (*to* DURVAL): Your enterprise was highly ill-conceived,
           And you deserved the beating you received!
           To fight a woman one must needs be clever.
           Men rarely win such fights, and husbands never!
           If you desire an outcome that is suitable,
           You'd best make sure your proofs are irrefutable!
           Yours were, as we have seen, completely toothless,
           And in such cases women can be ruthless!
           They don't much like each other, but just dare
           Accuse one, and the others will be there!
           The female population will arise;
           The tocsin's sound will echo through the skies!
           They'll rally round their sister and will feel
           Unprecedented tenderness and zeal.
           Pity comes first, and fury not much later,
           The husband's branded as calumniator.
           That's why I have avoided getting vexed,
           Treating my wife as honest as the next.
           That's my advice, though now a bit too late.
           You'll have to bow your head and take your fate!
           (*He goes.*)

DURVAL (*to* DAMON): You see I am both angry and dejected.
           The storm I raised was wholly unexpected!
           This cruel vengeance caught me unawares.
           All that I did was publish her affairs!
           What difference does it make what I may do
           If, after all, my wife is guilty too?
           Yet she's not blamed at all, while I'm berated!

DAMON: But don't you think that she's exonerated?

DURVAL: Nonsense! It's clear her guilt is past denying.
            For that I hate her! Still, there's no use trying
            To make her odious in others' eyes
            Who cannot pierce her virtuous disguise.

DAMON: I don't know why you still suspect your wife,
            But I know Constance. I would stake my life . . .

DURVAL: You'd lose, my friend! Constance, what pain is this!
            Seeking her heart, I opened an abyss!
            Did my example give her cause to fall?
            Might I be somewhat guilty after all?

DAMON: Whether that's true or not, you should reject
            A policy that's had such bad effect,
            And learn from this unhappy situation
            To exercise restraint and moderation!
            You paid your first impulses too much heed.

DURVAL: I did, and I have paid for it indeed!
            Inflamed against my wife, I tried to stir
            Up passions that harmed me instead of her.
            I dealt a deadly blow, and I am dead.

DAMON: I have forebodings worse may lie ahead.

DURVAL: They're wrong, and if you wish I'll promise you
            Full confidence in everything I do.
            I'll share my thoughts, but not in expectation
            This confidence will change my inclination,
            Rather I hope to win you to my case.
            There may be other enemies to face.
            In the upcoming battles I intend
            To fight, I hope to count on you as friend. (*They go.*)

ACT V

(DURVAL *and* DAMON *appear at the rear of the stage. They are wearing masks.*)

DURVAL: Damon, now is the moment. Almost all
            Our friends have been distracted by the ball.
            Tell me about this picture.

DAMON: I can show
            That it was stolen. Here is how I know.
            Around that studio Damis was lurking
            Just at the time the portraitist was working.
            The marquis seized the work, his theft unknown,
            To carry out a purpose of his own.
            One of his men, dressed in your livery,
            Came for the painting, intimating he
            Had come from you, a lie that was believed.
            This news, not comprehending, I received.
            I knew that painter asked Constance to sit
            But didn't know you had commissioned it.

DURVAL: What wickedness! Permit, my friend most dear . . .

DAMON: Yet wait! A lot of things are still not clear.
            I found the traitors near here in the yard
            Full of self-glory, but I pushed them hard.
            So gradually their foolish facade crumbled
            And this conceited duo, somewhat humbled
            Under my inquiries, illuminated
            The complex web of lies they had created.
            Around those diamonds both of them spun stories
            To try to bring to each of them new glories.
            After giving a lesson to these two,
            I bring the purloined picture back to you.
            (*Gives him the portrait.*)

I hardly think they'll dare to speak of how
They sought to damage you. They'll be gone by now.

DURVAL (*crushed*): Thanks to their folly, what mistakes I've made!
And what a frightful price we all have paid!

DAMON: You don't seem very pleased with your success!

DURVAL: Because I still am guilty of excess!
Amidst my happiness I always see
Another traitor, whom I cannot flee,
And that's myself, since I am well aware
Of the responsibility I bear.
Whether or not the others are to blame,
I'm weighted down by my own sense of shame!

DAMON: I understand your pain . . .

DURVAL: Say my despair.

DAMON: But now it's Constance who requires our care.

DURVAL (*touched, tears in his eyes*):
You're right! My dearest wife! Where is she now?
Can we be reconciled? Please tell me how!
I was her torturer and not her mate,
Withholding love and treating her with hate!
She's dead to me now, gone without a trace!

DAMON: You paint too dark a picture of the case.
Constance has saved you from your recent fury,
Concealed her shame and quite convinced the jury
Showing, in pain, the courage of a queen,
Extracting honor from this awful scene
Of which she was, unknown, the hidden source.
I tried, without revealing this, of course,
To calm her somewhat, hiding all the rest.
But come, let's find her. You don't want to test
Her strength much more. She may be near its end!

DURVAL: I'll do whatever you say, my dearest friend!
Be my sole emissary to my mate.
Paint my despair. You can't exaggerate
My suffering at all that I have lost.
Implore her pity, at whatever cost.

DAMON: Your own appearance would have more effect.
In this case my own motives are suspect.
Go on your knees, apologize, deliver
To her your heart. Think of the joy you'll give her!

DURVAL: Now when I need your friendship, you refrain.

DAMON: Why are you only bold when causing pain?

DURVAL: Can you expect me, when I have displayed
Such outrageous behavior, when I've made
Such cruel charges, baseless intimations,
With accusations piled on accusations,
That I could now present myself before her,
And hope that she'd feel anything but horror?
Shame holds me back.

DAMON: That's too severe a sentence.
Shame's in the act, and not in the repentance.

DURVAL: But what I've written how can I gainsay?
I've treated her in such a cruel way!
How can I seek her confidence once more
When I have broken every vow I swore?

DAMON: Love pardons all, and I can give you aid.
I am to meet with Constance. She has made
Such a proposal, doubtless to discuss
The same confusions occupying us.
Tonight's masked ball will give an opportunity
Of frankly speaking to her with impunity
Behind a mask.

DURVAL: Suppose I took your place!

DAMON: My very thought!

DURVAL: She needn't see my face.
             I'll keep my voice low. She will never guess,
             And all my inmost thoughts I can confess
             To win her back.

DAMON: I'll start a conversation
             While you discreetly watch the situation.
             Seeking the happy moment when you can
             Adroitly take my place and crown our plan!

DURVAL (*after some thought*): I'm fearful of my curiosity.

DAMON: I will prepare the way. Just follow me.

DURVAL: I fear the worst. Thinking she speaks to you,
             Constance may say more than I want her to.
             All the reproaches that she has suppressed
             In their full fury now may be expressed,
             And I, already weakened by remorse,
             May not be able to withstand their force!

DAMON: Recent events give you no cause for fear.
             Constance's gentleness is all too clear.
             What other spouse would treat you with such care?
             Your hearts are more attuned than you're aware.

DURVAL: My weakness is a flaw, but not a crime.
             Someone is coming! Help me one more time!
             (*He goes.*)

DAMON: Self-love controls us, making us afraid
             To rectify mistakes that we have made.
             Still I will try to help him as he asked,
             Though it's a difficult and thankless task!
             (*Enter* FLORINE.)

FLORINE: Madame's awaiting you. Didn't you vow
              To speak to her?

DAMON: Indeed, I'm going now! (*He leaves.*)

FLORINE: Who can predict where these events are tending?
              I fear the cloister! What a tragic ending!
              Shutting ourselves away, that would be hard!
              I don't hold solitude in high regard!
              To leave the world at twenty! What a thought!
              It soon will leave us, whether we wish or not,
              And since we all must ultimately perish,
              At least we should have memories we cherish
              In later years to give us consolation,
              But all I've known in life is deprivation.
              And if I've suffered so in high society,
              What can I hope from abstinence and piety?
              The hours will pass, as tedious as slow,
              Boredom the only pastime that we know.
              Society has irritations, true,
              But there is always something you can do —
              Coming and going, gossiping and chattering,
              Praising, condemning, slandering and flattering —
              Good moments come, and if they are but few,
              One keeps them in the mind for fond review.

CONSTANCE (*enters, wearing a mask*):
              Though I don't see him, Damon must be near.
              We have agreed that he's to meet me here.
              We need a spot secluded to insure
              A conversation open, yet secure.
              (A MAN *appears in a mask.* CONSTANCE
              dismisses FLORINE.)
              You're here at last. Perhaps we can complete
              Our conversation where it's more discreet.
              Damon, forgive my tears. I'm sure you know
              Only a trusted friend will see them flow.
              They will betray my state if others see;
              That's why today I was constrained to flee.

(*She wipes her eyes.*)
I still recall the time, far off but sweet
When Durval made my happiness complete.
Love flourished like the roses in full season,
A perfect union for the age of reason.
When we were married I of course assumed
That in two hearts where such a passion bloomed
Love would keep growing, widening its sway,
And giving greater pleasure every day.
The passion in my heart more strongly burned
In knowing that its feeling was returned.
What happened to those times? I hardly know
How circumstances could have altered so.
My happy fate became unfortunate,
My love was now rejected as importunate,
And seeing that he hardly could abide it,
I couldn't change, but did my best to hide it.
Worse still, I saw the man I still adored
Becoming colder, more distracted, bored,
And step by step departing from his wife.
Losing my love, I almost lost my life,
For all is lost when one cannot return
The tender fleeting glance, the sweet concern,
The gentle feelings that another shares,
The confident assurance someone cares —
All these the loving heart subsists upon,
And life itself grows dim when they are gone.
Silence was added to my other pain,
For I thought it was wicked to complain.
This is the first time I've expressed my woes,
But I've decided finally to disclose
My feelings and my fears alone to you,
Hoping you can advise me what to do.
I needn't give you details I assume.
You've seen my husband, in this very room
Express his rage and call down my disgrace.
I saw a look of pity on your face.
So I appeal to you. How could it be
That he's grown so contemptuous of me?

What have I done? Do you possess some facts
That would explain the cruel way he acts?
What unknown irritant makes him so zealous?
Since he's indifferent, how can he be jealous?
I'm lost, and yet I fear that he's aware
That his attacks upon me were unfair,
And if he now regrets, to some degree,
His actions, that gives no relief to me.
I fear that if he fears humiliation
That only will increase our separation.
If he's ashamed, that may prevent his speaking
The words to reconcile us I am seeking.
But maybe my fond hopes and expectation
Have caused me to misread the situation
And look for hope with a deluded eye.
You do not answer. What does that imply?
Yet if the hopes I cherish are correct,
And he'll come back to me as I expect,
What holds him back? Why doesn't he decide
To claim my love? My arms are open wide.
If only he were willing to appear
I'm sure my love would put to rest his fear.
What should I do? Should I go seek him out?
That's what I wanted your advice about.
I fear I may appear too circumspect
Or else too bold, and forfeit his respect.
Will he condemn me for anticipating?
But even so, I cannot bear this waiting!
My love and duty both insist I go
And gain my life or lose it at one throw.
You haven't said a word. I hear you sigh.
Am I mistaken, then, to even try?
Your silence tells me what I fear to know.
You do not dare . . .

THE MASKED FIGURE (*aside*): Alas, I suffer so!

CONSTANCE: What did you say? Speak! I don't understand.
          But wait, is that my portrait in your hand?

Why do you have it? I'm confused . . . You'd better . . .

THE MASKED FIGURE (*presenting a letter*): You must . . .

CONSTANCE: What?

THE MASKED FIGURE: Look at this.

CONSTANCE: Why, it's a letter!
          You tremble. I also, for I surmise
          This signals my rejection and demise.
          (*She opens the letter.*)
          The writing is Durval's, but it appears
          The lines have almost been effaced by tears!
          (*She reads.*)
          "The suffering you've felt has been in vain;
          The man you've wept for wasn't worth your pain.
          Dear spouse, there's nothing that I wouldn't do
          To make up for the pain I've given you.
          I first knew love in looking on your face,
          And I would die now to obtain your grace . . ."
          Why did I hesitate? Conduct me please
          To my beloved.

DURVAL (*taking off the mask and kneeling at her feet*):
                                He's here, on his knees!
          Here let me die! And may my tears provide
          Mute testimony of my vanquished pride!

CONSTANCE: Husband, arise! In giving to your wife
          Your heart again, you also give her life!

DURVAL: You pardon all the injuries I've done you?

CONSTANCE: I now feel only joy that I have won you!

DURVAL: Avenge yourself!

CONSTANCE: For what? It was a dream.

Now you are back!

DURVAL: But how can I redeem
            Myself?

CONSTANCE: If you insist on reparation,
            Forget that I once lost your admiration.

DURVAL: I should recall the faults I would repair.
            (*A sound of people approaching.* CONSTANCE *is
            concerned, but not* DURVAL.)
            Before the world I'm ready to declare . . .

ARGANT (*Entering with* SOPHIE, DAMON *and* FLORINE):
            So all are happy?

FLORINE: What a great surprise!

SOPHIE (*ironically, to* DAMON):
            Your friend succeeds in everything he tries!

DURVAL (*vehemently*): Appearance doesn't matter any more!
            In short, this is my wife, whom I adore!
            Like it or not, my happiness is ample.
            And maybe I can serve as an example.
            Others will follow me, for I am sure
            This foolish prejudice cannot endure!

ARGANT: I'm not sure what to make of this confusion,
            But I can find no fault with your conclusion.
            When women interest us we should pursue them
            Even if we have gotten married to them.

DAMON (*to* SOPHIE):
            The happiness our married friends now claim
            Leads me to hope we may enjoy the same.

SOPHIE (*to* CONSTANCE):
            Constance, I've often told you what to do,

Dear friend. (*They embrace.*)
Now I must ask advice from you.

ARGANT (*taking her hand and putting it in that of* DAMON):
Love does not need advice. The heart alone
Controls our pain and pleasure on its own.

END

JEAN LOUIS LAYA

Royalistes tremblez, tremblez républicains,
Tombez devant les loix, voilà vos souverains.

The Friend of
the Laws

by

Jean-Louis Laya

Dedicatory Epistle to the National Representatives

Citizen Legislators

In dedicating my comedy to you I am not so much paying a tribute as clearing a debt. *The Friend of the Laws* could not have appeared except under the auspices of its models.

Author's Foreword

I will not provide a preface for this work. That would require a whole book, and I need only to write a few reflections that appear to me indispensable. My success has not blinded me. It is due more to the subject I treated than to the talent of my treatment. All true citizens have had to declare themselves in favor of one who loves only them and nothing but them, and it is in that respect that I have presented these new actions for them. How impressive has been the mass of opinions which have been so energetically and unanimously offered in defense of the holy love of laws, of order, and of manners! How overwhelming its weight has been for the open and hidden enemies of liberty! You who condemn Paris, come and see it. It is not in those tumultuous assemblies where intrigue and crime triumph, where the most unreasonable or the most intemperate may carry the day. Come rather to see it in the gatherings of citizens drunk with liberty, but respectful of the laws without which liberty could not exist, all afire with the revered names, glowing with civic flame, turning their eyes and their hearts toward this Friend of the Laws, of which each of them is the model.

I will not respond at all to the many calumnies that have been brought against me. I fully expected them, and I have an unanswerable plea in my defense, that of having desired to do something good. Those who would condemn such a motive can feel free to do so, since I feel myself beyond reproach in that respect. I will be forever committed to my ideas, since I believe them useful. Unhappy the one who has possessions and who fears impoverishment if he distributes their benefits! His hand will reap little, since they have little sown. I will not bother to refute those miserable imposters who acknowledge only virtue which profits them, and who challenge disinterestedness as if they were pointing out some crime. I have only one response to this: I offer my entire life to their calumnious considerations, and if they can find a single instant in it which was not worthy of me, I will allow them to consider me their equal.

Some persons of singular merit, excellent patriots, have made observations to me which deserve a serious answer. The first is the reproach that I have made my Friend of the Laws a former nobleman. First, it would have been difficult for Versac, obsessed with his nobility and his titles, to be able to select for his son-in-law a man of a class he considered inferior to his own. But this motive would have been weak without another. Who have I depicted? A real philosopher. What did I want to make him value? A revolution which in the eyes of a wise man will always represent the triumph of humanity and reason. Would it require any great effort for a man coming from the oppressed classes to rally to the new order and to make war against the class of the oppressors? To speak in favor of the revolution should one only look for apostles among those whose existence and rights were expanded by it? No. But instead to show someone triumphing over his prejudices when those prejudices had provided him with a pleasant and comfortable existence, to show him breaking with his own hands those powerful bonds of self-esteem, sacrificing for his brothers his most favored prerogatives, to offer to the eye a truly free man, an exemplary sage combating evil and adversity, blessing on the debris of his fortune the revolution which has ruined him, before which he lived in peace and happiness, does not all this eternally sanctify that revolution?

What constitutes a commitment if it is not to embrace in the midst of disasters an extraordinary joy beyond the understanding of the vulgar, akin perhaps to those soft torments of love which render its favors the more intoxicating? The true love of liberty proves itself by its sacrifices. Who can doubt that this sentiment inflames the heart of Forlis? Molière in his *Tartuffe* makes his truly devout person only a moralist. That great author gave us, in the character of Cléante, a theory of true piety, although some contemporary humorists raised doubts about the practicality of his character in everyday life. But here the philosophy is practical; both preaching and persuasion are effected not only by speeches but by actions. Once my two antagonists are placed on stage, one of them is devoted entirely to rejecting the traits and the infamies of the other. I am well aware that our contemporary Nomophages, who have undertaken to honor as patriots incendiaries and assassins, have condemned as a moderate this Forlis, who has no desire for a liberty built on fury but rather does battle against its subverters and seeks order, manners, laws. He has by no means allowed his timid eyes to become accustomed to seeing blood flow, his weak hands to shedding it, his ears to hearing the cries of victims. Honest men see in his opponents only tigers devouring all about them, and in Forlis and in all those who resemble him, a race of friends and brothers.

One of the complaints some people have made against my work is that I have not made my aristocrat an imbecile or a monster, for, these deep thinkers have said, this shows that the author wants us to love the aristocracy. Thus what is perhaps the most moral dimension of my comedy has been slandered. Let me explain. I preach to convert, but I swear that I have never believed until now that insults were the best way to gain proselytes. One does not gain hearts by wounding them. I distinguished at the very outset (and anyone with a bit of sense would have already done this with me) between the aristocrat of Coblenz and the aristocrat of Paris, between the one who has taken up arms against his country and the one who has remained faithful to hearth and home. The one is guilty, the other is at worst blinded. Can it be believed that all those exaggerated portraits that are shown on the stage of aristocrats fighting as best they can in their fury and stupidity are particularly efficacious in curing those they are attacking? Such portrayals irritate them, and that is all. As I have said, I will have nothing to do with such portraits, an affront to both taste and reason. I have portrayed an aristocrat and a republican, if we make the first an honest man, the second will gain much more honor by appearing so. In the scene that I offer I will have attained a great deal already if I can make those blush who share Versac's opinions for not sharing his honesty. This is already the first step toward a conversion, but how can it be taken if not by making this honest but misguided man sympathetic? If on the contrary I made him a villain, those who merely favor aristocracy would accuse me of exaggeration and imposture, while the real villains would find in this representation an excuse for not changing their ways. What would I have accomplished? Clearly, nothing, and the goal of this work, which is to be useful, would have been missed.

As for the character of Filto, I can sum up all of his aspects in a single phrase, an axiom that wicked persons have abused: "virtue cannot be achieved by going backward." I wanted to provide by the example of this weak man a possibility for those who have only strayed.

The principle aim, the true aim of my work was to enlighten the people, but also to avenge those calumnies which have attributed to them all the crimes that brigands have committed. By continually reminding the people of their feeling of dignity it will be permanently fixed within them, but I have never dishonored my art by turning its comedy into satire, as some have claimed. I did not want my verses to become an arena for the struggle of animosities. Everything that they depict is drawn from nature, the source from which a poet must always take his colors. I have gathered scattered traits to compose my masses, true comedy being a mirror of human life, not of any individual. I began a prologue in which I developed these ideas, though I never finished it. Here are a few verses of it, a dialogue between the author and a friend in which the friend attempts to convince the author not to present his comedy.

> Yes [he says] monsieur, you have talent, I can see.
> Your work is good, but I can guarantee
> That it will fail. A thunderstorm of rage
> Will surely welcome it upon the stage.
> Even the title, should you dare announce it
> Will raise a host of zealots to denounce it.

THE AUTHOR: Let them be angry. I am not afraid.
> True citizens will rally to my aid.

THE FRIEND: Heavens! Such enemies!

THE AUTHOR: But I despise
> Such rogues, with honest men as my allies.
> Vice plays the tyrant only when one fears.
> Stand up to him, he quickly disappears.
> Molière would censure without hesitation,
> Never once stooping to accommodation.

He knew the mortal danger vice presents
Whenever someone's vigilance relents
And his immortal verse, his soul sublime
Will challenge vice until the end of time.
I want his courage.

THE FRIEND: Can you claim to share
His genius?

THE AUTHOR: Never! He's beyond compare.
But if I can't compete with him in art,
As citizen I still can do my part.
The way I love my country and I show it
In poetry can make of me a poet.

THE FRIEND: Many have called you spiteful and malicious.

THE AUTHOR: Rascals and fools will always be suspicious.
Of any work an honest man produces
That sees into their hearts and shames their ruses.
Comedy is but a mirror whose inspection
Provides for all the world a just reflection,
And yet how few who see it understand!

THE FRIEND: The portraits coming from the master's hand,
Tartuffe and Trissotin left little doubt
Of whom the dramatist was pointing out.

THE AUTHOR: Yes, he was scrupulous, and I must do
As he did, follow nature and be true
To her. My rogues, whatever be their race,
May have no hearts, but bear a human face,
And if that face and yours should be the same.
I but report the truth. Am I to blame?

    I cannot put down my pen without thanking those citizens who performed in my play and whose talent was inspired by their enthusiasm. I will not speak of anyone in particular, and I am sure they will forgive me for including in a single expression of praise the thanks I owe to each. They have all well merited the praise not just of the author but of the entire Parisian public, and perhaps of all Frenchmen, for establishing a work which has not been without its use.   To divide among them the congratulations that the entire group has earned would be to weaken the feelings that should be shared. Let me thus extend to them all my gratitude.

THE FRIEND OF THE LAWS

by

Jean-Louis Laya

Premiered at the Théâtre de la Nation
(formerly the Comédie-Française)
January 2, 1793

CAST OF CHARACTERS

M. DE VERSAC, a former baron

MME de VERSAC, his wife

M. DE FORLIS, a former marquis

M. NOMOPHAGE, a Revolutionary

FILTO, his friend

DURICRANE, a journalist

M. PLAUDE, a Revolutionary

BERNARD, FORLIS's financial manager

AN OFFICER and his followers

SERVANTS of M. DE VERSAC

ACT I

VERSAC: You've seen my daughter? I am glad to say
She's all right now, but while you were away
I strongly feared her health would be affected
By all these crowds. My house is now infected
By lords of misrule, who, if they were able,
Would seize the country, with my wife and table.
Their constant fuss my daughter can't abide
After the quiet of the countryside.
She's gone now to her aunt's for some respite
From these messieurs who chatter day and night,
These brash political non-entities,
These would-be lions, who are merely fleas.
In her retreat I'm sure she dreams of you,
But Forlis, you have catching-up to do!
You've been away two weeks and every hour
That you've been gone, your foes increased in power.
My wife they have enlisted and misled;
I fear a bitter struggle lies ahead.

FORLIS: I have your word and Sophie's.

VERSAC: That is true.

FORLIS: It means a lot if I can count on you.
I know that you are master of this place.

VERSAC: Those days are past.

FORLIS: Truly? What a disgrace!
What happened?

VERSAC: Everything is rearranged.
My wife was quite submissive. How she's changed!
She's now a pillar of strength and resolution.
It was, my dear Forlis, the Revolution

That quite deprived me of a husband's right.

FORLIS: A strange result!

VERSAC: I suffered in her sight
From two great flaws, neither to be endured.
First, I was noble.

FORLIS: Of that, we're both cured.

VERSAC: And then I was her husband, and you see
My family had no goods to leave to me.
My wife's relations, having little rank,
Made up for this with money in the bank.
It was a perfect match in the beginning,
I brought the honor, she the underpinning.
A double source of power I could claim:
The rank of husband and my noble name.
Now I command in vain; my haughty wife
Lets no one tell her how to run her life.
And since she holds the pursestrings, it is plain
She thinks the family now is her domain
And that her daughter's fate is in her hands.
If as her husband I should give commands,
I would be lost. Today's regenerators
In social customs have become dictators,
Opposed to all traditions. They, of course,
Find marriage less attractive than divorce.

FORLIS: It's true.

VERSAC: With rank and name alike defiled,
No wonder my wife treats me like a child.

FORLIS: As an aristocrat you take it well.

VERSAC: I am enraged, but nobody can tell.
I could complain, but never will, because
My wife won't change, and neither will the laws.

FORLIS: Is your home still a site of agitation?

VERSAC: Indeed, for all the seers of the nation.
            One, with a small constituency, calls
            For France to stay within the city's walls.
            Another scorns such limited expanse,
            Thinks Europe should be all absorbed by France.
            A third would split France into thirty states,
            Each with its king, high walls, and guarded gates.
            And all would change our customs and our manners
            Since all are obdurate and ruthless planners.

FORLIS: Between ourselves, your portrait fits them truly,
            But you should not alarm yourself unduly.

VERSAC: You do not know the threat . . .

FORLIS: Your wife . . .

VERSAC: She's mad!
            She's lost what little sense she ever had!
            Your lack of observation is appalling!
            You do not seem to know the sky is falling!
            You're like a drunken suitor in the way
            You love the Revolution! Can you say . . .

FORLIS: Please don't attack me. If I must defend
            Myself, we'll come to quarrel in the end.
            Is your wife likely to surprise us here?

VERSAC: I'm by myself today. You needn't fear.

FORLIS: And she?

VERSAC: She's at her club, her favorite scene.
            Meanwhile read this. (*Giving him a letter.*)

FORLIS (*looking at the address*): Coblenz! What does this mean?

VERSAC: They're only . . .

FORLIS: Who?

VERSAC: Supporters of the King.

FORLIS: You frighten me! What is it that they bring?

VERSAC: The rule of law, which surely you agree,
               Is what is wished by the majority.
               A chorus of angry voices now expresses
               How Europe is alarmed by our excesses.

FORLIS: Indeed.

VERAC: There have been detailed declarations
               Published about the rights of men and nations,
               And armies have been raised to guarantee
               That all may live their lives secure and free.

FORLIS: What sort of laws and liberty are those
               That cannonfire and armies can impose?

VERAC: They come not to destroy but elevate.
               You dream of tearing down. They will create.
               Industry, commerce, arts are near their end.

FORLIS: And foreign armies will reverse this trend?

VERSAC: They'll first restore our rights.

FORLIS: You mean restore
               Our privileges, at the cost of war
               In which the blood of Frenchmen will be lost.

VERSAC: No, I reject all honors at that cost.
               I see myself as an aristocrat
               But I'm an honest man for all of that.
               Your claimed equality I find despotic.

So I'm conservative, but patriotic.
Though I approve of much of what they've said,
I haven't joined the others who have fled,
Though as a gentleman I must confess
I wouldn't be displeased with their success.

FORLIS: They won't succeed.

VERSAC: You think this ancient nation,
Of monarchy the very incarnation,
Can change to a republic?

FORLIS: We shall see.

VERSAC: Come, now! A state without nobility?
Society needs ranks, something to gain.

FORLIS: We walk together on a level plain.

VERSAC: You mean in this new state the lowest scum,
Without a name or patron can become
The equal of those men of highest station?

FORLIS: Indeed, without resistance. In this nation
The ranks that separate us don't exist!
All that is gone!

VERSAC: You foolish optimist!

FORLIS: You're angry.

VERSAC: Yes, and I could not be wearier
Of all this cant. Beneath a French exterior
You seek a Roman soul, but just recall,
Cato also loved Rome, before his fall!
Inflamed by passion, that unhappy sage
Thought to restore to Rome its golden age.
Perfect equality was what he sought,
And he was not content with what he got.

Driven by virtue to achieve perfection,
He suffered for his pains complete rejection.
His vision didn't set the Romans free
But opened them to Caesar's tyranny.
My friend, I hope this lesson will be ample.

FORLIS: There are a few defects in your example.
In freedom's cause half-measures are unsound;
The fruitful seed is lost on rocky ground.
Cato, no doubt, is much to be admired.
His dreams for Roman glory were inspired,
But he was wrong. What error caused his fall?
Virtue he knew, but nature not at all.
In a degenerate, exhausted time
He acted as if Rome were in her prime.
And ended as a fool and not a sage
In looking for a vanished golden age.
Are we like that? No, all our ancient faults
Are buried, with our kings, in dusty vaults.
No more sepulchral pomp, no feudal night.
We've left them to emerge into the light.
Those faithful guiding torches, time and reason,
Brought us from winter into spring's sweet season,
Revealing the old system's many flaws
And building a new edifice of laws.
A common spirit . . .

VERSAC: Common? What about
All the intriguers?

FORLIS: There are some, no doubt,
But soon or late, excesses are forsaken;
Men dozing in the sun's pure beams awaken.
Occasionally one or two may stray
Out of the well-defined appropriate way,
But reason's soft immortal voice will guide them.
They'll hear its admonitions deep inside them.
And realize their steps have been mistaken.
False guides will then be punished and forsaken.

VERSAC: Fine words, indeed! If only they were true!
           But clearly there's no reasoning with you!
           We'll say no more. Acquaintance soon will show
           You whom I fear.

FORLIS: Who is it? Might I know?

VERSAC: Doubtless you've heard their names.
                              There's Monsieur Plaude,
           Who's not intelligent, although he's loud.
           Demosthenes he'd like as his cognomen,
           But he's no speaker, either Greek or Roman.

FORLIS: Nor French, I think.

VERSAC: He is a sorry case,
           Seeing dark plots in everybody's face.
           The thought of treason gives him constant fright,
           Denouncing daily what he dreams at night.
           He worships politics to the degree
           That no one's as ridiculous as he.

FORLIS: I know him well.

VERSAC: You also know the rest.
           Plaude's friend is Duricrane, another pest,
           A journalist who's feared but not respected;
           His heart and brain have never been detected!
           Then Filto and his colleague Nomophage
           Filto's the least committed in that lodge,
           Lacking alike in scruples and authority,
           He only wants to be in the majority.
           And Nomophage, ah, there's a man indeed
           An Attila in power and in creed,
           Potentially a dangerous opponent,
           Sowing discord as we have never known it,
           A partisan . . .

FORLIS: Not dangerous.

VERSAC: Who knows?
             He fears you.

FORLIS: And I scorn him, and all those
             Who follow him.

A SERVANT (*entering*):   Monsieur, your wife is back.

VERSAC (*to* FORLIS): My friend, prepare for an attack!

FORLIS: I'm ready. (MME VERSAC *enters*.)

VERSAC: Madam, Forlis has returned!

MME VERSAC (*coldly*): Good day, sir.

FORLIS (*aside, to* VERSAC):   Your suspicions are confirmed!

VERSAC (*to* MME): I've told Forlis him that you are now inspired
             To give up what you formerly desired,
             The advantageous union that we planned.
             Can you explain? He doesn't understand.

MME VERSAC: Whether he understands or not, it's true.

VERSAC: Madam has spoken. I'll bid you adieu.   (*He goes.*)

MME VERSAC: This union, Forlis, doesn't suit my ends,
             Although I hope that we can still be friends.
             If all your talents had been turned to action,
             You might have been the leader of a faction.
             Young men should be audacious at your age,
             Instead of which you chose to play the sage.
             That never was the role in which I'd cast you.
             Others of far less merit have surpassed you.
             Despite your talents, they have seized the prize.
             I favored you before, but now my eyes
             Are opened and I realize you lack
             Distinction, like my dear Monsieur Versac,

Who thinks as baron he should be addressed,
When now he's just as bourgeois as the rest.
Since you two haven't kept up with the nation,
Others have risen in my estimation.

FORLIS: I would be frightened, Madame, but I dare
               Believe that in the end you will be fair.

MME VERSAC: You really think your rivals can be bested?

FORLIS: I do.

MME VERSAC: Well, if you don't mind being tested,
               They'll soon be here. I think they will debate
               The current plans to subdivide the state
               In thirty parts.

FORLIS: Indeed!

MME VERSAC: I'm quite annoyed!
               Our cherished unity will be destroyed!
               The plan seems foolish, but I don't disdain it.
               Good Nomophage is coming to explain it
               To me at dinner. He, I realize
               Is one of those whose prowess you despise.

FORLIS: I'm proud to say I do.

MME VERSAC: Perhaps you'll say
               Just why.

FORLIS: Of course! The one who's duped I may
               Forgive, but not the one who dupes.

MME VERSAC: Although
               You jest about them, I would like to know
               If you would dare engage them face to face?
               Tomorrow perhaps?

FORLIS: Madame, save me a place!

MME VERSAC: Four of our party's leaders will be here.

FORLIS: Such adversaries cause me little fear.
               I won't gain laurel wreathes for victories
               Over such petty enemies as these.
               There's only one condition I impose,
               And that's in the debate, however it goes,
               I'm free to speak my mind without offense.

MME VERSAC: Of course! They're men of probity and sense.

FORLIS: Madame, I must admit to some surprise
               At how they've pulled the wool over your eyes!

MME VERSAC: Believe me, they're all patriots!

FORLIS: Madame!
               No one's more patriotic than I am!
               A patriot! There is no title, clearly,
               That has such virtue or is loved so dearly,
               But nothing of the patriot resides
               In these poltroons, these closet homicides,
               These would-be Solons, these reforming fools
               Who out of dreams weave their destructive rules.
               They'd turn this whole vast country on its head
               Reviving classic customs, long since dead.
               Do not confuse the very different hearts
               Of the true citizens with these upstarts.
               They are not patriots, though that's their claim.
               The others are, but do not boast the name.
               They do not, like your fellows, take offense
               At the heart's true and honest sentiments.
               Domestic virtues are the source, they feel,
               Of civic virtues. Someone will reveal
               How good a citizen he'll likely be
               By how he treats his friends and family.
               He knows the ills we all have suffered, yet

He looks upon all blood shed with regret.
He sees in all a spark of that same fire,
That love of virtue to which all aspire.
That is the sort of patriot we need.
Your fellows are a very different breed.
Which of the two deserves your approbation?

MME VERSAC: Neither one yet.

FORLIS: Why not?

MME VERSAC: My inclination
Is not yet to decide who's right or wrong.

FORLIS: But some day you must choose!

MME VERSAC: It won't be long.
You can confront your rivals, and if they,
As they presume, should carry off the day,
My daughter's theirs, for, as you realize,
The suitor who's the best deserves the prize.

FORLIS (*kissing her hand*): I'll be your son-in-law!

MME VERSAC: That, time will show.
As for my husband, he must come to know
All are susceptible to fortune's wheel —
One's up, one's down, and there is no appeal.
His once great rank and honors now have flown,
While I aspire to honors of my own.
I'm looking now for politicians, since
My daughter can't aspire to wed a prince.

FORLIS (*laughing*): A fairy-tale conclusion, I must say!

MME VERSAC: It is indeed, but now, I cannot stay.
My husband waits.

FORLIS: May I conduct you to him?

I'd love to see what good your tidings do him!
(*They go out.*)

ACT II

FORLIS: Come in, Bernard.

BERNARD: Monsieur, I bring to you
                The list you asked of me.

FORLIS (*taking it*):   Yes, this will do.
                Let's see—consider twenty sou a day,
                Two hundred louis in a month, let's say—

BERNARD: Less twelve, Monsieur.

FORLIS: Less twelve—

BERNARD: And you must add
                Four pounds to that.

FORLIS: Four pounds.

BERNARD: Monsieur, I've had
                Misgivings. It's a great amount to spend.

FORLIS: It costs a bit, but it will put an end
                To friends' financial troubles.

BERNARD: Few would be
                Capable of such acts.

FORLIS: Please don't judge me
                By others. Is my secret quite secure?

BERNARD: It is, but when your motives are so pure,
                Why hide it?

FORLIS: Dear Bernard, you surely know
                Virtue is tarnished when it's done for show.

The good deeds that we do we really ought
To hide. A reputation can't be bought.
Good is its own reward, it seems to me,
And further recompense is usury.
Goods can be sold, but good is given away
Without a thought of profit or display.
But here come people I've no wish to see!
Filto and Nomophage. Come, follow me.
(*They go out.*)

NOMOPHAGE (*seeing them go*):
What! Forlis back! Now there'll be hell to pay!
I must alert the papers right away!
But we are safe for now.
(*They sit.* NOMOPHAGE *spreads out a paper.*)
                              Here's the proposal
For all that we will have at our disposal.
You know the plans are virtually completed.

FILTO: I also know how well you have been treated.

NOMOPHAGE: I let them know what good I've done the nation.
Self-interest always fuels my inspiration.
There's been some opposition . . .

FILTO: I've no doubt.

NOMOPHAGE: A little blood spilled, though, can bring about
Conviction, and the backing that we need
If we expect our projects to succeed.
For, speaking frankly, friend, in times gone by
We both were less than nothing, you and I.
We had no debts, but that was cause for sorrow,
Since, having nothing, nothing could we borrow.
Now we, bred up in misery and shame,
Without a shred of honor to our name,
Will be endowed with spacious territory,
Subjects and treasure, influence and glory.

FILTO (*reading the paper and consulting a map*):
>Let's see the spoils. Here's Macon, Beaune, they say
>That's good wine country.

NOMOPHAGE: Best for some gourmet.

FILTO: They've given me Le Maine.

NOMOPHAGE: No wine, but still,
>Good chicken country. You can eat your fill.

FILTO: I'm satisfied, and Poitou goes to you.

NOMOPHAGE: Not bad, though I'd have rather had Anjou.

FILTO: Does Plaude get nothing?

NOMOPHAGE: No. He sows confusion
>Promoting his agrarian illusion,
>Seeking to build a commune where we'd toil
>Together for the glory of French soil.

FILTO: Didn't you join him once?

NOMOPHAGE: I did, but briefly.
>I used him as an instrument and chiefly
>For my own ends, to get a bit of land.
>I was agrarian, but understand,
>Plaude's farms have lost their interest for me since
>An entire province now may call me prince.

FILTO: The plan is excellent, but I've some doubt
>It can successfully be carried out.

NOMOPHAGE: Why not?

FILTO: We cannot win without debating
>Forlis, who's gifted . . .

NOMOPHAGE: And infuriating!
            The next eight days must see that man's demise!
            His fall is needed if we are to rise!
            He and the followers that he empowers
            Befriend the public. They're no friends of ours!
            A man like Forlis, lacking all ambition,
            A foolish patriot, can destroy our mission!
            He is a monster, who, without impunity,
            Would force our fractured nation into unity
            And thwart our goals. Ambition needs a state
            Divided for its power to operate.

FILTO: Virtue impresses me, though I don't know
            Exactly why it stimulates me so.
            Between ourselves, I'd like to change my view,
            Be more like him, and rather less like you.

NOMOPHAGE: You are a fool. Once settled on the track,
            Must you betray yourself by looking back?
            Full speed ahead if you would gain the prize,
            Judge for yourself and not with others' eyes.
            Strong walls may long contain the fire's fierce blast,
            We're startled then, when it breaks forth at last.
            I understand, but hearts that men admire
            Move bravely forward and defy the fire.
            Success goes only to the one who dares.
            The fearful soul delays and then despairs,
            Losing his way, by circumstance beguiled,
            He must be led as one would lead a child.
            Virtue's quite admirable, I suspect.
            I've always treated it with great respect,
            But in this world goods give a man control,
            And so, like others, goods have been my goal.
            I think that Duricrane, who hates Forlis,
            Will soon remove him and restore our peace.
            Virtue's faint urgings he won't even hear,
            And their last echoes soon will disappear.

FILTO: Perhaps, but oftentimes the voice we swore

To stifle comes back stronger than before,
And don't we run some risk collaborating
With Duricrane?

NOMOPHAGE: No. He's exasperating,
But we can manage him.

FILTO: Yet, frankly speaking,
How good is this republic we are seeking?

NOMOPHAGE: Quite good, for us!

FILTO: My friend, when I'm with you
I can't escape the image of those two
Satiric Roman priests that Cicero
Made laughing stocks so many years ago.

NOMOPHAGE: We'll laugh ourselves, when others bow to us.
But we have other matters to discuss.
Do you still have your eye on Versac's daughter?

FILTO: Somewhat.

NOMOPHAGE: Well, forge ahead. I've quite forgot her.
In my new state kings will be my allies,
I have no interest now in bourgeois ties.

FILTO: You're right, and with a province of my own,
Why shouldn't some infanta share my throne?

NOMOPHAGE: Yes, but my friend, though she appeals to neither,
Make sure that Forlis doesn't get her either.
Remember after all she's still an heiress,
And if some cruel demon should embarrass
Our plans, and we don't get what we deserve,
It would be well to have her in reserve.
If that should happen, I do not see how
You wouldn't win. (*Aside*) I have the mother's vow!

FILTO: I feel the same, and would be pleased to see
                You win the prize. (*Aside*) Her hand is promised me!

(DURICRANE *enters.*)

NOMOPHAGE: Here's Duricrane, and clearly he's delighted.
                Speak up, my friend, what has you so excited?
                You're like the cat who swallowed the canary!

DURICRANE: Oh, I have every reason to be merry!

NOMOPAGE: I'll wager, since your pleasure is so great,
                You've come across some plot against the state!

DURICRANE: Indeed, and you won't guess the traitor's name.

NOMOPHAGE: Traitors are traitors. They are all the same.

DURICRANE: No, this one's worth a hundred lesser fry.

NOMOPHAGE: Tell us, you temptor!

DURICRANE: Heaven cast its eye
                Upon me! Once again I've saved the nation!

NOMOPHAGE: Let's have less boasting and more information!
                Leave heaven and the nation out of it;
                Give us a bit more matter and less wit.

DURICRANE: It was as if some strange, mysterious force
                Led me.

NOMOPHAGE: To where?

DURICRANE: Why, to this park, of course.

NOMOPHAGE: To see what?

DURICRANE: You, who think you are so clever,

> In sniffing out intrigues and plots, would never
> Given a thousand guesses have discovered
> The malcreant whose guilt I have uncovered!

NOMOPHAGE: Enough! Give us the traitor's name and cease
　　　　　　This banter!

DURICRANE:　　　　　　　What?

NOMOPHAGE:　　　　　　　　　　His name!

DURICRANE:　　　　　　　　　　　　　It is Forlis!

NOMOPHAGE: Forlis!

FILTO:　　　　Impossible! It cannot be!

DURICRANE: It's true, Messieurs. You can rely on me!

NOMOPHAGE: And yet he's powerful. We must take care.
　　　　　　What evidence have you of this affair?
　　　　　　We must provide ourselves sufficient clearance
　　　　　　We need, if not some proof, at least appearance.
　　　　　　We'd be delighted . . .

DURICRANE:　　　　　　　　　What! Appearance? Fie!
　　　　　　A full-blown plot that he cannot deny!
　　　　　　Five hundred enemies that he supports!
　　　　　　In my own pocket I have the reports!

NOMOPHAGE: Don't keep us waiting! Speak!

DURICRANE:　　　　　　　　　　I beg your pardon.
　　　　　　In brief, then, I was strolling in the garden.
　　　　　　An ill-appearing fellow came in view
　　　　　　Walking beside another whom I knew.
　　　　　　This was Monsieur Forlis, and, being observant,
　　　　　　I soon was sure the other was his servant.
　　　　　　Forlis' abrupt return, his unknown mission,

Both gave me ample reason for suspicion,
And to myself I said, "This fellow speaks
Of being out of Paris several weeks
Yet he here he is returned when least expected.
Some mystery is here to be detected."

NOMOPHAGE: Your reasoning is flawless; there is not
A shred of doubt that you've sniffed out a plot!

DURICRANE: I have a gift for spying, as you see.
The subtlest plots are all too clear to me.

NOMOPHAGE: What happened next?

DURICRANE: I quietly drew near,
Treading so softly that they could not hear,
And hid behind a hedge, as still as death,
On high alert, fearing to draw a breath.
I listened, saw, and fully won my gamble.
After a short and meaningless preamble
"Good," Monsieur Forlis said, "Your lists are done.
I'll take this now." Then, quickly, seizing one,
He left, but think of my delight to find
That in his haste, he'd left the list behind!
Out of my hiding place at once I leapt
To seize this damning list, which I have kept!
Look here! Peruse it! In it you will see
Five hundred names reduced to poverty
During the Revolution. Forlis's task
Has been supporting them. Why, one must ask?

FILTO: This doesn't prove a lot. You really need,
If you're condemning him, to prove . . .

DURICRANE: Just read!

NOMOPHAGE (reading): "I, Charles Alexandre Forlis, swear
To take the names which follow in my care,
Give twenty sols a day if they agree

Not to reveal the money comes from me.
Other conditions are for them to set."

DURICRANE: As close to a confession as you'll get!

NOMOPHAGE: We must denounce him!

DURICRANE: It's already done!

NOMOPHAGE: Good work!

DURICRANE: I think so, but it's just begun.
              I'll need support. He's cunning, I'm afraid.

NOMOPHAGE: Fifteen or twenty copies must be made
              And sent to friends.

DURICRANE: Good!

NOMOPHAGE: There's enough of us,
              Armed with this list, to raise an awful fuss!

DURICRANE: We can stir up a devil of a row.
              Rely on me. I'm in my setting now.
              No one knows better how to manage fights.

FILTO: But don't forget, accused men still have rights.
              We still have laws and still must honor those.

DURICRANE: Still this, still that! You sound just like our foes!
              With judges who are strong and prone to action,
              The laws can best be viewed as a distraction.
              Justice, not law, the honest patriot seeks!

NOMOPHAGE: Well said!

DURICRANE: I have denounced, within two weeks,
              Eight separate plots, that's four a week, and most
              Good citizens, I think, would likely boast

If they found four a month. Yet some are wary.
They dare to call my fears imaginary!
My plots are chimerae, they love to say;
Those I accuse are freed the self-same day!
Some call me mad, but their protests are vain!
This new affair recharges me again!

NOMOPHAGE: Lead on! I'll follow and support your word.
Two voices are more likely to be heard.
Filto, we shall return.

(NOMOPHAGE *and* DURICRANE *leave.*)

FILTO (*alone*):   Pray, don't make haste.
I view this whole affair with great distaste.
I have no wish to join. If they're committed,
Let each pursue the course to which he's fitted.
These madmen, Nomophage especially,
Have tried to make a madman out of me!
I was born poor but honest and I'm very
Much drawn to being quiet and sedentary.
I'm in the serpents' nest now. It seems wrong,
But what to do? My character's not strong,
And though I feel I'm not one of their sort,
I have no other sources of support.
What kind of world is this, where if he's wise,
The honest man must live by compromise?
(*He exits.*)

ACT III

(*Enter* FILTO *and* NOMOPHAGE.)

FILTO: I warn you once again, my friend, be wary.
                This Forlis is a clever adversary.

NOMOPHAGE: Wariness is the style for which you're known.
                Don't worry, we have weapons of our own.
                What's the worst situation that you fear?
                We think him guilty but his record's clear?
                Are his accusers wrong? That would be new!
                Their zeal, we know, drives them to what they do.
                Even when Terror errs it's right because
                The public's good stands higher than the laws.

FILTO: Although you think it salutary, fear
                Can be defended only if sincere.
                The public will not long support its use
                If they think it is subject to abuse.

NOMOPHAGE: Morals and caution! We've no need of those!

FILTO: Your actions are all legal, I suppose,
                But still the secret measures you've pursued,
                Distributing that list, could that be viewed
                As legal also?

NOMOPHAGE: Stop there! Don't you see
                Our plan's protected by its secrecy?
                The course we took was dangerous, I know,
                But what respect to traitors do we owe?
                The list was just distributed to those
                We carefully selected, and we chose
                With care. The list was only circulated
                To men whose virtue cannot be debated.

FILTO: Each one of them your own position shares.
                How can they judge Forlis and his affairs?

NOMOPHAGE: You're too late. We've already spread the word,
                Electrifying everyone who's heard,
                And so the story circulates, increasing
                In power and detail, thanks to the unceasing
                Efforts of those who share our public spirit.

FILTO: This gossip is abuse and all should fear it.
                It glories in corruption and in lying.

NOMOPHAGE: I see you find perfection terrifying.
                Should we restrict our vision for those few
                Who find it too utopian, like you?

FILTO: But don't your hearts grow hardened?

NOMOPHAGE: Yes, of course.
                Prodigiously!

FILTO: And you feel no remorse?

NOMOPHAGE: None whatsoever! Forlis has such gall,
                Such arrogance that he's condemned to fall!
                It warms my blood to think he'll be confounded
                With all the rogues by whom he is surrounded!
                In earlier days this Monsieur, nobly born,
                Dared to give Nomophage contempt and scorn!
                Now, Monsieur Forlis, you're about to find
                That damaged pride retaliates in kind!

FILTO: Must wounded pride give rise to inhumanity?

NOMOPHAGE: My hatred is the fruit of his own vanity.
                Besides, his fall enhances our position.
                Guilty or not, he's not above suspicion.
                The case against him is already made.

FILTO: Let justice do its work then.

NOMOPHAGE: With my aid.
                Is that so bad?

FILTO: You call it aid, perhaps,
                To force a verdict?

NOMOPHAGE: Dear Filto, your lapse
                In vision may destroy you. You're about
                To join the moderates! There's little doubt
                Your spirit's hardened. You refuse to see
                Forlis is still a noble, therefore he
                Can never bear to let the people win.

FILTO: But Forlis . . .

NOMOPHAGE: True, the snake may shed its skin
                But it remains in character a snake!
                Consider then, Filto, what stands you take,
                Or you will find your own name compromised.
                One final word of warning: Be advised.
                When Duricrane is here you would be wise
                To watch your step. Don't let your air, your eyes
                Betray you. Your friend Forlis may already
                Be under guard.

FILTO: What?

NOMOPHAGE: As I've said, be steady!
                Don't show that you are open to attacks.
                Quiet! Someone's coming in.

FILTO: It's the Versacs!

(*Enter* VERSAC, MME VERSAC *and* FORLIS.)

MME VERSAC (*aside, to* NOMOPHAGE):
                I hope to see the plan that you're proposing.

You have it?

NOMOPHAGE (*aside, to* MME VERSAC): In my pocket.

MME VERSAC (*aside, to* NOMOPHAGE):   Its disclosing
                    Will take some time, and not with all this crowd . . .
                    Then there's your marriage . . . (*Aloud*)
                                        Ah! Here's Monsieur Plaude!

(PLAUDE *enters.*)

VERSAC (*aside to* FORLIS): It's like a visit from the Inquisition!

MME VERSAC (*to* PLAUDE): We've missed you!

PLAUDE: Madame, one in my position
                    Must serve the public first.

MME VERSAC: Ah, you're excused!

PLAUDE: My time, of course, was profitably used.
                    This dissertation, once it's circulated, should
                    Turn France upon its head, for its own good!

FORLIS: For its own good, Monsieur?

PLAUDE: Monsieur, of course!
                    I've traced our country's evils to their source.
                    There's only one, however it's disguised.
                    It's property!

FORLIS: Why am I not surprised?

PLAUDE: All social evils and injustice flow
                    From property; we've learned that from Rousseau.
                    Ban property and theft will disappear —
                    No crime, no punishment. It's all quite clear.
                    No misers, since there's nothing to acquire,
                    No plotters, since no reason to conspire,

No libertines, all women being free,
And not another form of property.
No gambling, and therefore, in a trice,
No manufacturing of cards or dice.
Possession fuels these evils, as we see,
So dispossession is their remedy.
Doors, windows, walls — we will destroy all these,
Leaving men free to go wherever they please.
What good possession does is still unsure.
If some are rich, others must needs be poor.
In your republic every poor man pleads
For all. In mine, he takes whatever he needs.
If you own nothing, robbers cannot hurt you.
Vice will be gone if we abolish virtue.

FORLIS: It seems you have no use for moderation.

NOMOPHAGE: It is no longer useful to the nation.

FORLIS: If "moderate" you use to designate
                Those egoists who undermine the state
                By their indifference, their lack of passion
                For anything but idle fads and fashion,
                Whose cold indifference and lack of care
                Add to the burdens that we all must bear,
                I hate like you these rascals, who remain
                Indifferent to abuses that are plain.
                But if by moderate you mean the man
                Who seeks to be as honest as he can,
                A citizen by heart if not by name,
                Defending truth, and sometimes taking blame
                For doing so, determined to maintain
                The people's rights, for love and not for gain,
                I'm not the sort of "patriot" you see
                Up on the rooftops, shouting "Liberty!"
                But one of those who, without grand effects,
                Promotes the law that he himself respects.
                If that is how a moderate is known,
                Then it's a title I will gladly own.

PLAUDE (*aside*): He is a former nobleman. That's clear.

NOMOPHAGE (*aloud*): It's men without a party that I fear.

FORLIS: It's modesty, I'm sure, and not conviction,
    To fear the ones devoted to that fiction.
    I won't name names, but if you look around
    I'm sure more fearful figures could be found.

NOMOPHAGE: I know of none.

FORLIS: I'd name some if I chose.

NOMOPHAGE: Those foreign mercenaries, I suppose.
     Those paladins who constantly design
     Plots to invade us from beyond the Rhine.

FORLIS: The ones I'm thinking of are far more near.
    You needn't look beyond our own frontier.
    They're all too often found within our ranks,
    The soap-box patriots, the mountebanks,
    Their faces all aglow with civic pride.
    Idealists without, tyrants inside,
    Ambitious hypocrites who sow disaster
    Bowing before an image made of plaster.
    While heaven's greatest gift, sweet Liberty,
    They've sought to make us hate, pretending she
    Is blood-thirsty as they are. It's not so!
    For Liberty, a god they scarcely know,
    Has her eternal throne within our hearts!
    So let these charlatans, these rude upstarts,
    These wild-eyed zealots who disgrace the name
    Of patriot, be purged, and let's proclaim
    Eternal war with every anarchist,
    Whether republican or royalist!
    All now should dwell in harmony because
    We all accept one sovereign, the laws!
    Those brigands of misrule we used to fear
    Should see their time is past and disappear.

NOMOPHAGE (*somewhat embarrassed*):
        I know of no one such as you describe.

FORLIS: Surprising! I know many of that tribe.

NOMOPHAGE: I beg to differ.

FORLIS: Yes, you would. It's plain
        The blind man looks into the mirror in vain.

NOMOPHAGE: You hesitate to give us names, I see.

FORLIS: I've tried to purge them from my memory.

NOMOPHAGE: The evidence for those you blame is spare.

FORLIS: Their writings and their deeds are everywhere!

NOMOPHAGE: Friends of the people always have deplored
        Extremists, but they're easily ignored.

FORLIS: The honest man shows much less toleration,
        But treats such rogues with scorn and detestation.

NOMOPHAGE: If they're as ruthless as you say they are,
        Why have they held their zeal in check thus far?

FORLIS: Those with pure motives do not feel the need
        To trumpet endlessly about their creed.
        True virtue's never openly expressed,
        Those who speak of it least display it best!

(*Enter* DURICRANE.)

NOMOPHAGE: Ah, Duricrane! I think that you display
        The traits Monsieur condemns!

DURICRANE (*aside, to* NOMOPHAGE):   They're on their way!

NOMOPHAGE (*aside, to* DURICRANE): Silence!

PLAUDE: Enough of this! Each person sees
With his own eyes, and factions such as these,
Make it unlikely we'll be subjugated.

FORLIS: Yet Liberty alone is over-rated
Unless it's bound by law. This is because
The freest man also respects the laws.
Unhappy is the state where mere caprice
Threatens each man's security and peace.
Brutus to bloody action was not moved
Till Caesar's guilt was absolutely proved.

PLAUDE: Brutus, suspecting Caesar of ambition,
Should have arrested him on that suspicion.
Nothing gives more protection to a nation
Than does detention and incarceration.
There's no need for judicial interference.
We can rely entirely on appearance.
Take me, sir, for example, I arrest
Whenever I am sure it's for the best.
It's black or white with me, no shades of grey,
And if I'm told some suspect got away,
I'm after him at once!

FORLIS: A fearful trade!

PLAUDE: It's a demanding task. One must be made
Of iron, Monsieur. It is a constant fight—
A traitor every day—there's no respite!
A new arrest is scheduled for today;
The order's out; the troops are on their way.
He's rich, he's noble, and he is aloof.

VERSAC: I understand. You're overwhelmed with proof.

PLAUDE: But I have more.

VERSAC: Indeed?

PLAUDE: In my possession
    I have a note as good as a confession.

DURICRANE (*aside*): We are undone!

PLAUDE: So I expect today
    A nice arrest.

VERSAC: So soon!

PLAUDE: Yes. Why delay?
    He'll serve as an example, and I swear
    I'll give this fine monsieur my utmost care.
    His doom is sure. The process is complete.
    The court's instructed.

NOMOPHAGE (*aside*):   This is indiscreet!

VERSAC: He is a noble?

PLAUDE: Yes, whose name no doubt
    The town will know before the day is out.
    He's one Monsieur Forlis, who's a marquis.

MME VERSAC: Forlis?

FORLIS: What's that? It cannot be!

PLAUDE: Yes, Monsieur de Forlis.

FORLIS: Are you delirious?

PLAUDE: No, Monsieur, that's the name. I am quite serious.
    I worked all morning on the case, I'm pleased
    To say.

FORLIS: Good lord!

PLAUDE: The traitor should be seized
               At home by now.

FORLIS: No, Monsieur, I can swear
               When they arrive, Forlis will not be there.

PLAUDE: You know him?

FORLIS: Yes.

PLAUDE: I am surprised. How can
               You have relationships with such a man?

FORLIS: Monsieur . . .

PLAUDE: A rogue, a rascal.

FORLIS: I deny
               Your charges, sir. This Forlis, it is I.

PLAUDE: Can this be so? Monsieur, I'm quite ashamed.
               Perhaps it's some mistake for which you're blamed.
               You may stay here, or come along with me.

FORLIS: Monsieur, don't worry. I would never flee.

PLAUDE: I'm truly sorry for this. It is clear
               You're a brave man, sir.
                 (THE OFFICER *and his* MEN *arrive.*)
                                    Ah, my men are here.
               Sirs, here's Monsieur Forlis, so my commission
               Is done. Farewell. (*He goes.*)

FORLIS (*to* THE OFFICER):   I'm at your disposition,
               Messieurs.

THE OFFICER: Here are our orders.

FORLIS: So I see.

When laws themselves deny us liberty
They are a travesty. Still, the accused
Will naturally claim he is abused
And right or wrong, I will respect the law.

VERSAC: Such improprieties I never saw!
That liberty, which promised us such bliss,
Can it be compromised as much as this?
Between the law and freedom what disparity
When the law operates with such severity!
For my friend's innocence I will attest.
Let him remain here under house arrest.

FORLIS: No, no, the law should tolerate no wavers,
I would not dream to ask for special favors.
No rank exists in crime or punishment
I must submit, guilty or innocent.

THE OFFICER: Monsieur, your thoughtful words, your decent air
Suggest your innocence in this affair.
Though as you know I've promised to uphold
The law and always do as I am told,
The law itself should always act with charity
So I can also temper my severity.
I'll go at once and see what I can do
To let your friend have custody of you.
Until that's done, I must remain in charge,
And ask you not to roam about at large.
Stay with these people here and wait for me.
I'll be as quick in this as I can be.

VERSAC: Such nobleness! It's not what I'd expect!

THE OFFICER: Citizen-soldiers, sir, deserve respect.
In them, compassion is combined with zeal;
Their virtue isn't cruel, but it is real.
Unhardened by the tasks they must fulfill,
Common humanity inspires them still.

FORLIS (*to the departing* OFFICER):
>   Forlis is ready for whatever transpires.
>   Mercy he neither asks for nor desires.
>   (THE OFFICER *and his* MEN *exit.*)
>   (*To* MME VERSAC)
>   Madame, forgive this unexpected blow.
>   What it may mean I'm at a loss to know.
>   There's some imposture here time will reveal.

MME VERSAC: And had you no suspicion?

FORLIS: None. I feel
>   As mystified as you, but it may be
>   These gentlemen are more informed than we.
>   They all are very close to Monsieur Plaude.
>   Among such friends few secrets are allowed.
>   Doubtless they all know something.

NOMOPHAGE: No, not I!

DURICRANE: I'm at a loss.

FORLIS: Well, still, I can rely
>   On strong support to counter this design.
>   Many a heart is less tranquil than mine.
>   My enemies seek vainly to disguise
>   That tell-tale light of triumph in their eyes,
>   But let them taste their triumph while they may
>   They'll weep tomorrow for their success today!

NOMOPHAGE: I'd act as you do, sir, or very nearly,
>   Were I accused, but let me say sincerely,
>   A reputation tainted by suspicion
>   Is tarnished always.

FORLIS: Sir, with your permission,
>   My reputation will remain intact.
>   It's not as feeble as you think. In fact,
>   Your false concern is something I can spare.

Your tone reveals how much you really care.
Why not for once be honest in your dealings?
Attack me openly, show your true feelings!
I hold you in contempt, I'm proud to say,
And I'm quite certain that you feel that way
About me.

NOMOPHAGE: Can you think . . .

FORLIS: The more that you
Deny it, that's more evidence it's true!

NOMOPHAGE: Monsieur . . .

(A SERVANT *appears with a napkin.*)

FORLIS: Dinner is served. While we're at table
Let's put aside this subject, if we're able.
This ugly mystery will soon be clear.
Only my enemies have need to fear!
(*He gives his hand to* MME VERSAC *and all exit.*)

ACT IV

(*Enter* FILTO *and* NOMOPHAGE.)

FILTO: Monsieur, one word!

NOMOPHAGE: Not now. I'm in a hurry!

FILTO: We'll see!

NOMOPHAGE: See what? My dear Filto, you worry
          Too much.

FILTO: I will not leave you till we talk.

NOMOPHAGE: All right, Filto. That means that you must walk
          Where I do. What is it?

FILTO: I think we're wrong
          About Forlis.

NOMOPHAGE: Impossible!

FILTO: That's strong
          And confident.

NOMOPHAGE: Now I've heard your opinion.
          Good lord, Filto! If he were just some minion,
          A fellow like yourself, we could surprise
          His caution, catch confession in his eyes.
          But he's too clever.

FILTO: Yet, I must insist,
          What is the evidence of guilt?

NOMOPHAGE: The list!

FILTO: The list? Of what? Some names nobody knows!
                It could be innocent!

NOMOPHAGE: The names are those
                Of discontented nobles he is paying.
                What is his motive?

FILTO: Still, would you be saying
                All this about him were you not in league
                With Duricrane, that master of intrigue?

NOMOPHAGE: What, me? A journalist? Since when are you
                The moral judge of anything I do?
                You used to be less honest.

FILTO: To my shame.

NOMOPHAGE: If you're concerned with saving your good name,
                I tell you frankly, Filto, you've converted
                A bit too late. The soul that's been perverted
                Never regains the good that it's renounced.
                Know that a villain, open and pronounced,
                Is worth more than those unpretentious creatures,
                Good men or bad, without distinctive features!
                Remove commitment and distinctions cease.
                You'll have no Nomophage and no Forlis!

FILTO: What must I do then?

NOMOPHAGE: You must play your part.
                You're already corrupted to the heart.
                You've made your choice; you've given us your vow.
                Your very blood's contaminated now.
                The fever of ambition, once contracted,
                Cannot be cured, cannot be counteracted.

FILTO: Take back those feeble honors I've attained.
                I've paid too high a price for what I've gained.

NOMOPHAGE: You will have nothing.

FILTO: Yes.

NOMOPHAGE: Since all you own . . .

FILTO: Has come, alas, from crime.

NOMOPHAGE: You'll stand alone.
          Of all you hoped for, nothing will remain.

FILTO: Not even innocence.

NOMOPHAGE: You stood to gain
          Whole provinces. Would you cast those aside
          Out of repenting zeal? Where is your pride?
          Forget these fancies! They can greatly hurt you,
          My newly rediscovered man of virtue!
          You'll pay the price, and it will not be pretty!
          And yet, despite your folly, I'll have pity
          On you, my friend. I will try not to blame you.
          Despite your folly, I'll try to reclaim you,
          To turn away your steps from the abyss.
          I've some responsibility in this.
          You're my creation, though you may deny it.
          If you're disgraced, I'll suffer somewhat by it.
          You're not repentant, Filto, you're just weak.
          It isn't good, but peace and quiet you seek.
          Look, on this globe each person runs his race,
          Wise man or fool, and leaves but little trace.
          Our vain pretensions science has exposed.
          We're only matter, randomly composed.
          Atoms pursue their universal dance
          Fleeing or joining others quite by chance.
          The many germs that populate the earth
          Monstrous embryos may bring to birth
          Or just as whimsically may combine
          Producing bodies that we call divine.
          Life doesn't care what forms it may produce

Since any form of life may have its use.
The major thing is movement and it makes
No difference what direction movement takes.
Let mighty kingdoms crumble through the ages
Let fearful shipwrecks mark the ocean's rages,
Water retreats in time and fires will burn,
Then fire dies out and water has its turn.
Nature transforms with every passing minute.
Each structure hides a different one within it.
Nothing is ever lost, each new position
Reveals another one in opposition.
The sun distributes its illumination
On everything without discrimination.
Whatever men decide to praise or blame.
The earth will go on turning just the same.

FILTO: The man in whose life virtue is respected
Sees in his universe virtue reflected.
And in his heart he honors that great being,
The author of creation, the all-seeing,
Whose wisdom and beneficence appears
Throughout the world. In the celestial spheres
This heavenly harmony man has been shown
So he may seek perfection of his own.
But vicious man, indifferent to good,
Would make the whole world evil, if he could.
Attempting to make Nature take the blame
For crimes that he commits in Nature's name.

NOMOPHAGE: Filto, adieu.

FILTO: Wait, my unhappy friend.
Think for a moment where your course may end.
This conflict is important! On one side,
A righteous man, without a thing to hide,
And on the other, vice and treachery.
What will the outcome very likely be?
You may well lose.

NOMOPHAGE: So be it. I'm past caring.
                     A man like me must live and die by daring.
                     Tempt all, risk all, without a trace of fear,
                     In short, behave quite unlike you, my dear.
                     Adieu, Filto. (*He leaves.*)

FILTO (*alone*):   Ah, what corruption! How
                     Could I have followed him? And can I now
                     Somehow aid Forlis? Is there any way
                     That I can help him and yet not betray
                     My benefactor? Though there's every reason,
                     I can't begin an honest life with treason.
                     The benefits he's given me created
                     A sacred bond that can't be abdicated.
                     Forlis is coming back! I must depart.
                     His very presence cuts me to the heart!
                     The Versac house is near. There I can hide!
                     (*He exits.*)

VERSAC (*entering with* FORLIS):
                     We are alone. My wife is occupied.
                     In confidence I beg you, friend, confess
                     What you have done to cause all this distress?

FORLIS: Surely you don't believe these idle thoughts.
                     These fairy tales of non-existent plots?

VERSAC: Excellent. You deny it. Though I never
                     Took silence for confession. You're too clever.
                     And yet, dear friend, with me there is no need
                     For such dissimulation. No, indeed
                     A noble is a noble to the soul
                     Custom and habit teaches us our role,
                     Not nature, and our training makes us fit,
                     If we are forced, to play the hypocrite.
                     A patriotic bearing we may keep
                     But still be wolves while we appear as sheep.
                     The pompous praise that you have been so quick
                     To give the revolution was a trick

> To cover your real secrets, I'm relieved
> To see.

FORLIS: Indeed.

VERSAC: I really was deceived.
> Your jealous enemies cannot begin
> To rival you. I'm certain you will win.
> Let me congratulate you in advance.
> Forlis, the savior and the hope of France . . .

FORLIS: Versac, you've let your fantasies deceive you.
> If we weren't friends . . .

VERSAC: My friend, I do believe you.
> Forgive me.

FORLIS: I deny your intimation.

VERSAC: What are these charges then?

FORLIS: Pure fabrication!

SERVANT (*entering*): Monsieur!

FORLIS: What's this?

SERVANT: A horrible surprise!
> A servant, ashen-faced, with rolling eyes
> Has run to tell you, with the utmost fear,
> New horrors!

FORLIS: What has happened?

SERVANT: You will hear
> From his own lips. He's here!

BERNARD (*running in*):   Good lord!

FORLIS: What fright!

BERNARD: Pardon, I am distracted!

FORLIS: Why?

BERNARD: The sight
          Of those grim furies I cannot escape!

FORLIS: What furies were these?

BERNARD: Brigands, in the shape
          Of fiends from hell, all bristling with arms
          Their fearsome looks as fit to give alarms
          As those firebrands they carried. I suppose
          They were not French. We have no men like those,
          Savage as tigers, mindless in their wrath,
          Destroying every object in their path.
          On your poor house these furies have descended.
          No one was spared, nothing could be defended.
          There's not a tower standing, not a wall.
          It's an inferno. All is burning, all.
          With tears and prayers I begged with them to halt.
          Nothing could stop their murderous assault.
          Helpless I watched as your possessions perished,
          Furnishings, paintings, everything you cherished
          Reduced to ashes by the fearful ravages
          Of these mysterious and heartless savages.

VERSAC: The villains!

BERNARD: Nothing, sir, would have been saved,
          But with the fire on every side, I braved
          Its fury. Risking death, I ran inside.
          An opening among the flames I spied.
          It was the secret passageway which led
          Into your cabinet. Down its length I fled.
          The brigands and the flames so far had spared
          This sanctuary. Driven by fear, I dared

To burst inside, determined to commit
A crime against you for your benefit.
I seized your papers, but with eyes tight closed.
None of your secrets therefore were exposed.
Theft I committed, only to restore
The theft. I grieve that I could do no more.
(*He gives* FORLIS *papers.*)

FORLIS: This is worth more than all my goods restored!
I know, Bernard, that there is no reward
That I can give to match the satisfaction
In your own heart from such a noble action.
Was any servant wounded in this hateful
Attack?

BERNARD: No one.

FORLIS: For that we must be grateful.
(FORLIS *makes a gesture and* BERNARD *retires.*)

VERSAC (*after a moment of silence*):
You're thoughtful, friend. Perhaps you've now decided
Your trust in this new order was misguided.
Here's what remains of that enchanting dream!
That golden age where law would reign supreme,
Those visions of a state just and eternal,
Produced instead a system quite infernal!
You're silent.

FORLIS: Silent, yes, but not defeated.
Your arguments don't need to be repeated.
However men may think or men may act
Good remains good. They cannot change that fact!
My reason comforts me. I swear I would
Endure all suffering for the common good.
When good and excess have become confused,
Must good be cast aside when it's abused?
Or must we call the law to task because
Men justify their evil deeds with laws?

No, let those fearsome brigands out of hell
Destroy my dwelling and myself as well.
By fire and sword all else they may control,
But I remain the master of my soul.
Living or dying, fear will not decide
My actions. Reason will remain my guide.

VERSAC: I never thought a man as wise as you
Would dare defy these villains as you do.
Why don't you flee? Why will you not reject
A world where reason's given no respect?
When error's raging flood attains its crest
Your vessel will be shattered with the rest.
I would remain your friend, and yet I hate
Your cause. What's the foundation of this state?
The sovereign people, whom you so respect
Reign over all, unchallenged and unchecked,
Fond of excess, resistant to instruction,
All of its power built upon destruction!

FORLIS: The people are to blame! I know that song.
All evil comes from them and every wrong,
But would you be so passionate to mention
Their virtue if that came to your attention?
People are good, although you cannot bear it,
They hate injustice, they would never share it.
Of course they make mistakes, and yet they stay
Innocent even when they go astray.
Crime can enlist them, by deceit and lies,
But they reject it when they realize
Their error, and they mourn crime's grim effect.

VERSAC: Often too late, alas.

FORLIS: Still, I respect
And love the law as you do, and I'm grieved
To see the law abused and men deceived.
But is the law to blame if it's abused
Or is the fault in how the law is used?

Accuse the agents, they're the ones to blame.

VERSAC: The agents or the law, it's all the same,
When all goes badly, and yet, why should I
Complain when such abuse has passed me by?
You've suffered, but you'd rather have it so.

FORLIS: You just don't understand me. Let it go.

VERSAC: So be it. May I ask what you intend
To do now, how you're planning to defend
Yourself?

FORLIS: I will do nothing, but remain
Quietly at your house. It would be vain
To challenge my arrest.

VERSAC: Yes, that is clear.
But as your friend, there's other things I fear.
Those papers Bernard saved. Do they provide
Material it would be best to hide?

FORLIS: I haven't looked. (*He looks through the papers.*)
                    Oh, brave Bernard! Just see!
Banknotes and assets are restored to me!

VERSAC: Why keep them? Give your people a bequest!
Reward the honest folk who burned the rest!

FORLIS (*ignoring him*):
This paper, worth much more, I nearly missed!

VERSAC: Your claim to title?

FORLIS: Not at all. A list
Which you must hold in strictest secrecy,
Though innocent, it may not seem to be
It cannot compromise you, but my foes
Could harm me greatly with it, if they chose.

VERSAC: Give it to me. I'll keep it under guard.

FORLIS: Wait! There's another list! Today Bernard
            Brought it to me. I folded it inside
            My tablets, til I had a chance to hide
            It better.

VERSAC: Let me have it. I've designed
            Some hiding spots the devil couldn't find!

FORLIS: Good lord, I'm lost!

VERSAC: What has disturbed you so?

FORLIS: The paper's missing!

VERSAC: What! Another blow!
            You're sure it's gone?

FORLIS: I can't think what I did
            With it!

VERSAC: Think hard!

FORLIS: Wait! I recall I bid
            Bernard to bring it to me. I would bet
            I left it in the garden where we met.

VERSAC: We must run there at once.

FORLIS: No, it's too late.
            For Nomophage was lying there in wait.

VERSAC: Then you are lost indeed!

FORLIS: No, I'm relieved!
            I know what evidence they have received.
            The plot they've laid is clear and now I know
            From whence and why I have received this blow.

VERSAC: What is this list? What secret does it hold?

FORLIS: Patience, my friend. It's time that you were told.
               But with the other gone, I must retain
               This copy.

VERSAC (*handing it back*): Here it is. But please explain.

FORLIS: Know then . . .

MME VERSAC (*entering, with* FILTO, *in great haste*):
               Good Heavens! I'm in such a state!

VERSAC: What is the matter?

MME VERSAC: Ah, most cruel fate!

VERSAC: Explain, I pray you! What is all this fuss?

MME VERSAC: We're doomed, Monsieur! What will become of us?

VERSAC: Control yourself and tell us what's occurred!

FILTO: One of your servants, sir, has brought us word
               That troops of men at arms have been observed
               Advancing on your home, but what unnerved
               Him more were all the furious groups
               Of citizens who followed up these troops.
               (*To* FORLIS) It's time you fled!

MME VERSAC: I'm trembling with fear!

FORLIS: I am the only one they're seeking here.
               I'll go and meet them.

VERSAC: No! I took my oath.
               Whatever happens now concerns us both.
               Forlis, however much we disagree,
               Friendship binds us together, you and me.

If I can't change your fate, then I will share it.
My shame would be so great I couldn't bear it
If I betrayed a friend in his distress.
I will protect you. I can do no less.

FORLIS: I'm not afraid. My innocence is clear.
Only the criminal gives way to fear.

VERSAC: Just be assured, whatever may befall,
You have a faithful friend on whom to call.

MME VERSAC: Some say they saw an angry mob descend
On Nomophage's house, the people's friend,
Accusing Nomophage, what could be stranger?
Of sheltering his friend Forlis from danger,
And torch in hand, they sought to make him pay
For sheltering a traitor in this way!

FORLIS: His friend Forlis! This is the very first
Charge that has hurt and it's by far the worst!
This vile intriguer I have always hated,
Treated with scorn and constantly berated,
This rascal whom all honest men will shrink
From dealing with, could anybody think
We're friends?

(NOMOPHAGE *enters*.)

FILTO: He's coming!

VERSAC: Can he dare appear
Before us?

FORLIS: I'm appalled!

FILTO (*aside*):   Why is he here?

NOMOPHAGE: My presence here surprises you, I see.

FORLIS: What do you want?

NOMOPHAGE: To save you.

FORLIS: You? . . . Save me?

NOMOPHAGE: Yes, from injustice. Here is my proposal:
                To put my services at your disposal.

FORLIS: After the morals, sir, that you've displayed,
                I'd rather have your hatred than your aid.

NOMOPHAGE: At least give me a hearing. Then decide
                The value of what help I can provide.
                Just listen.

VERSAC: Listen, Forlis.

NOMOPHAGE: You're accused.
                The people, acting justly, or abused . . .

FORLIS: You know they are abused.

NOMOPHAGE: They want your head!
                I've calmed the tempest briefly, and instead
                They've turned on me, so I have dearly paid
                For this mistake those honest people made.
                The few words that I spoke in your support
                They took as friendship speaking and, in short,
                Carried away, they sought to link us two.
                The charge was false; though I would have it true.
                If I'm your friend, then there is every reason
                To think me an accomplice in your treason.
                I cannot claim this liaison, alas.

FORLIS: Indeed you can't.

NOMOPHAGE: This tempest, though, will pass.
                The people's cause I have personified.

Their wrath I've both directed and defied.
It was my work that made you first suspected.

FORLIS: Indeed?

NOMOPHAGE: I also got those blows deflected.
But you're accused.   The law, which still endures,
Must judge between the people's will and yours.
I've held the people off a bit, but they
Will soon be here.   Monsieur, you can't delay.
You can't hide here, but neither can you flee.
What friend could offer you security?

FORLIS: These are vile options, all of which I shun.
What is your point then?

NOMOPHAGE: I have only one.
You have one hope, if it is not too late.

BERNARD (*rushing in*):
Time's running out! The mob is at the gate!
I hear their cries!

NOMOPHAGE: Forget our enmity.
I know that you have never cared for me,
And yet the public leans in my direction.
Allow me then to offer you protection.
For me at least, our enmity is waived.
Appear before them with me and you're saved!
The people still have such regard for me
Our friendship will be your security,
Or our feigned friendship, if that's your position.
I offer you my aid without condition.
Your safety is my paramount concern.

FILTO (*aside*): Great heavens, what a change! Can this be true,
Or does he have some evil end in view?

VERSAC (*to* NOMOPHAGE):

Monsieur, your offer's generous to a fault.
Go with him, Forlis. Don't be difficult!

FORLIS: Sir, I decline.

VERSAC: Forlis! Are you insane?

NOMOPHAGE: You're lost, Monsieur, if . . .

FORLIS: Please, let me explain.
Your power with the people I would praise
If it had been attained in honest ways.
Then I would have been honored, yes, and proud
To stand as one with you before the crowd.
You say the public's swayed by indirection
And I must trust in that for my protection,
That my just enmity must now be waived
And I must seem your ally to be saved?
How marvelous! Monsieur, it seems to me
You've lost your mind, or else your memory.
You have most inconveniently forgotten
The people's wrath when they sense something rotten,
The rage that just now led to demonstrations
Before your own house, seeking explanations!
For my own honor and humanity
Your secrets have so far remained with me.
Illegal power, though, I can't abide.
The people summon me. I cannot hide.
(*To* VERSAC)
Restrain him here. My absence will be short.
Spare me, Versac, the shame of his support.

NOMOPHAGE: Monsieur, I beg you . . .

FORLIS: Those are my conditions.

NOMOPHAGE: Monsieur . . .

FORLIS: Enough! You're rousing my suspicions!

VERSAC: I'm coming too!

FORLIS: Picard! Lafleur! Duval!
               Come here at once!

VERSAC: What's all the fuss? Why call
               Your servants?

(FORLIS's SERVANTS *appear*.)

FORLIS (*to* THE SERVANTS):
               Friends, you couldn't have been faster!
               Take this reward. (*He distributes money*.)
                          I know you love your master.
               Guard his escape. Farewell. (*He leaves, alone*.)

VERSAC: Forlis! Please wait!
               I'm wasting breath. He's gone to meet his fate!
               (*He leaves the opposite way*.)

MME VERSAC: What will become of him? Why this attack
               On you? It's strange. His soul is not so black
               That . . .

NOMOPHAGE: Suffering, no doubt, has dimmed his reason.
               So he sees everywhere intrigue and treason.

MME VERSAC: Ah, what injustice! I am quite unnerved.
               Still one can't say his fate was undeserved.
               Let's go and watch what this encounter brings
               To Forlis, sadly born for better things.
               (*To* FILTO) You, sir, go after Forlis. Bring us word,
               I fear it won't be good, of what's occurred.

ACT V

NOMOPHAGE (*alone*): An hour passed, and Filto not returned
    To let us know whatever he has learned!
    Three lackeys also gone. It's all so tiring!
    It's the first time since I began conspiring
    That I have met a man with such acumen.
    Filto was right. Forlis is hardly human.
    I thought he'd follow me without exception
    But he at once rejected my deception.
    (*He looks offstage.*)
    No one. Where's Filto? Have I been betrayed?
    Filto's a fool. Why should I be afraid? (*He listens.*)
    They're shouting still! All this was my creating.
    Accursed Filto, keeping us all waiting!
    I cannot flee. Already I'm suspected,
    And fleeing is precisely what's expected.
    Forlis, I sought to trap you and instead
    I've trapped myself. That's where my plotting led.
    The denouement approaches. I must be
    Steadfast. I have strong people under me,
    And there's no proof . . . but here come the Versacs!

VERSAC (*entering with* MME VERSAC):
    Madame, forgive my anger. My attacks
    Stemmed from the sufferings I have endured.
    Neither the soul or heart is well insured
    Against the shocks that life so often brings
    In friendship's joys or friendship's sufferings.
    I've sought him high and low, I had no choice,
    Summoning Forlis in a trembling voice.
    No one I met had anything to say.
    So frightful silence ends this fearful day.
    Ring for the servants. Though God knows I fear
    The horrible reports that I may hear.
(MME VERSAC *rings. A* SERVANT *appears.*)

MME VERSAC (*to the* SERVANT): Has anyone returned?

SERVANT: What? From the riot?
           No, not a soul. But everything seems quiet,
           Thank God! (*He goes.*)

VERSAC: All quiet! But my relief is hollow.
           Knowing another, greater storm may follow.

MME VERSAC: Listen!

VERSAC: Someone comes, running. What disaster
           Is this?

(A SERVANT *and* FILTO *enter, in great excitement.*)

SERVANT: He's saved! He's saved!

VERSAC: Who's saved?

SERVANT: My master!

VERSAC: Forlis?

FILTO: Himself!

MME VERSAC: Oh, happiness!

NOMOPHAGE: Oh, fury!

VERSAC: Justice has triumphed! Heavens, I must hurry
           To be the first to make him my amends.

FILTO: The first you cannot be. A thousand friends
           Among the people gave him their embrace!

VERSAC: Among the people! Heaven!

FILTO: It's a place

Of honor he now holds. He's venerated!
An innocent who's been exonerated!

VERSAC: I long to see him.

FILTO: Monsieur, please allow
The people to surround and love him now.
Respect their transports, let them feel the power
Of joy and of respect. It is the hour
For him to taste his glory. Friendship will
Have its own time, which will be sweeter still.

VERSAC: What prodigy has brought this strange release?

FILTO: First the prodigious courage of Forlis,
Matched by prodigious judgement on the part
Of people sensitive in mind and heart.
I've never seen such fairness, such nobility,
Such a display of warmth and affability
As Forlis and the people have exhibited!
Their mutual regard was uninhibited.
Forlis was saved, and he deserved to be!

NOMOPHAGE (*aside*): Saved by the people! Who will rescue me?

FILTO: I ran, as you commanded, to the spot
Where Forlis was surrounded. He was not
In danger at the moment, but the crowd
Around him, quiet at first, was growing loud.
"It's him!" I heard a thousand voices cry.
Above the din he shouted, "Yes, it's I!
I am here, citizens, because accused,
But you and I are equally abused.
I've come here to denounce a fearful plot.
Citizens, listen!" Silence! There was not
A sound! He went on: "I know you are just.
But guilt and innocence alike have gained your trust.
And sometimes blood of innocents is shed,
The blame for which may fall upon your head,

While those assassins, the initial cause
Of such dark crimes, scorn and defy the laws.
You do not share their crimes, their love of force.
Reject them, so the law can take its course."
These daring words had scarcely been pronounced
When some of the assassins he denounced
Rushed toward him, daggers drawn.

                                    He was surrounded!

VERSAC: Great heaven! Did he fall?

FILTO: No, he astounded
Them all by seizing two and with an oath
Of rage he shouted: "I arrest you both
As traitors whose devotion to your cause
Has mocked the people, heaven, and the laws!"
The rest of the assassins were so cowed
They tried to fade away into the crowd,
Yet six were seized by the outraged spectators
Who readily subdued and jailed these traitors.
Forlis then headed for the court to face
The magistrates and to present his case.
"Judges," he said, "the people, whom you serve,
Have heard me charged with treason. I deserve
To hear those charges, and if I dispute them,
To offer evidence that will refute them."
One document was offered. "Yes," he said,
"That is my writing. Read it!" It was read.
It was a list of names, which many thought
Was evidence sufficient of a plot.
Why did Forlis in secret give support
To some five hundred people, asked the court.
What was his aim? What did he have to hide?
The honest Forlis hastened to provide
Another copy to confirm the first.
It was the best of tactics, or the worst.
As they were reading, cries were heard outside.
"You're seeking proofs. Those proofs we can provide!
The traitors you are seeking, we are here!

Ours are the names that on those lists appear!
Victims of crime and misery, we came
To clear the blot on our protector's name!
Embrace him, Frenchmen, praise him for his care!
Without him, we'd be driven by despair,
By our resentment, jealousy, and hate,
To crimes against your persons and your state.
His generosity removed our wrath
And firmly fixed our feet on virtue's path.
His generous payments were the instigation
That saved our hearts and spirits for the nation.
Can you dare punish actions such as these,
Creating citizens from enemies?"
No poet, no painter ever could have rendered
The transport that these heartfelt words engendered.
First an astonished silence struck our ears,
Followed by cries of joy and floods of tears.
The day is his. His enemies are cowed.
Surrounded by a huge admiring crowd
He stands triumphant, noble and erect,
The focus of love, honor, and respect.

VERSAC: My troubled soul is still, my heart is freed.

MME VERSAC: I think Forlis is here.

FILTO: He is indeed!

(*Enter* FORLIS *and* SERVANT.)

VERSAC (*throwing himself into* FORLIS's *arms*):
            Forlis!

NOMOPHAGE (*at the rear of the stage*):
            How awkward!

VERSAC: Friend, once more we meet!

FORLIS: My friend! My happiness is now complete!

The victory I sought I have attained,
But glory was the only thing I gained.
The friendship that I feel here in your arms
By far surpasses glory's fleeting charms!
(*He sees* NOMOPHAGE.)
But who is this? Good heavens, is it he?

NOMOPHAGE (*aside*): My only hope lies in audacity.

FORLIS (*to* NOMOPHAGE):
How can you dare to look us in the face?

NOMOPHAGE: Why not?

MME VERSAC:　　　　　What boldness!

FORLIS:　　　　　　　　　　He has not a trace
Of shame. Pretending friendship, he but waited
A chance to see Forlis assassinated.
He planned my death and would have even led
Me to the spot to make sure I was dead!

VERSAC:　　The villain!

FILTO (*aside, to* NOMOPHAGE): Flee!

NOMOPHAGE (*aside, to* FILTO):　　　I am not one to flee!
I am no Filto! (*To* FORLIS) Sir, your calumny . . .

FORLIS:　　Your colleagues have confessed. The crowds assemble.
The people know you now. Hear that and tremble!

NOMOPHAGE: You think those mobs you've conquered with such ease
Won't listen to another, if they please?
Are they assembled? Good! Are they enraged?
I'll speak to them. Their wrath will be assuaged.
For such presumption I may pay a price,
But I will trust the throwing of the dice.
The danger of a course does not concern me,

But only what advantage it may earn me.
I play to win, but if I lose instead,
I never waver once I've placed my bet.
I show no hesitation, nor regret.
Monsieur Forlis, the game is yours. Adieu.
I hope I've proved a worthy foe for you. (*He goes.*)

VERSAC (*to a* SERVANT): Follow that man and see if any choose
To trust him still and listen to his views.
(*The* SERVANT *goes.*)

FORLIS: How sad such gifts can be so misapplied!

FILTO (*aside*): To think I once considered him my guide!

MME VERSAC: I blush, Forlis, at my naivete,
To let myself be fooled in such a way.
From now on this new order I'll abhor
As much as I embraced it all before!

FORLIS: No, no! Avoid such excess! Love it still!
But love what's good about it, not what's ill!
Don't make the generous people bear the blame
For crimes that are committed in their name.
(A SERVANT *enters*.) What news?

SERVANT: No longer does the villain reign!
He tried to win the people back in vain.
His treacherous words, once loved, they now despised,
And greeted them with loud, reproachful cries!
Still speaking, he was seized, his hands were tied,
His once feared sword was taken from his side.
He was not harmed, the people would not shed
His impure blood with their pure hands. Instead,
They bore him to the prison to await,
Quite rightly, for the law to judge his fate.

MME VERSAC: Too good for him! His evil deeds must sever
All bonds between us and his kind for ever!

(*To* FILTO)
Monsieur, your presence, I need hardly say,
Sadly recalls . . .

FORLIS: No! No! Let Filto stay!

FILTO: Monsieur, I swear . . .

FORLIS: Filto, we realize
You were the victim of those villains' lies.
Madam, forgive his past mistakes! See, I extend
My hand to Filto, calling him my friend!

VERSAC: I can't believe it!

FORLIS: I know Filto's heart
Is good.

FILTO: Monsieur, I swear that for my part
You're now my model!

FORLIS: Anyone confessing
His errors and repenting has my blessing.
Give me your hand, my brother!

FILTO: Once the prey
Of vice, to virtue I am won today!

FORLIS: You feel its power?

FILTO: Your consoling voice
Supports me and confirms me in my choice.
In this new path your helping hand I'll need.
Allow me that. I'll follow where you lead.

VERSAC: Miraculous! It's like a work of fiction!
If I were not so firm in my conviction
The Revolution's wrong, I would be for it!

FORLIS: You'll come to love it!

VERSAC: I?

FORLIS: Indeed, adore it!

VERSAC: Were I to heed you, then I'm sure I must!

FORLIS: Your soul is generous, your heart is just.
                You'll come to love it.

VERSAC: Ah, my friend, you flatter!
                (*To* MME VERSAC)
                But Madam, there's another pressing matter!
                To give my daughter . . .

MME VERSAC: To Monsieur Forlis,
                Of course!

VERSAC: Although the union won't increase
                Our wealth.

MME VERSAC: No matter. Rather I expect
                More sacrifice from you. You must reject
                Your titles!

VERSAC: Let them go! They're out of date.

MME VERSAC: Monsieur Forlis, our debt to you is great.
                My head was turned, my foolish heart was lured
                By dreams of wealth and glory. You have cured
                My errant soul. The help that you've provided
                Reminded me to let my course be guided
                Again by reason. Now with open eyes
                I see once more the light and I despise
                The darkness. From its bondage I am free.
                The laws of blood and those of family
                Will be my constant care and occupation.
                That's how a woman best can serve the nation!

The citizens who most deserve applause
Are honest men who are the friends of laws!

END